Walsall Borough Police

101

Historic Cases

from
1832 to 1898

Paul Reeves

First Published in the United Kingdom in 2023

All rights reserved. No part of this publication may be reproduced, stored in a retrieval system, or transmitted in any form or by any means, without the prior permission in writing of the publisher, nor be otherwise circulated in any form of binding or cover other than that in which it is published and without a similar condition including this condition being imposed on the subsequent purchaser.

ISBN: 9798868066764
Imprint: Independently published by Paul Reeves.

Text copyright © Paul Reeves 2023

The right of Paul Reeves to be identified as the author of this work has been asserted by him in accordance with the Copyright, Designs and Patents Act 1988.

Although the author has made every effort to ensure that the information in this book is correct, the author does not assume and hereby disclaims any liability to any party for any loss, damage, or disruption caused by errors or omissions, whether such errors or omissions result from negligence, accident, or any other cause.

Every reasonable effort has been made to trace copyright-holders of material reproduced in this book, but if any have been inadvertently overlooked the publisher would be glad to hear from them.

Paul Reeves
Burntwood
Staffordshire

A TwoP Publication ©
2023

email - twop8540@gmail.com

WARNING

This historical work contains the graphic details of real violent and sadistic crimes, which by their very nature can be disturbing, horrific and painful to read. These 101 nineteenth century incidents are all in some way connected to Walsall Borough Police. I must warn you now, that some elements of police work, were then and are now, not for the squeamish or faint hearted. Even after the passing of over one hundred years, these crimes retain their gruesome and hard hitting impact and for educational reasons, I have made no attempt to dilute them. This book was not designed to intentionally shock, upset or offend, but please be aware, some of these stories are sad and hauntingly unsettling in nature, so read at your own peril! - Paul R.

Contents

	Introduction	Page 1
1.	The Caldmore Iron Thieves - July 1832	Page 5
2.	The Parliamentary Election - December 1832	Page 8
3.	The Burglars Final Farewell - Stafford Assizes July 1833	Page 10
4.	The Wall End Bridge Baby Murder - July 1833	Page 13
5.	The Mysterious Demise of John Vickers - January 1836	Page 19
6.	The Emerald Isle & Lady Smashers - November 1836	Page 21
7.	The Bilston Market Clobber Snatchers - December 1836	Page 26
8.	The Absconding Apprentice - January 1837	Page 27
9.	Shoplifters Seven Years Bad Luck - February 1837	Page 27
10.	The Peculiar Insanity of Mr. Brace - February 1837	Page 28
11.	A Conniving Couple of Conmen - June 1837	Page 29
12.	Wisemore Sheep Rustlers - July 1837	Page 31
13.	Lifting the Lichfield Larceners - January 1838	Page 32
14.	The Hue and Cry for Gaol Breaker - March 1838	Page 33
15.	A Gentleman's Duel at Ryecroft - May 1838	Page 34
16.	Picking A Pocket or Two Boys - June 1838	Page 35
17.	Admonished Vagrants - August 1838	Page 35
18.	Trí Crooked Tanner's - September 1838	Page 36
19.	An Unvirtuous Bloxwich Wench - May 1839	Page 36
20.	A Test Case for Burglar's Footwear - May 1839	Page 39
21.	Irish Blarney and Seduction - October 1839	Page 40
22.	Life for the Lamb Thieves - November 1839	Page 41
23.	Bloxwich Breakers Win Five Bob Trip - November 1839	Page 43
24.	Sleight of Hand, Costs Liberty for Life - November 1839	Page 44
25.	Two Days In Gaol for Girl of Fifteen - February 1840	Page 46
26.	Taking Stock - March 1840	Page 46
27.	Drink Induced Drunken Fit - May 1840	Page 47
28.	Silent Victim with Something to Hide? - May 1840	Page 48

29.	Kill A Nag to Escape the Nagging - June 1840	Page 48
30.	Wild Cat Lady Breaker in Little Bloxwich - June 1840	Page 49
31.	The Unlucky 7 Till Snatch - June 1840	Page 50
32.	Six Months 'Bird' for Fowl Play - September 1840	Page 51
33.	Flight of the Harden Duck Snatcher - November 1840	Page 51
34.	More Tea Vicar? - February 1841	Page 52
35.	Severity and Mercy - August 1841	Page 53
36.	Tracking Down the Gailey Lee Burglars - August 1841	Page 54
37.	The Murderous Hatherton Burglary - October 1841	Page 55
38.	The Dastardly Delves Bank Murder - December 1841	Page 58
39.	A Long Time for Watch Shop Heist - March 1842	Page 75
40.	'Boney Jack' and the Rioters - September 1842	Page 76
41.	The Burntwood 'Ménage à trois' Murder - November 1843	Page 77
42.	The Sabbath Day Bloxwich Brawlers - March 1845	Page 90
43.	The Mayor's Melancholy and Murky End - July 1845	Page 91
44.	Discreditable Deceit - August 1847	Page 95
45.	The Bilston Bacon Burglars - June 1848	Page 96
46.	Confidence Tricksters on the Hop - July 1848	Page 98
47.	Blue Lane Beer House Burglary - December 1849	Page 100
48.	A Poultry Family Arrangement - December 1849	Page 101
49.	Highwaymen In Violent Attack - April 1850	Page 103
50.	Justice for Turnips and Handkerchiefs - September 1850	Page 104
51.	Enlisting Embezzler - September 1850	Page 105
52.	Crime Cutting Police Cutlass - March 1851	Page 106
53.	Irishmen's 'Mayor of a Mistake' - June 1851	Page 108
54.	The Indecent 'Wise Man of Walsall' - March 1852	Page 109
55.	Return of the Irish Shenanigans - April 1852	Page 110
56.	An Epitome of Misery the Old Pit Murder - May 1853	Page 112
57.	Moore's Tailor Made Trouble - 1853 & 1854	Page 122
58.	Baby Body Stuck Up Turk's Head Chimney - 1854	Page 125

59.	Riot and Tumult At The Pits - March 1855	Page 127
60.	The Flawed Handling Case - September 1855	Page 130
61.	Lady 'Jack Sheppard' at Walsall - 1855	Page 132
62.	Violent Bobby Bashings - 1856	Page 133
63.	The Leaping Darlaston Burglar - March 1856	Page 135
64.	The Cheese and the Pigeon - May 1856	Page 136
65.	Walsall Wood Wrong'uns - September 1856	Page 137
66.	Judge Hacked Off with the Flour Case - December 1856	Page 138
67.	Second Shot at the Pigeon - December 1856	Page 145
68.	The Notorious 'Tom Duck' of Bloxwich Road - April 1857	Page 148
69.	Two 'Brummie' Smashers - April 1857	Page 149
70.	Irish Hotheads' and the 'Disfigured Man' - June 1857	Page 150
71.	No Mercy for the Post Office Thief - June 1857	Page 151
72.	Despicable Treatment of a Child - October 1857	Page 153
73.	The Ex-Cop & His Minder's Manslaughter - August 1858	Page 154
74.	Confounding the Cock Fighters - May 1859	Page 159
75.	A Superintendents Good Thrashing - February 1860	Page 160
76.	The Lewd Snappers Ultimatum - March 1860	Page 161
77.	Mr. Ebsworth's 'Prize Fight' Revenge - May 1860	Page 162
78.	Another Post Office Thief - October 1860	Page 163
79.	The Wilful Murder of James Flynn - December 1860	Page 165
80.	St. Peter's Macabre Baby Bodies - March 1862	Page 168
81.	The Wilfully Woeful Child Murder Case - 1866	Page 170
82.	A Plague of Street Arabs - February 1867	Page 175
83.	The Remarkable Thompson and Simpson - October 1869	Page 175
84.	Old Man Miller the Long Acre Killer - January 1870	Page 181
85.	The Dead Prisoner Who Failed To Appear - July 1871	Page 187
86.	Attempted Sweetheart Murder - February 1872	Page 188

87.	Tipsy Prisoner Drops Down Dead - October 1874	Page 190
88.	The Slaying of 'Hampton Jack' - February 1875	Page 192
89.	Doveridge Scrap Ends in Disaster - August 1876	Page 197
90.	The Sadistic Pleck Baby Slayer - May 1879	Page 199
91.	A Serial Gaol Breaker - April 1884	Page 208
92.	Brutal Attack on a Walsall Detective - April 1885	Page 211
93.	A Murderer's Wife, a Constable and a VC Winner - 1887	Page 215
94.	The Ablewell Street Hoard of Gold - January 1889	Page 221
95.	Brutal Bridge Street Wife Stabbing - October 1891	Page 222
96.	The Walsall Anarchists - January 1892	Page 227
97.	Matrimonial Misery, Murder & Suicide - December 1892	Page 227
98.	The Park Street Bomb - October 1894	Page 234
99.	Murderess or Melancholy Mother? - May 1895	Page 236
100.	Storm in a Teacup - Reddick v. Evans - December 1896	Page 241
101.	The Mysterious Constable Conundrum - March 1898	Page 251
	About the Author - Paul Reeves	Page 259
	Dedication	Page 260
	Acknowledgements	Page 261
	Further Reading	Page 262
	Signposts to the Past - Source Records	Page 263

Introduction

The year of 1832 was significant for many reasons in the history of Walsall. The fortunes of the town were on the up, the Reform Act confirmed Walsall's borough status, awarding them with a Member of Parliament at Westminster. An air of civic pride and respectability descended on Walsall and the Council was keen to show off their success and prosperity to neighbouring towns and villages. To put 1832 into context, William IV was king and it was only seventeen years after the decisive Battle of Waterloo, that brought peace to Europe.

Times were still very different and difficult, for example a serious outbreak of cholera swept through the town in 1832, claiming the lives of eighty-five people. Industry was growing at a phenomenally fast pace, opening the floodgates for new arrivals and an influx of outsiders. In spite of the atrocious mortality rate for infants and the abysmally short life expectancy for adults, the population of Walsall was rapidly rising. The atmosphere of the old rural market town, inhabited by well established local families was slowly being eroded away. For years the country had lived under the threat of a European invasion and now the indigenous people were being invaded by outsiders from all around. The introduction of so many new people, caused living conditions to fall, with overcrowding and the inevitable spread of disease like cholera.

Many came for work, but not all the people who came to the town were decent or honest and there was an eerie feeling of mistrust, uncertainty and the potential for crime and unrest. There was no regular law enforcement or police back then and the towns people were concerned about protecting their life and property with so many transient types passing through. Although the judicial system was a brutal deterrent to stop most committing crime, poverty tempted even the most righteous to stray from the path of honesty. At the turn of the nineteenth century, there had been a system of 'Watchmen,' who were basically local citizens who patrolled the streets during the hours of darkness keeping things secure, but this had been largely abandoned by 1832.

On the 29th of September, 1829, Sir Robert Peel introduced a new policing concept in London, when the Metropolitan Police became the first regular force of its kind in England. At first the Metropolitan Police was commanded jointly by two Commissioner's, Sir Charles Rowan and Sir Richard Mayne. Rowan who served under the Duke of Wellington at Waterloo provided the structure and discipline and Mayne an accomplished barrister looked after the legal business. Many of the early officers were ex-servicemen with fighting experience and a good proportion of them were Irishmen, which was still part of the United Kingdom.

Walsall Mayor Thomas Dickenson and the Council wanted to ensure that the forthcoming election for their first Member of Parliament under the new Act ran smoothly. There was a history of disturbances during elections, even though only a selective number of men could actually vote the spectacle attracted the masses. The idea was born to create a new Walsall Borough regular police force, which would certainly be one up on their neighbours as it would be the first in the region.

Walsall's figurehead was the Mayor who was elected annually every November. He held all the real power over the Council, the Courtroom and the Borough Gaol and this new planned regular police force would also fall under his command. There would be a superintendent in charge of the men, but he would take his orders from the Mayor.

When Walsall looked for a man to take charge of the Borough Police, there was only really one place you could go for someone with the relevant experience and that was to London. The first ever Superintendent appointed for Walsall Borough Police was Frederick Henry West, who had served as an Inspector in the Metropolitan Police since it began three years earlier. To have achieved this rank, Frederick West almost certainly had an influential sponsor, most likely an army officer and he must have been well connected to get the Walsall job.

Walsall Borough Police was established on the 6th of July, 1832 and it was the earliest pioneer force to be set up in the Midlands region. It was older than Birmingham (1839), Wolverhampton (1837) and Staffordshire (1842). This new embryonic organisation consisted of one superintendent, Frederick West and three full time constables, all sworn in by the magistrates, to maintain law and order and to keep the King's Peace. Like most brand new things, the police were viewed with suspicion by the Walsall public as nobody really understood their remit or role in society and the new men were outsiders with no attachment to the community. The new Borough Police Force consisted exclusively of tough, formidable, determined lawmen and were large and imposing in stature. To many these men were intimidating, but Walsall men did not frighten easily. The policemen were disciplined, no nonsense types, taking their orders from the Mayor, whose authority in the town was second only to the King. One thing is certain, policing in 1832 was a very different beast than people know it today. The laws were strict and the punishment was harsh and the new 'Coppers' were in the thick of it. Walsall had its own Magistrates Court to deal with everyday crime and a gaol for the prisoners. A Quarter Sessions Court was held every season and for the most serious of crimes it was off to Stafford Assizes to see a Judge.

It is important to understand that history by its very nature is a thing of the past, an unchangeable sequence of events cast in stone. While we can criticise what happened, the value is in examining and scrutinising the detail, all in the hope that we can collectively make things better for the future. We inherited the past, but we don't own it, we can look and learn, but never change it, nor should we feel responsible for it. Those times belong to our forefathers, the good and bad, right and wrongs all belong to them. Whatever happened in those days of old, everything was just part of the natural progression of society. Historical events such as public hanging or transportation to Australia can look atrocious by applying today's standards, but remember those standards were only achieved by learning from the mistakes of the past and changing things for the better. I make these observations, because as you read through this book you may ask yourself, "how cruel was that?" Or "how could they have done that?" But it was just the way of the world at that time and future generations might well say the same of us.

This book is a chronological collection of 101 nineteenth century real life stories, closely connected to the men of the Walsall Borough Police Force. I have put them together in date order to show how crime and punishment changed over the years between 1832 and 1898 and how policing kept pace with the ever changing landscape.

These incidents are just a small selection of historical snapshots, some very short and simple and others very serious and devastating. I have endeavoured to give a balanced view of justice from both sides of the fence, from the side of authority and from the offender point of view. There are thousands of stories, these are just a sample, dedicated to the memory of the officers and men who served in those early days.

The characters in this book were all real people, who may still have living descendants in the town today. Some will have done bad things, I just hope I have fairly portrayed them. I would love to hear from any interested parties who have something further to add.

1. The Caldmore Iron Thieves - July 1832

Frederick Henry West, the first Superintendent of Walsall Borough Police and his three uniformed constables, took up their duties on Friday the 6th of July, 1832. These individuals were hard men, employed to enforce the law and keep the King's Peace on the streets of pre-Victorian Walsall. No doubt when they started, they had good and honourable intentions, but even back then, Walsall was no sleepy hollow and Frederick West was about to find out the calibre of the people he was paid to keep in line. Only a few weeks after starting his new job, Frederick West got the first opportunity to stamp his new found authority on wrongdoing Walsall parishioners.

On the morning of Wednesday the 25th of July, 1832, together with his three policemen and some other deputised men, West rode out to Caldmore, where he sought out and arrested five local men suspected of being iron thieves. Having the element of surprise on his side, the suspects were seized and taken to the borough gaol, where the quintet of suspects were all remanded in custody by a magistrate named Wood until the next day. It was a gross understatement to say elements of the townspeople were unhappy, the temperature on the streets was about to be turned up. When the police officers left the Guildhall to go to their lodgings at the Royal Oak, they were surrounded in Digbeth by a hostile crowd, who had gathered in protest. The Mayor sent out some special constables to relieve the situation, but by ten o'clock that night the mob had returned, surrounding the Royal Oak and pelting the officers with stones and other missiles from outside. When the Mayor found out, he was furious and personally returned to the Oak with twenty or so men and an officer from the local militia. Upon his arrival the police officers had already managed to arrest a local man, but had retreated back inside. The Mayor demanded the mob disperse immediately and used his official powers as authority. The dissenting crowd refused to leave and a scuffle broke out. In desperation, the Mayor struck a man named Harrison with his staff and they were forced to arrest him and three others. As the mob surged baying for blood, the Mayor also retreated to the parlour of the Royal Oak, where they now held five prisoners. After an hour and a half of stalemate and being pinned down at the Royal Oak, the Mayor was forced into taking a tactical decision. In a compromise, he was forced to reluctantly release all but one of the prisoners, when they agreed an oath of good behaviour. This broke the deadlock and finally the crowd began to disperse, allowing the lawmen to take their sole remaining prisoner to the Borough Gaol

The following day on Thursday, the five Caldmore iron thieves were frog marched and paraded before the magistrates. Due to the trouble and for fear of further reprisals the victims of the iron thefts now refused to prosecute and inevitably the five suspects had to be discharged. In those times it was the victims responsibility to prosecute crimes, police prosecutions were still a thing of the future. Harrison, the prisoner from the Royal Oak, appeared before the Mayor and was given bail pending trial at the next Assizes.

That night the rioting and stoning continued outside the Royal Oak against the policemen. Although several people were taken into custody, they were released again after promising not to reoffend. Frederick West and his men must have wondered what kind of job they had taken on, but these were tiny steps in a trust building exercise, between the public and the police. It must be remembered that this was a period even before the time of Queen Victoria and long before the American Wild West. This was Wild Walsall in the day's of West.

On Friday morning, Superintendent West and the Mayor travelled to Birmingham, where in anticipation of further trouble they purchased two blunderbusses, a number of pistols, several sets of handcuffs and three wooden rattles. Rattles were used before the introduction of the police whistle and had been issued to all Metropolitan officers. The clacking noise they made was to attract other officers attention to a request for assistance. This clearly demonstrates that the use of firearms is not a new idea for policing and also shows that the police perceived a real threat to their lives. Walsall could be a raucous turbulent place and that afternoon, several special constables were sworn in to help keep law and order.

Later that night, about one thousand people converged on the Royal Oak, throwing stones directed at the police officers inside. The Mayor attended with an officer from the militia and in no uncertain terms read the mob the 'Riot Act,' giving them one hour to disperse, under threat of the soldiers breaking them up. Several of them were taken prisoner with four taken to the gaol. The truth was the public knew that militia troops followed orders, they were not interested in taking prisoners and sometimes their methods were bloody and brutal. On this occasion the desired effect was achieved, the crowd was persuaded to go home and dispersed before the hour was up.

On the Saturday morning, two of the four men from the previous night were bailed and Cotterell the churchwarden took several of the detained men including Harrison to Stafford Gaol, to be tried at the summer Assizes.

That night the Mayor received information from various local sources, that locals planned further disturbances against the police. He sent out orders instructing local men to ensure their servants, apprentices and children were kept indoors all night. At ten o'clock, the police officers, bolstered by more than sixty special constables attended at the Guildhall in readiness of any disturbance breaking out. As they assembled, small groups began to appear in the street outside and abusive and foul language was directed towards them. Just after eleven o'clock some large stones were thrown at the Guildhall and some tried to force entry into the building. The police divided into three sections of about twenty-four men each, two groups went out into the streets, while the third remained to protect the Guildhall building. Some smaller groups that had assembled outside were persuaded to disperse, but there was a hard core who outright refused to listen to reason. In the period of negotiation, a large stone crashed through the window of the Mayor's parlour. He again read them the 'Riot Act' from the window above and sent out constables to clear rioters away. One of the police groups arrived back, reporting they had been stoned near the top of Rushall Street. They detained the man who incited the gang and brought him back with them. Things slowly quietened down and at about two o'clock that morning the special constable's were stood down. The officers and specials went home that night very unhappy, that for all their efforts, the Mayor didn't have a word of thanks and they ended up having no refreshments during their tour of duty.

On Sunday the sabbath day, everything was quiet except for one special constable named Bennett being threatened. The man responsible was brought into court on the Monday and bound over to keep the peace. The local custom of magistrates meeting on a Tuesday was cancelled that week and although large groups formed outside the Guildhall all was peaceful. On Wednesday morning at ten o'clock the magistrates reconvened and things settled back to normal. [1]

2. The Parliamentary Election - December 1832

Polling to elect the new Member of Parliament for Walsall was all scheduled for December, 1832. A local banker and former mayor, Charles Smith Forster, was standing as the Tory party candidate and the election was being contested by George De Bosco Attwood, from the Unionist Party. He was the son of Thomas 'King Tom' Attwood, leader of the Birmingham Unionist Party, who was also standing for election in Birmingham. Mr. Forster made his election headquarters at the George Inn on The Bridge and Mr. Attwood at the Dragon Inn on High Street.

On Tuesday the 11th of December, 1832, 'King Tom' Attwood, led a large procession from Birmingham into Walsall town centre in support of his son's campaign. The Unionist's travelled in carriages, on horseback and by foot with the Birmingham Union Band playing music along the route in a carnival spirit. They marched straight into Walsall town and terminated outside their headquarters at the Dragon Inn. Speeches were made from an upstairs window to the onlookers below, who came to witness the spectacle.

Later that day several of Attwood's supporters congregated intimidatingly outside Mr. Forster's headquarters at the George Inn. Whatever the intention, the effect was to provoke Mr. Forster's party inside. At about eleven o'clock, the Tory supporters and several special constables, went outside to drive Attwood's men away, but this only served to pour fuel on the flames of tension. When the Unionist's realised what was going on, their reinforcements started to arrive and scuffling broke out. Eventually Forster's outnumbered men had to make a hasty retreat back into the George Inn. What happened next is confusing, but in the commotion that followed all the front windows of the George Inn were smashed. Attwood's supporters said that rocks and stones were thrown out from the upper windows onto their heads, while Forster said they only returned the missiles thrown at them first. Tempers were reaching a fever pitch, so a magistrate expecting the worst, sent for a detachment of infantry to attend the George Inn. Just as the volatile situation began to simmer down, enthusiastic infantrymen with bayonets fixed marched onto The Bridge, forcing their way through the crowd. In the turmoil that followed about a dozen people were injured, one of them seriously. The infantrymen formed a defensive line outside the George Inn and held their ground until a cavalry troop of Scot's Grey's arrived from Wednesbury. [2] [3] [4]

The next day, Thursday was polling day and a temporary polling station was erected on The Bridge for eligible people to cast their votes. Men with wealth and property were included, but certainly not the poor and definitely not women, whatever their status. Voting commenced promptly at eight o'clock that morning, but as further trouble was anticipated the Mayor swore in a large number of special constables and had a detachment of the 33rd Regiment of Foot ready to maintain the King's Peace.

Several thousand of Mr. Attwood's supporters congregated on The Bridge with the apparent intention of disrupting the proceedings. Mr. Forster made an appearance at the broken windows of the George Inn to address his supporters. Several of Mr. Attwood's men in the street below, jeered and shouted as he tried to speak. Mr. Forster persevered to make a short speech, concluding by asking his supporters not to delay from registering their vote. Mr. Cotterell, who was Mr. Attwood's chief campaigner also addressed the crowds on behalf of the Unionist's.

At around two o'clock that afternoon, the sound of horses hooves echoed from the cobbles, as an imposing detachment of Scot's Grey's rode on horseback onto The Bridge. The troopers with their swords drawn, formed a defensive line in front of the George Inn.

Mr. Attwood was infuriated, declaring the military interference and intimidation as undemocratic. He said that the voting was illegal and void and told his supporters to return home.

The final outcome was, 304 votes for Mr. Forster, against 231 votes for Mr. Attwood. Despite the appeals from Attwood, the Tory candidate was duly elected as the first new Member of Parliament for Walsall. [5]

3. The Burglars Final Farewell - Stafford Assizes July 1833

Back in 1833 housebreaking, or burglary was considered a very serious crime, so serious in fact that you could receive the death penalty if convicted. These are two cases heard at the Stafford Assizes in 1833.

Between ten and eleven in the morning, on Sunday the 7th of April, 1833, silver refiner Richard Marlow and his housekeeper Jane Perry, left his house in the Foreign of Walsall to attend chapel. Watching for them to leave with a view to breaking and entering, were twenty-five year old Joseph Lewis, a goldsmith from Birmingham and twenty-seven year old Richard Bluck, a lapidary from London. As soon as the coast was clear they seized their chance to break in. They crudely rummaged through the cupboards and drawers in the house, ransacking the place for anything of value. They stole nine silver teaspoons, three tablespoons, some crop silver and various other items. As they left the premises at just after eleven o'clock that morning, a neighbour Thomas Guest spotted them and gave chase. Guest caught up with Lewis, grabbing and detaining him. By the time Lewis was handed over to Police Constable William Foxall at the police office, Bluck had also been apprehended and Thomas Guest identified him as the other man he saw leaving Richard Marlow's house. When Constable Foxall searched the two suspects, he found all of the stolen property belonging to Marlow in their possession, pretty well equally divided up between them. He also found picklock keys in both their pockets, used by burglars to break in.

Both defendants appeared before Judge Baron Gurney at Stafford Summer Assizes on Tuesday the 23rd of July, 1833. Mr. Corbett conducted the prosecution and Mr. Lee was counsel for the prisoners. The Judge asked them if they had anything to say in their own defence, to which Lewis said "if the verdict be against us, I hope you will shew us mercy, and the prayers of the unfortunate shall be offered up for you." Bluck said they had already been in gaol for four months while they were awaiting trial. Both men were found guilty of burglary and the ultimate judgement of death was passed.

The Judge however, said he would recommend His Majesty to spare their lives, but no further mercy could be shown to them. The Judge was then informed that Lewis had a previous conviction. He sternly told him, "If I had known earlier that you, Lewis, had been convicted before, I don't know that I could have recommended you to mercy. You must both expect to spend the remainder of your lives in a very miserable manner indeed."

The death penalty was commuted to transportation to Australia for life, never to return. Prisoners awaiting transportation were taken to what were called prison hulk ships. These were old unseaworthy vessels moored off the coast, converted for temporarily holding prisoners in miserable conditions, until the convict ship came alongside to pick them up. Bluck was taken to the hulk ship 'Ganymede' at Woolwich and Lewis to the 'York' at Portsmouth to await transportation. When the transportation ship 'Fairlie' arrived on the 14th of October, 1833, both men were picked up for the long voyage. They arrived in Australia for their new lives to begin on the 15th of February, 1834. Joseph Lewis was later conveyed to Norfolk Island, arriving there on the 9th of September, 1834. The men would have served a whole life sentence as convicts, until it was deemed safe to release them. Richard Bluck was pardoned on the 30th of July, 1847, on the condition that he didn't return to the United Kingdom ever again and Joseph Lewis received his pardon on the 30th of September, 1847, on the same terms. Richard Bluck died on the 11th of January, 1875 and was buried the following day at Rookwood General Cemetery. [6] [7] [8] [9] [10] [11] [12] [13] [14] [15] [16] [17] [18]

Our second case involves a break in at the cottage of Samuel Woodcock in Huntington on the morning of Wednesday the 5th of June, 1833. Labourer Samuel Woodcock left for work at about six o'clock and his wife Elizabeth, left at half past seven. As she was leaving, she saw James Bailey, a nineteen year old chimney sweep from London outside her cottage. Bailey said he was thirsty so she gave him a cup of water before leaving the premises secure. She was surprised to see another man, eighteen year old John Emmerton, hanging around a short distance from the house. Elizabeth Woodcock didn't know either of the men, they were both strangers in the area.

When the couple returned to the property sometime between ten and eleven o'clock that morning, they found the window shutters uncovered and the window open. The floor inside the house was covered in soot, the thieves having apparently entered the premises by means of the chimney. A check revealed that two loaves of bread, three parts of a cheese, two handkerchiefs and a lady's garment had been stolen.

At about half past two that afternoon, Police Constable William Foxall saw James Bailey and John Emmerton, carrying a bag in High Street, Walsall. He thought they both looked dirty, scruffy and suspicious characters, so he followed and detained them. Inside their bag he found part of a cheese, two loaves of bread, two handkerchiefs and a lady's garment, all later identified by Elizabeth Woodcock.

Their case was heard at Stafford Summer Assizes on the same day as the last case, again before Judge Baron Gurney. Mr. Corbett prosecuted, Mr. Lee was counsel for Emmerton and Bailey entered a guilty plea before the case commenced. Emmerton was found guilty and both men were sentenced to death, although again the Judge spared their lives. He told them that they must expect to spend the remainder of their days, living in a very miserable manner transported for life to a distant country.

The Judge recalled Constable Foxall and commended him for his diligent police work, rewarding him with five pounds for his conduct in this matter.

Bailey was taken to the hulk ship 'Ganymede' and Emmerton to the 'Justitia.' Bailey boarded the 'Fairlie' on the 14th of October, 1833 and travelled with those from the previous case, arriving in Australia on the 15th of February, 1834. There is no mention of Emmerton going to Australia and although I have found no record, it is likely he died in the awful conditions on the hulk, prior to leaving. [19] [20]

4. The Wall End Bridge Baby Murder - July 1833

This is the tragically sad and melancholy tale of Mary Smith, who in July, 1833, was just a young woman aged twenty-three and worked as a live in servant girl for her sixty year old master, James Harrison. It seemed evident that Harrison wanted a bit more from his servant girl than a few domestic chores, as she was pregnant and this was not the first time he had fathered an illegitimate child with her.

In the middle of May, 1833, Mary Smith met with Ann Fowler the local Bloxwich midwife, who had delivered previous children for her. Mary Smith asked her if she could suggest a place for her confinement and the birth of her child. Ann Fowler introduced her to a neighbour called Maria Cocking, who agreed to take her into the family home for the confinement and birth in June. On the 21st of June, 1833, Fowler delivered a healthy full term baby girl, ordinary in every way, except for a distinctive cleft lip.

Mary Smith and the baby left her confinement on Wednesday the 3rd of July, 1833, telling Maria Cocking that Harrison's sister was collecting the baby to be nursed in Birmingham. Wearing a distinctive red cloak and a white straw bonnet, she set off carrying the baby in her arms. At about nine o'clock that night, William Cocking, Maria's husband, saw a woman carrying a baby and wearing a red cloak and white bonnet pass by his workshop as he locked up. Although he had to look twice, he was almost certain it was Mary Smith, who was walking along the canal towpath towards Wall End Bridge.

A boatman named John Shipton also saw Mary Smith with the baby near to Pratt's Bridge, again wearing the distinctive red cloak. She asked him directions to the Pleck and he advised her to take the turnpike road, but she insisted there were two men she had to meet along the canal. He thought her behaviour was odd, for the best part of an hour he watched her senselessly pacing up and down the towpath, with no particular purpose.

Mary Smith then asked another man named James Dean the way to Darlaston. Dean advised her to go home as he was concerned about her and the baby's safety so late at night. She said again there were two men she had to meet first.

Eventually Mary Smith walked off into the darkness, her shadowy figure disappearing along the towpath in the dead of night. What terrible painful event happened can only be imagined, but she went off towards Wall End Bridge with the baby and when she came back she was alone. Wall End Bridge carries Fryers Road in Bloxwich over the Wyrley and Essington canal.

At ten o'clock that evening, Mary Smith returned to James Harrison's house, where his other servant girl, Hannah Cocking heard her outside and went downstairs to let her in. Mary Smith walked in alone and went straight upstairs to Harrison's room. His room was next to Cocking's bedroom and through the thinly plastered walls, she heard Harrison ask Mary Smith where the child was. She assured him that the child had been left safe with a nurse. Harrison told Mary Smith that she should bring the child home and he would pay for a nurse to look after her. That night Mary Smith stayed in Hannah Cocking's room with her, but hardly a word was spoken.

In the morning the two girls were to go and collect Mary Smith's belongings from the Cocking's house. Hannah Cocking, suggested they walk along the canal, but Mary Smith awkwardly refused, saying that the sight of water frightened her and insisted on the road.

On a nice summer evening on Saturday the 6th of July, 1833, farmer, Luke Head was strolling along the towpath, near to Wall End Bridge. His attention was drawn to a strange bundle of rags floating on the water, so when curiosity got the better of him he stretched out with his hay fork and dragged the mysterious object to the bank. To his absolute horror, he discovered the gruesome package contained the lifeless corpse of a new born baby girl.

Police Constable William Foxall from Bloxwich was alerted to the incident and the unfortunate child's body was taken to the Spread Eagle public house. It was usual in those days for inquests to be held at the nearest public house and the coroner was informed of the death.

Constable Foxall commenced inquiries immediately, starting with all the local midwives. Ann Fowler attended the Spread Eagle to look at the body and instantly identified the dead baby when she saw the cleft lip. The baby was quite well when she saw it last, so she told Foxall the mother was Mary Smith, a servant who worked for Harrison.

Constable Foxall wasted no time and made his way to the home of James Harrison, who was arrested on suspicion of the baby's murder. There was no sign of Mary Smith or any baby, confirming that his suspicions might be right. Harrison was taken to Walsall gaol where Foxall informed Superintendent West that Mary Smith, the mother had already fled the town.

The following day Superintendent West and Constable Foxall set off on horseback in hot pursuit of Mary Smith. This was a time before trains, when it wasn't easy to get anywhere quickly on foot. Mary Smith had taken the main road towards Birmingham and by asking a few simple questions, it wasn't difficult to track a woman walking alone. Near the town of Birmingham she was captured and arrested for the baby's death. The two burly officers returned to Walsall with Mary Smith, but she hardly said a word all the way back.

At Walsall gaol, Mary Smith saw Harrison who said to her, "Mary, what a disgraceful situation you have placed me in," to which she replied, "I had no wish to get you into any trouble, for you are as innocent of the crime as the child itself."

Mary Smith later made a confession to the policemen that she had, "been tempted by the devil himself" and had put the child in the cut under Wall End bridge. She admitted watching as the child desperately struggled for life by trying to survive in the water and that terrible haunting sight made her want to drown herself as well. At one point she realised the grim reality of what she was doing, so she made a forlorn and futile attempt to grab the child back, but it was too late, it began to sink and then disappeared out of her reach. She told them that Harrison knew nothing about what she had done.

The body of the girl was subjected to a post mortem examination by surgeon Henry Paget, who concluded that the two week old baby girl was a healthy child, whose death was caused by drowning. He noted that there was some external bruising on the body, but thought it may well have been caused in the water after death from boats passing by.

The coroner opened the inquest at the Spread Eagle public house on Tuesday the 9th of July, 1833, where the lifeless and silent body of the baby was laid out on a table in the bar, like a macabre stage prop for the jury to see. The unforgettable sight of the infants corpse appeared to greatly disturb Mary Smith, with the reality of things understandably having a traumatic effect on her. At the end of that day, the inquest was adjourned until Saturday the 13th of July, 1833.

When the inquest reconvened the remaining evidence was heard. In summing up the Coroner said there was no evidence to incriminate Harrison at all, so he was acquitted. The jury retired to consider their verdict against Mary Smith, but they only took a few minutes to return their solemn verdict of 'Wilful Murder'. The Coroner committed her to stand trial for murder at the next Assizes. [21]

Mary Smith appeared before the Summer Assizes at Stafford on Monday the 29th of July, 1833, charged with the murder of her child. In the crowded court room all the evidence was heard again. It was a relative speedy process and the jury returned a guilty verdict without much deliberation.

Mr. Godson who defended Mary Smith raised a point of law, because the indictment said the child's name was 'unknown.' He questioned whether the charge was valid and asked for it to be considered before sentence was passed.

This legal challenge on a technicality delayed the judgement somewhat cruelly for eight months, until Mary Smith appeared back at Stafford Lent Assizes on the 17th of March, 1834.

The courtroom was full of people anticipating Mary Smith's fate, including an unusually high number of women. As the Judge, Mr. Justice Patteson entered the room everyone stood and he called for Mary Smith to be brought to the bar.

The Judge told her that ultimately the judiciary had decided that the legal technicality raised by her defence could not be upheld and their decision was against her. Mary Smith began to sob loudly as the Judge continued to speak over her. When Mr. Justice Patteson told her that she had been found guilty of murdering her twelve day old daughter, she broke down and the sound of her wailing cries echoed all around the courtroom. The Judge placed the notorious black coif on his head, which must have been a fearful experience for those watching especially the woman, as it could mean only one thing, certain death.

The Judge could see Mary Smith was not only in a bad state of health, she was becoming hysterical so he did not want to prolong her agony. Struggling emotionally to deliver the sentence himself, he told her that she had been convicted on overwhelming evidence, but he would not dwell on the enormity of the case. He concluded by saying that she would be executed on Wednesday morning. Many of the women attending were openly and inconsolably crying loudly as Mary Smith was led away for the very last time.

Her execution was fixed for eight o'clock on the morning of Wednesday the 19th of March, 1834. That morning Mary Smith got up at six o'clock, by which time huge crowds had already started to come from miles around, filling the narrow streets of Stafford all around the gaol. Literally thousands flooded to witness the macabre spectacle of a triple public hanging. Mary Smith was to swing with Charles Shaw and Richard Tomlinson, both convicted of murder. When Mary Smith was led into the prison chapel, she was totally speechless and her whole body was agonisingly quivering and shaking with violent and uncontrollable tremors. Mrs. Seddon, the prison matron, had to support her throughout, but the sight of seeing Tomlinson enter, literally made her sink to her knees. Mr. Dibbs, the head turnkey had to physically help her back to her feet as the Reverend Buckeridge conducted the sacramental religious service. He delivered this final sermon, in an impressively emotional way, in a hope of distracting them from the inevitable end.

As the service concluded the heavy chapel door opened and the twenty-two year old Tomlinson was taken out into the corridor. He was pinioned out of the sight of Smith to spare her the agony. Mary Smith saw her pinion cords in the hands of Mr. Brutton, who calmly told her they were essential to spare her from pain during the act of death. Overwhelmed by her tormented mind, Mary Smith dramatically shivered in expectation of what was to come. The night before the executions, Stafford's Governor received a last minute reprieve for Shaw, he was not to be hung, but cruelly nobody told him until just before the proceedings began.

Tomlinson and Smith were led away, their doomed souls stricken with an almost unsupportable anguish. On the final walk towards the scaffold the silence was only broken by the sound of Smith's mournful sobbing. Standing near to the lodge door, was the shadowy figure of the executioner, wearing his clean smock frock and brown cap pulled down across his eyes. He was the grim reaper that every prisoner hoped never to see. Tomlinson walked up to the drop, but the unsteady Mary Smith was assisted to her place by the warders. Each had the noose of their respective hanging rope carefully adjusted around their neck, before the white sack was put over their head. Awkwardly Tomlinson's sack was slightly too small and had to be stretched over his head, still revealing his facial features. With one swift movement the two bodies dropped, twanging the ropes as the slack was taken up and sending their souls quickly to the next world. The almost hypnotised eyes of the onlooking public, stared in an eerie silence as the final curtain fell and the show was over. At the conclusion of the prescribed time the lifeless corpses were cut down, placed in their coffins and taken to the dead house for burial in unmarked graves within the confines of the gaol. [22] [23] [24] [25] [26]

5. *The Mysterious Demise of John Vickers - January 1836*

Twenty-five year old John Vickers and his twenty-six year old common law wife Ann Price, lodged in a doss house belonging to chair maker Henry Sherratt in an unsavoury part of town.

John Vickers father, John Vickers senior was the licensee of the Castle Inn in High Street. He didn't approve of his son's totally improper three year relationship with Ann Price, who he thought was a woman of the town. John Vickers junior was however, partial to more than the odd pint and had gone off the rails as far as his family were concerned.

During the afternoon of Thursday the 26th of November, 1835, Vickers was out drinking at a public house in Park Street, getting 'three sheets to the wind' and when he didn't come home Ann Price went looking for him. He refused to return home with her when she found him, but promised to follow her shortly.

Vickers finally staggered back drunk to the lodgings sometime between eight and nine o'clock. All the ingredients were there for the unavoidable domestic argument and of course, unsurprisingly it happened. In a rage Vickers aggressively threw his boiled ham supper into the fire. Ann Price was no shrinking violet and when Vickers stood up, she swung an under handed 'cog winder' into the pit of his stomach, completely knocking the wind from his sails.

Sherratt the landlord heard things cracking off so went into the back room to check every thing was alright. He opened the door slowly, Ann Price was sobbing in the corner and Vickers was sat in the chair with his head in his hands looking exceedingly ill. The concerned Sherratt asked Vickers what was wrong, he told him he felt very bad. Sherratt knew he'd had a skin full, so told him he would feel better in the morning when he had sobered up. Sherratt helped him up the stairs to the bedroom and Vickers told him that she had hit him on an old wound.

The next day on Friday, Vickers was no better, in fact he was in excruciating pain. His father heard he was unwell and promptly sent two people around to bring him to the Castle Inn. When he arrived it was obvious he was seriously ill and immediate medical help was required. John Swift a surgeon from High Street was first to attend, but soon after a second opinion was sought from Benjamin Arthur Kent another surgeon from George Street. John Vickers senior employed Jane Burton to nurse his son and she kept a vigil as he was confined to bed. Vickers remained in total agony and sensed his own impending doom. In his final few days, he began to give away his possessions to family and friends and he died in the arms of Jane Burton on Tuesday the 26th of January, 1836.

John Vickers senior, never liked Ann Price and was extremely suspicious about his son's untimely death so he contacted the police.

As a result of the allegations made Police Constable William Foxall apprehended Ann Price. On the way to the lock-up she admitted striking Vickers, but said she never meant to hurt him.

An inquest was opened then immediately adjourned to facilitate a post mortem and for other enquiries to be conducted. The inquest continued on Saturday the 30th of January, 1836. The surgeon Benjamin Kent, who conducted the post mortem found that Vickers died from a ruptured gall bladder, which was split in a transverse direction and greatly lacerated. The inquest took the best part of two days to hear all the evidence and concluded with the jury returning a verdict of manslaughter against Ann Price. The Coroner committed her to the County Gaol to await trial at the Assizes.

On Tuesday the 15th of March, 1836, Ann Price appeared at Stafford Assizes, charged with killing and slaying John Vickers at Walsall, in the county of Stafford. The Judge was Mr. Justice Williams, counsel for the prosecution was Mr. Lee and Mr. Allen defenced Price.

Henry Sherratt was the first witness who gave his account of what happened in his house, back in November, 1835.

He was followed into the witness box by John Vickers senior, who gave a very emotional account of how he had tried in vain to help his stricken son back to health.

Jane Burton, the nurse told how in the days before his death, he told her the end was near and 'that he had given up all worldly affairs.' She said he died in her arms in tremendous pain. An objection was raised to any dying declaration being admissible, but this was overruled. Jane Burton went on to say that Vickers told her that Ann Price gave him an under handed blow.

John Swift the surgeon who first attended Vickers said in his opinion the blow from Price ruptured his gall bladder, which eventually caused his death.

Thomas Graham an apprentice to the surgeon Mr. Kent, said he was present at the post mortem and observed the ruptured and lacerated gall bladder.

A third surgeon, Edgar Ashe Spilsbury from Park Street was called for the defence. He stated on oath that he had never seen a gall bladder burst and believed it was impossible to cause such an injury with a single blow. Spilsbury conducted experiments to test his theory and concluded he was right, it couldn't be done. Furthermore if Ann Price did cause such an impossible injury, Vickers would have certainly died within thirty-six hours of receiving it.

His evidence was very convincing and enough to provide the jury with reasonable grounds to give Ann Price the benefit of the doubt. When the verdict arrived, they found her 'Not guilty' and she was released from custody and allowed to leave the dock.

John Vickers grave and that of several of his family are in the churchyard at St. Matthew's Church. His father died the following year on the 9th of November, 1837. [27] [28] [29] [30]

6. *The Emerald Isle & Lady Smashers - November 1836*

Walsall was a convenient stop off for travellers passing along a major coaching route through the Midlands. Some of these transient types looked for late night adult entertainment and found it hidden away in the murky back streets of Walsall. Travellers went to these courts and yards where the poorest and sleaziest underbelly of society lived, to be entertained by prostitutes or buy stolen wares.

Plying their crooked trade were a couple of 'Emerald Isle' risk takers, twenty-eight year old Patrick Cosgrove and thirty-one year old Elizabeth Wilson. These partners in crime were from a devious class of people, who operated on the periphery of serious crime by preying on the addicts and users of the vice trade. They devised a cunning scheme to turn dirty money clean, by relying on the premise that their victims held higher morals than them.

Elizabeth Wilson, was about five feet five inches tall with a freckly ruddy complexion, dark brown hair and grey eyes. She was the late night bait, who would loiter near a dimly lit alleyway opposite the Swan public house in Dudley Street. She used her seductive charms to lure unsuspecting men who were after some late night action into her lair.

Sometime between midnight and one o'clock on the morning of Saturday the 26th of November, 1836, William Bowen a labourer working for the Grand Union Railway Company, just so happened to be in the area. He saw her dusky figure in the alley by the Swan, where she offered him certain sexual favours for money and an agreement was made. She enticed him to follow her down the dark entry, through a brewhouse and up a ladder into a storeroom above. He unwittingly fell into her trap, the dimly lit room had a fire in the hearth and from the light he could see it contained a bed, a table and some chairs. The going rate of a half crown was handed over by Bowen, with a further sixpence for a glass of rum for 'Dutch courage.' As he took the last few sips of rum, Wilson reneged on their business arrangement and withdrew her promise of the services offered. It was all part of the plan, Bowen disgruntled and disappointed demanded the return of his cash. Wilson at first refused, but when he got more threatening she handed over two shilling coins. Her job was done, she had slipped him two forged shillings and hoped he wouldn't notice, or if he did he didn't have the nerve to go to the police and tell them the truth. Right on cue

Bowen heard the voice of a man getting closer and closer. He realised he was in a precarious even dangerous position and fearing for his personal safety made a hasty retreat. Clambering back down the ladder, Bowen made for the light and safety of Dudley Street at the end of the alleyway. At the point of exit, Patrick Cosgrove almost bumped into him on the way to make sure he left. This was a clever and devious form of money laundering, a different take on the old crime of punters being robbed by unsavoury pimps. The crime relied on the respectability of the victim, the hope being they would be too ashamed to admit being with a prostitute.

When Bowen was far enough away from danger, he looked closely at the two shilling coins given to him by Elizabeth Wilson and realised he had been done, they were both counterfeit. Unfortunately for Wilson and Cosgrove, Bowen had no shame or high morals, all he wanted was his money and he immediately went to see Superintendent Jonathan Rider at Walsall Borough Police in his quest for compensation. It just so happened that Superintendent Rider had received many complaints recently of counterfeit currency turning up in the town and the prospect of eliminating the source was just what he had been waiting for.

Superintendent Rider and Constable Raymond went with Bowen, retracing his steps back to Wilson's den of iniquity in Dudley Street. The officers knocked the front door of the house and instantly entered when they heard some rustling going on inside and Bowen identified Elizabeth Wilson as the woman responsible. She denied the allegation and Patrick Cosgrove started to slip away up the stairs. Superintendent Rider followed him and watched as he suspiciously trod amongst the ashes in the fire, as if he was to trying conceal something. His furtive behaviour called for a closer inspection, which proved worthwhile when the superintendent saw two pieces of metal lying near the fireplace. These two pieces when joined together made a complete counterfeit shilling. Wilson and Cosgrove were both arrested and Police Constable Raymond conveyed them back to the custody house. The dark room was searched for the rest of that night and resumed in the morning, when there was better light. Fragments of metal were found in the ashes, together with plaster of Paris for making moulds. Constable Raymond found a counterfeit shilling in the room and a sixpence in the bed. They found an old tobacco pipe with traces of molten metal and the bowl of an iron spoon that had evidently been in the fire. There were two iron files with minute traces of metal in the grooves and a good half crown with some sixpences concealed in the roof.

Cosgrove and Wilson, appeared before the Judge, Baron Bolland at Stafford Assizes on Saturday the 11th of March, 1837. Mr. McMahon and Mr. Corbett prosecuted the case against the two defendants who were undefended. They both adamantly denied the offence of having possession of objects to make a mould for counterfeiting silver coin of the realm.

Edward Joseph Powell from the Royal Mint told the jury, that they possessed all the instruments for making and milling counterfeit coin and also proved the two shilling coins given to Bowen were counterfeit.

Cosgrove avidly listened to the court proceedings and frequently interrupted by asking a series of foolish or irrelevant questions, which only made him look more guilty. At the conclusion of the evidence, Cosgrove finished his defence by rambling and talking a load of ludicrous nonsense.

The Jury found them guilty and the Judge sentenced them to be transported to Australia for seven years each. The Judge said he had little doubt that Cosgrove's profession as jewellery hawker, was a mere cover for him to pass as much counterfeit as he could manufacture.

Cosgrove went to the prison hulk 'Ganymede' at Woolwich on the 15th of May, 1837 and boarded the 'Neptune' prison ship on the 27th of September, 1837. It sailed on the 4th of October, 1837 and docked at Van Diemen's Land on the 18th of January, 1838.

Wilson left England on the 14th of July, 1837 aboard the 'Henry Wellesley II' together with another 139 women convicts and reached New South Wales, Australia on the 22nd of December, 1837. [31][32][33][34][35]

'Smasher' was a term used to describe people who passed off counterfeit currency and 'Uttering' was the act of passing the coins on.

At the same court of Assizes, two further ladies, Charlotte Eggington, twenty-two years and Elizabeth Homer, twenty-nine years were charged with uttering counterfeit coin in Walsall.

The circumstances of the crime were that on Monday the 28th of November, 1836, two lady 'smashers' were out in the town, intent on uttering their fake coinage. A popular modus operandi at the time was for two respectably dressed women to go out and work in partnership, changing forged shillings for small items. On this particular day, Charlotte Eggington bought a penny herring from fishmonger Sarah Worrod's in Digbeth, with a counterfeit shilling. A short time later, Elizabeth Homer did exactly the same thing. Eggington then bought a penny pie from Michael Folkes shop, using another fake shilling. Superintendent Rider and Police Constable Raymond were alerted that the 'uttering duo' were on a shopping spree and went in search of the culprits.

Constable Raymond arrested them both and found in their possession, seven counterfeit shillings, five of them secreted in a special pocket of Homer's purse. They also had fifteen shilling, t'pence ha'penny in copper in Eggington's basket, the proceeds of their crimes.

At the Assizes, Mr. Powell from the Royal Mint confirmed all the coins were counterfeit.

A man named Fulford came to court to give good character references for both women. He turned out to be a blatant liar and conceded when cross examined that Homer had a previous conviction for a like offence at Warwick Assizes. It also transpired that Homer's husband was Eggington's brother and he had already been transported for the same crime. The Judge was furious at Fulford's deceit and severely reprimanded him for trying to conceal the facts.

Charlotte Eggington was sentenced to nine months imprisonment for each offence to be served consecutively and Elizabeth Homer was sentenced to twelve months imprisonment.

The Judge made it very clear that the severity of the sentences were designed to deter other offenders and also protect the public from such devious thieves. [36] [37]

7. The Bilston Market Clobber Snatchers - December 1836

William Downing a Brierley Hill tailor and draper regularly sold his wares on the local market stalls. He spent all day at Bilston market on the 19th of December, 1836, until the close of business when he began to pack away his wares. Whilst he was busy loading up his cart, one of his bundles of clothing, containing eighteen pairs of trousers, twenty waistcoats, two pair of breeches, three pair of gaiters, one jacket and a wrapper was stolen.

The following day, William Carpenter saw two suspicious looking characters carrying baskets up an entry in Upper Rushall Street. Leaving a friend to keep watch, Carpenter lost no time in going to see Superintendent Rider at Walsall police station. Returning together Carpenter pointed out the men to Superintendent Rider, both standing outside a house belonging to Ann Cushing with two baskets full of clothes next to them. The two men, thirty-two year old John Richards and his nineteen year old nephew Edward Richards, denied all knowledge of the baskets when Superintendent Rider asked them. They explained they were travellers lodging at Ann Cushing's house, but Superintendent Rider was unconvinced with their explanation and arrested them both and took them to the police cells. Superintendent Rider returned to Ann Cushing's house where she consented to a search of her premises. Several items of stolen clothing were found concealed in the loft above the top room and Ann Cushing was arrested on suspicion of handling stolen goods.

All three suspects appeared at Walsall Quarter Sessions on Saturday the 8th of July, 1837, before the Recorder Edward Lloyd Williams. Having heard all the evidence the jury acquitted Ann Cushing of receiving stolen property, but found both the Richard's guilty.

Despite a letter from a local Bilston priest in their favour, the elder prisoner got three months and the younger one two months imprisonment, both with hard labour. [38] [39]

8. The Absconding Apprentice - January 1837

During the nineteenth century apprentices were legally tied to their masters contractually for the duration of the apprenticeship and it was an offence to leave their employ without permission.

On the 30th of January, 1837, eighteen year old Thomas Palmer appeared at Walsall Magistrates Court charged with absconding from his harness maker's apprenticeship with John Horton. This was apparently the fifth time he had left his employer and each time he was returned. On a previous occasion, Superintendent Rider discovered that Palmer had run away to enlist with the 80th Regiment of Foot and had to travel all the way down to Chatham barracks to get him back from the army. John Horton forgave him at court on that occasion and took him back. This time Palmer was sentenced to one month's imprisonment combined with hard labour to teach him a lesson. It must have worked because Thomas Palmer was still a harness maker at the time of the 1841 census living in Hill Street, so he must have stuck at it. Incidentally, I found out that John Horton was my great/great grandfather, what are the chances! [40] [41]

9. Shoplifters Seven Years Bad Luck - February 1837

Ann Yates owned a little shop in Walsall selling cutlery, knives, scissors, razors and the like. In early February, 1837, she was visited by two dubious youths, twenty-one year old Hiram White and sixteen year old John Wean, who asked her loads of bamboozling questions, but never intended to purchase anything. It was all a well worked scam to distract her away, while they helped themselves to a number of her things.

On Wednesday the 6th February, 1837, Hiram White went to a man named John Bush at his home in Portobello, trying to offload some of the stolen razors and scissors. White was totally unaware that Bush was in fact Ann Yates brother-in-law, who knew the property being offered was stolen from her shop. Bush didn't let on he knew, but followed

Hiram White back to Walsall and he watched him enter the Lion Inn in Park Street where he met up with Sarah White and John Wean.

John Bush wasted no time in giving the facts to Police Constable William Foxall, who went straight to the public house and apprehended the three ne'er-do-well's, Hiram White, Sarah White and John Wean. Foxall also recovered the stolen property in a basket on the floor next to them, all of which was later identified by Mrs. Yates.

In addition to the theft from Ann Yates, the same three were also charged with stealing several pairs of shoes from Harriet Green's market stall on Saturday the 4th of February, 1837 and stealing second hand trousers from David Schir, a foreign Jew who had a shop in Berry Street, Wolverhampton.

The magistrates committed them to stand trial at the Assizes, where on Wednesday the 8th of March, 1837, Hiram White and John Wean, were found guilty and Sarah White was acquitted. Both men were sentenced to be transported for seven years each.

On the 21st of March, 1837, they were placed onto the 'Ganymede' hulk at Woolwich. An appeal was raised to reduce the sentence of John Wean on account of his age, but his sentence was upheld. Both White and Wean departed from England on the 4th of October, 1837, aboard the 'Neptune' which arrived in Van Diemen's Land in Tasmania on the 18th of January 1838.

It's very unlikely that they ever stole from another English shop with seven years bad luck. [42 43 44 45 46 47 48 49 50 51 52]

10. The Peculiar Insanity of Mr. Brace - February 1837

John Brace, aged sixty-five years was an unmarried and retired draper from Bromsgrove, whose health had not faired too well in his old age. John's delicate mental state had unfortunately deteriorated, to the point where he was forced to reside with his brother Henry, at his home in Elmore Green, Bloxwich.

John Brace was suffering from severe capiophobia, a deluded and irrational belief that the police were after him. His brother, Henry

Brace was a saddlers ironmonger, who was in a business partnership with another man named Henry Box. It just so happened that Henry Box was a personal friend of Superintendent Jonathan Rider and he suggested to him that he might be able to reassure John Brace about fears. Superintendent Rider met John Brace, with the intention of putting his mind at ease and reassuring him that everything was alright as far as the police were concerned and initially things seemed much better, but it turned out to be only a temporary fix.

On the 23rd of February, 1837, John Brace got up as normal and ate his breakfast with the rest of the family. A short time later one of the servant girls went down into the cellar and saw John Brace kneeling down in a very strange and odd position. As she approached him, through the dimly lit space, she shockingly realised he was hanging suspended from a thin rope attached to the door casing. There was a desperate and frantic attempt to revive him, but despite their best efforts it was too late, he was beyond all help.

At the Coroner's inquest the jury returned a verdict of suicide during a period of insanity. John Brace was buried in Bath Street cemetery, until his grave was exhumed by the local authority in 1959, when the graveyard was cleared. [53] [54] [55]

11. A Conniving Couple of Conmen - June 1837

On the 20th of June, 1837, Robert Parker an elderly gentleman farmer was strolling alone along the main road on his way to Walsall, blissfully unaware that two well versed conmen and confidence tricksters, had singled him out to be their vulnerable and elderly victim. As twenty-four year old Peter Wilson approached Robert Parker he pretended to find a purse lying in the road. Inside was a gold chain and two seals, which Wilson said they could share as joint finders. Just then as if by magic, thirty-eight year old Ambrose Martin walked towards them. Wilson told Robert Parker that the man coming towards them was the brother of Thomas Dutton a well known and established watchmaker with a shop in Walsall High Street, but that was a lie. Wilson asked

Martin what the items might be worth and he told them about fourteen pounds. Robert Parker believed that Martin knew what he was talking about, but it was all a big con the items were worthless. Martin also told Robert Parker that anything found on a road belonged to the finder, another lie. Martin then quietly offered Robert Parker a deal he could not refuse, he said if he could buy Wilson's half share from him, he would give him £18 when they got to Walsall. Robert Parker knew Thomas Dutton's shop, so thought everything would be alright, he fell for the trick and paid Wilson a five pound note and two sovereigns for his share. Having got the money, Wilson went his own way leaving Robert Parker following Martin to Walsall.

When they reached the town, Martin confusingly walked past Mr. Dutton's shop telling Robert Parker that he needed to see a friend at the Turk's Head. At this point he became suspicious, insisting that the deal be settled immediately. To pacify him, Martin gave him two sovereigns as a deposit towards what he was owed. Robert Parker was still five pounds out of pocket and began to smell a rat. When Superintendent Rider entered the Turk's Head, he told him what had occurred and Martin was arrested. It didn't take very long for Police Constable Foxall to find Wilson, who still had the purse in his possession, with a joke hairdresser's one hundred pound note from the Bank of Fashion in it.

Wilson and Martin appeared at Stafford Assizes on Tuesday the 18th of July, 1837, where Superintendent Rider and Constable Foxall both gave evidence. The Judge, Mr. Justice Coleridge pointed out that the circumstances did not constitute a felony as Robert Parker bought and paid for the items under a false representation of their value. He considered that the charge was not made out, so acquitted both men. Wilson and Martin must have thought their luck was in, until the prosecutor Mr. Beadon asked for a new indictment for conspiracy to be drawn up. The Judge consented to this course of action and on Thursday the 20th of July, they both appeared back before him, charged with conspiracy. This time, at the second bite of the cherry they were found guilty the Judge sentenced them to two years imprisonment each.

56 57 58

The old saying that, if it looks too good to be true, it probably is, was as true then as it is today!

12. Wisemore Sheep Rustlers - July 1837

In the 1830s Walsall was still very much a farming area, where a variety of livestock were kept within the town boundaries. Thomas Heath used a field at Wisemore to graze his sheep, tended for by his shepherd, Charles Jordon.

Overnight between the 3rd and 4th of July, 1837, Jordon noticed one of the lambs had gone missing from the field and suspected the animal had been stolen for meat. Jordon made a search and found the lambs entrails a short distance away in the Town Brook, which ran from Hatherton Street towards Darwall Street and eventually to The Bridge. This confirmed Jordon's suspicion that sheep rustlers had been at work stealing the animal for food.

On the 4th of July, John Small visited forty-one year old John Martin who was an acquaintance, at his home. Small became very suspicious when he observed nineteen year old Henry Holden, feasting on freshly cooked lamb, as this wasn't a time when working people could afford best lamb. Small later told Thomas Heath the owner what he had seen, who at once contacted the police. Constables Foxall and Raymond went to Martin's house to make a search for the stolen meat and as they walked in they could smell lamb cooking in the oven. In the cellar they found a leg, a shoulder and a loin of lamb, so Holden, Martin and eighteen year old John Wagster who was also present were arrested. Holden was heard to say to the others, "They may transport us, but they cannot hang us." This was probably a reference to the death penalty being removed for the offence in 1832. Henry Holden and John Wagster were charged with stealing the lamb and Martin, with receiving stolen property.

At Stafford Assizes on Monday the 17th of July, 1837, Holden and Wagster were sentenced to transportation for life and Martin was imprisoned with hard labour for two years. An appeal was set up for

John Wagster, but this eventually ended in failure. Wagster left England on the 7th of November, 1837 on board the 'Moffatt' arriving at Van Diemen's Land, Tasmania on the 1st of April, 1838. Henry Holden never made it, he died at sea aboard the 'Lord Lyndoch' on the 31st of July, 1838, whilst being transported to Australia.

John Martin had been very lucky to escape transportation this time, but his luck ran out on the 2nd of July, 1844, when he was convicted of larceny and sentenced to be transported for a period of ten years. He went to Van Diemen's land on the 'Sir Robert Peel' on the 6th of September, 1844. [59] [60] [61] [62] [63] [64] [65] [66] [67] [68] [69]

13. Lifting the Lichfield Larceners - January 1838

Shady travelling felons often frequented Walsall, where there was a good market to fence their dodgy wares to poor and impoverished buyers looking for a deal. As a consequence Superintendent Rider and his men were constantly on the lookout for shifty strangers drifting in and out of town with bags on their back.

On Saturday the 13th of January, 1838, there was a burglary at a laundry in Beacon Place, Lichfield where the light fingered thieves stole, two pairs of trousers and five shirts belonging to Hugh Woodhouse Acland.

Soon afterwards eighteen year old Frederick Wilshaw and twenty year old Joseph Brookes, two very well known villains in Lichfield started selling shirts around Walsall hostelries. Superintendent Rider and Constable Foxall got to know about it and went out on the hunt. After only a short space of time, they were both spotted and arrested with the stolen property from the burglary in their possession.

As this crime was committed outside the jurisdiction of the Borough, Wilshaw and Brookes were handed over to the authorities at Lichfield. The Mayor of Lichfield committed both men for trial at the ensuing county sessions. The following day, a third man, James Nickson, alias Derry, aged eighteen years was also arrested and he too was committed for trial.

The trial took place on the 20th of February, 1838, before Deputy Recorder J. Jervis at Lichfield. Nickson was charged with the burglary at the laundry and Wilshaw and Brooks with receiving the stolen property. Wilshaw entered a plea of guilty and the other two were found guilty by the jury. Nickson and Wilshaw were sentenced to be transported for seven years and Brookes was imprisoned for one year with hard labour. Neither men ended up being transported, James Nickson was taken to the hulk ship 'Leviathan' at Portsmouth on the 6th of June, 1844, having already served over six years and received a pardon from there on the 1st of July, 1844. Wilshaw was placed on the hulk 'Ganymede' on the 23rd of February, 1838 at Woolwich and received a pardon on the 2nd of August, 1841. [70] [71] [72] [73] [74] [75] [76]

14. The Hue and Cry for Gaol Breaker - March 1838

John Jones, alias Armstrong was a twenty-five year old man, who was arrested on Friday the 2nd of March, 1838 for stealing a wood plane, valued at two shillings from Richard Murray, the cabinet maker in Digbeth. Jones decided that the inside of Walsall gaol was not to his taste or liking and at sometime between three and four o'clock on the afternoon of Sunday the 4th of March, he managed to force one of the iron bars above the entrance. He squeezed through the gap gaining access to the Guildhall, where he simply opened a window and jumped down into the street and ran off towards the general direction of Wednesbury. Although his absence was quickly detected, a thorough search of the area failed to find him, he was well away.

Walsall Police sent out a 'Hue and Cry' a wanted descriptive report in the Police Gazette for the felon in an attempt to trace and locate the absconder from gaol. In September 1838, the Mayor of Walsall received a letter from the Governor of the Southwell House of Correction in Nottinghamshire, saying that John Jones was there serving a two months sentence for being a rogue and vagabond.

Taking no chances on him escaping again, Constable John Raymond was sent to Southwell to gate arrest the man and bring him back to the cells at Walsall. He appeared before the magistrates on Monday the 1st of October, 1838, who committed him to the County Gaol at Stafford.

Jones was tried for larceny and prison break at Walsall Quarter Sessions on Friday the 12th of October, 1838, where luckily for him he was found 'Not Guilty' and released without needing to break out. [77] [78] [79]

15. A Gentleman's Duel at Ryecroft - May 1838

On the evening of Thursday the 10th of May, 1838, two well known and respective Walsall gentlemen, solicitor Mr. William Cotterill and surgeon Dr. Henry Hamblin met to indulge in a game of cards. The gambling got too serious and the two men dramatically fell out, when one of them, challenged the other to a duel at dawn. Whatever happened, the gauntlet being throw down was a fight to the death, so it must have been a grave insult to their honour.

At five o'clock the following morning they met with their seconds in a field at Ryecroft as arranged, ready to vindicate insulted honour. Just as the pistols were about to be drawn, the imposing silhouette of Constable John Raymond was seen arriving on horseback. They all immediately knew who the large man was, everyone in Walsall knew him and his very presence caused them to think again. He was not a man to be trifled with and the proceedings were promptly brought to a swift end.

Constable Raymond had both men hauled up in front of the court, where they were bound over to keep the peace in the sum of one hundred pounds each.

His intervention allowed them both to go on to enjoy successful careers. On the 23rd of November, 1843, Hamblin arrived in Port Louis on the Falkland Islands to become the colonial surgeon at a salary of £300 per annum. He died at sea on his return journey on the 23rd of June, 1864, after twenty-one years on the island.

William Cotterill, whose brother, Charles Foster Cotterill was Mayor of Walsall between 1834-1836, became the Walsall Borough Coroner. He died in 1851, whilst still in office. [80] [81]

16. Picking A Pocket or Two Boys - June 1838

Wombwell's travelling menagerie was a show of exotic animals that came to Walsall on the 4th of June, 1838. The zoological spectacle was not only a sight to behold, it drew in pickpockets who came to Walsall to steal some money. All shows attracted these artful criminals eager to practice their craft, but this time Constable John Raymond would be ready and waiting for them. On this particular day, Constable Raymond observed five Birmingham lads, Joseph Fownes, John Haywood, Richard Hughes, Charles Avery and Joseph Village, dipping their hands into unsuspecting pockets. In return for their crime, they soon felt the hand of the law firmly on their collars.

The five Brummies appeared before the Mayor at Walsall Court on Wednesday the 6th of June, 1838. He sent them all to the Stafford House of Correction for three months each as convicted rogues and vagabonds. [82] [83]

17. Admonished Vagrants - August 1838

At three o'clock in the morning on Tuesday the 29th of August, 1838, Constable John Raymond was alerted to a possible break in taking place at the premises of Mr. T. Chawner in Bridge Street. He immediately made his way there and found four men within the enclosed stable yard. One of the men, Robert Richardson worked for the owner Mr. Chawner and claimed to be providing lodgings for the others that night. The other three were William Jackson, Samuel Guest and William Clarke, but the whole situation about their gathering seemed suspicious. Constable Raymond apprehended all of them under the Vagrancy Act of 1824, for being found on enclosed premises with an unlawful purpose.

They appeared on Wednesday before the Mayor who enquired about the mens previous character. Constable Raymond told them, Clarke had appeared three times previously, convicted once and acquitted twice, Jackson was on bail for stealing a watch, Richardson was of very good character and nothing was known of Guest.

After some deliberation the Bench discharged the prisoners with a severe reprimand and warning about their future conduct. [84]

18. Tri Crooked Tanner's - September 1838

On Saturday the 1st of September, 1838, Patrick Kirby, a thirty-seven year old Irishman from Castlebar, County Mayo, went into the Dolphin Inn, in George Street. In payment for his ale, he passed a fake tanner (sixpence) to the landlord Edmund Denham. Not wishing to miss an opportunity and having apparently got away with it once, Kirby returned to the Dolphin Inn on Wednesday the 5th of September, 1838, where he passed another counterfeit sixpence. This time he certainly didn't have the luck of the Irish on his side, it had run out, because Denham contacted the police.

When the huge figure of Constable John Raymond arrived at the Dolphin, Kirby was arrested and it was found he was responsible for passing a third tanner at a shop in Dudley Street.

Kirby appeared before Walsall Magistrates on Wednesday the 5th of September, 1838, charged with uttering three sixpences and was remanded until the following Monday. At the second court appearance he was committed to Stafford Gaol to await trial.

At Stafford Assizes on the 12th of October, 1838, Kirby was imprisoned for six months, two months for each tanner. Turned out to be an expensive drink after all! [85] [86] [87]

19. An Unvirtuous Bloxwich Wench - May 1839

Elizabeth Edge was a thirty-seven year old Bloxwich mother of twelve, married to Titus Edge an awl blade maker.

On Monday the 6th of May, 1839, Elizabeth Edge went into Birmingham and returned to Walsall later that day by horse drawn coach, that dropped her off at the George Inn. From there Elizabeth decided to walk back to Bloxwich and that's where the saga begins. The road from Walsall to Bloxwich took her past numerous licensed premises, which proved an impossible temptation to resist and she took refreshments at regular intervals.

Her first known watering hole was the White Lion in Green Lane, run by John Norris, where she ate some bread and cheese, helped down with a nice glass of ale. After finishing her snack, Elizabeth walked to the Spread Eagle, owned by Phineas Somerfield, where she partook of a small gin and peppermint. Refuelled and ready to go again she reached her final destination at the King's Arms, kept by Richard Thomas on High Street at Bloxwich. By half past seven that evening, Elizabeth Edge was falling over drunk, drinking and dancing with a man named Charles Welch. The landlady thought her behaviour was disgraceful and improper for a married woman, so turned her out.

What happened outside on that night is anything but clear, but the story has all the hallmarks associated with drunkenness. The accusations that came out of the alcoholic haze are very inconsistent and indiscriminate. What we do know is that on the following Tuesday morning, Titus Edge went to the police station at Bloxwich and reported a crime to Constable William Foxall. He told him that Charles Welch, John Ray and Daniel Wilkes were responsible for raping and assaulting his wife. As a consequence of his complaint all three men were rounded up and charged with the serious crime.

Sometime after the initial report was made the story changed, Ray and Daniels were removed for the indictment and another man, named Charles Bradbury was accused instead. Twenty-two year old Bradbury, was the landlords son from the Spotted Cow at Bloxwich and he now stood charged with ravishing and carnally knowing Elizabeth Edge, while Charles Welch, thirty-two was charged with being an accessory.

Both men appeared at Stafford Assizes on Monday the 22nd of July, 1839. Rape at this time was a capital offence and they could have been sentenced to death and hanged if found guilty. The Judge was Mr. Justice Williams, Mr. Godson appeared for the prosecution and Mr. Lee defended Bradbury and Welch.

The first witness called was Elizabeth Edge, who claimed to have known Bradbury for nine years. She accused Welch of pushing her to the ground allowing Bradbury to jump on top of her where he committed the crime of rape. After the deed was done, Bradbury left the scene and she saw two men, who she thought were Ray and Wilkes laughing at her. She walked as far as Bloxwich Green with Welch, where she accused him of trying to rape her. It was there that she called out "murder" and her husband heard the screams and came to her aid and then Welch ran off.

Mr. Lee for the defence suggested that Elizabeth Edge dropped her case against Ray and Wilkes, only after receiving a payment of two pounds from Ray's mother. He also accused her and Titus Edge of conspiring to frame Bradbury. She denied any conspiracy, but eventually acknowledged to having taking a payment of two pounds from Ray's mother.

Titus Edge was called and described how he saw Welch run off when his wife shouted "murder." He denied being involved in any conspiracy to frame Bradbury, implying that Constable Foxall never asked him about Bradbury, when he first made his complaint.

Constable William Foxall, said that when Titus Edge visited the police station to make the first complaint, he never mentioned Bradbury, either for assault or rape.

Richard Thomas, the landlord of the Kings Arms said that Edge was falling over drunk at quarter past eleven at night and was forcing Welch to dance with her. He knew Bradbury, but he was not at his house that night at all.

Richard Cooper said he was at Bradbury's father's pub the Spotted Cow, with Charles Bradbury all night until after midnight.

Joseph Tuston was at the King's Arms and saw Edge drunk, drinking all night from anyones glass. He did not see Bradbury that night, but saw Edge with Welch.

Charles Pardrill saw at least two men plying Elizabeth Edge with ale at the White Lion earlier in the day.

Two witnesses Isaac Fowler, a Bloxwich awl blade maker and William Radnall a clerk from Norton's at Birchills, both gave evidence about the alleged conspiracy between Titus and Elizabeth Edge. They claimed Titus Edge was in the passage of the Green Dragon in High Street and said to his wife, "You must swear against Charles Welch and Charles Bradbury, right or wrong, or we shall have the expenses to pay."

Three further witnesses, Job Wood, William Tew and John Birch all attended court to alibi Bradbury, placing him at his father's pub at the time in question and they also gave him a good character. Thomas Gripton a miller and John Paddock a farmer both from Cannock together with Phineas Somerfield from the Spread Eagle, all described Charles Bradbury's character as 'unimpeachable.'

The Judge summed up the case, but it only took the jury ten minutes to return a verdict of 'not guilty.' The jury were asked to consider a further offence of attempted rape against Welch, that occurred after Bradbury supposedly left the scene. Mr. Godson the prosecutor, said that under the circumstances he did not intend to offer any evidence in what would be a capital case and both men were released. [88] [89] [90]

20. A Test Case for Burglar's Footwear - May 1839

On the same day as the above case and again at Stafford Assizes, twenty-three year old, William Pritchard and William Jones, who was nineteen appeared charged with a burglary at the home of Thomas Hildick in Goodall Street on the 14th of May, 1839. They were accused of forcibly entering the property and stealing about twenty shillings and other items.

William Foxall, who was then described as Police Superintendent, said he apprehended both suspects in the Wolverhampton area and that a shoe print found at the scene of the crime matched one of the suspects footwear. Mr. Keating who addressed the jury on behalf of the prisoners, questioned the reliability of such evidence and this resulted in their acquittals. [91] [92]

It is fair to say that crime scene investigation was very much in its infancy.

21. Irish Blarney and Seduction - October 1839

In a sleepy little village called Sawley in Derbyshire, lived a labourer named Edward Turner and his wife. To make ends meet, they took in a twenty-six year old Irish lodger named Daniel Rook (alias Anthony Luke), who worked on the railways.

When Edward Turner returned home from work on Saturday the 26th of October, 1839, he found the house empty, his wife was gone together with two sovereigns, three gowns, a flannel petticoat and various other articles. The mystified Edward Turner made some of his own enquiries and it soon became apparent that his wife was having an affair with the lodger. He was told that they may have gone to Walsall together, so on the Monday morning he travelled to the town and spoke to Constable William Foxall. From the description Turner gave, Foxall put out the usual alerts to trace them.

That night, Daniel Rook booked into the lodging house of Ann Price in Rushall, where he claimed Mrs. Turner was his wife. Ann Price had seen Rook before and thought he was single, but he told her that he had recently got married. They stayed together at Mrs. Price's that night, but the next day Foxall found out and picked up their trail. Two miles from Walsall on the road to Stafford, Constable Foxall caught them up. Rook had some of the items reported stolen by Mr. Turner in the bundle he was carrying.

The case was heard at Derby Court on Thursday the 31st of December, 1839. Rook conducted his own defence in a rich Irish brogue, insisting that it was Mrs. Turner who inveigled him away not the other way around. He denied stealing anything at all from Turner, claiming it was his own wife who took the items. His manner and delivery caused fits of laughter in court and he called Edward Moore and several other Irishmen as witnesses. Despite his tomfoolery, it did not impress the jury, they found him guilty and the Judge sentenced him to four months imprisonment. [93] [94]

22. Life for the Lamb Thieves - November 1839

Sheep rustling was a serious problem around the Walsall area in 1839. The police received numerous complaints about animals going missing, but they made little headway to identify or capture the main culprits.

Richard Moore Fletcher from the George Hotel on The Bridge owned a flock of sheep, which he kept in his field off the Birmingham Road. On the evening of Thursday the 21st of November, 1839, John Meers, his shepherd counted the herd of sixteen sheep and everything was correct. On the following morning, Meers found one of the flock was missing and discovered that the offenders had made a gap in the hedge leaving footprints and traces of blood.

Superintendent William Foxall and Constable John Raymond were eager to follow up any leads to track down the sheep rustlers as soon as possible. At about nine o'clock that morning, their enquiries took them to the aptly named John Lamb's house in Freeth's Yard, just off the High Street. They searched the house and found a small piece of mutton thrown in the coal hole and a sheep's head behind the door. From information they received, they moved on to another house in Lower Rushall Street, where they found Thomas Cattell, Mary his wife and another man Richard Yates casually eating mutton chops. Lo and behold, they found a left hind quarter of mutton hanging in their pantry. Cattell was put in handcuffs, but in an attempt to save his own skin, he disclosed that a man named George Slater was currently on his way to Wolverhampton to sell the rest of the animal.

George Slater was a notorious local villain, who had evaded the law for years. If they could catch him, it would be considered a feather in the cap of any lawman. Foxall and Raymond commandeered a cart and went off in hot pursuit of Slater. He was spotted just the other side of

Willenhall, where the officers brought him to a stop. Sure enough in a basket on his cart, there was a leg, a shoulder, a loin and a breast of mutton all from a recently killed lamb.

Back at Walsall, Foxall and Raymond removed the shoes of Slater and Yates and returned to the scene of the crime. As if by magic their footwear exactly matched the footprints left in the mud and blood, near to the gap in the hedge. Foxall had tried and failed to use footprint evidence previously (story 20), but he was determined to try again. In a pool near to the field, Foxall found the lambs hide, weighted down in the water by two large stones. Two local butchers, Cornelius Stanton and Samuel Manley, were prepared to say that the hide recovered, belonged to the mutton found in the possession of the prisoners. Foxall and Raymond believed they had finally smashed the sheep rustling crime team, bringing their nefarious activities to an end once and for all. Within one and a half hours of the complaint being made, all suspects had been arrested and the remains of the animal recovered. That's what you can call a good bust in policing terms.

George Slater had a infamous reputation as a thief, extending over thirty-five years, which created a great deal of interest in the case when it came to court on the morning of Monday the 25th of November, 1839. A large crowd from all around the area gathered outside the Guildhall hoping to see him in person. At the hearing before the Mayor, the sagacity of the police officers in apprehending the gang was highly praised. George Slater, Thomas Cattell, Richard Yates, John Lamb and Mary Lamb were all committed for trial at the Assizes.

When the case came to trial at Stafford Assizes on Tuesday the 10th of March, 1840, fifty-eight year old George Slater and twenty year old Richard Yates, were both charged with stealing the lamb. Thomas Cattell, who was twenty-seven and John Lamb, who was forty-four, were charged with dishonestly receiving stolen property. The case against Mary Lamb had been discharged.

The evidence in the case was given and then the Judge said he thought the evidence against John Lamb was very thin. After a short deliberation the Jury found Slater, Yates, and Cattell guilty and acquitted Lamb.

Both Slater and Cattell had previous convictions and the Judge reminded them that until recently, they could have been sent to the scaffold for such a crime. As that option had been removed, he told them not to expect any mercy from the court. Both men were sentenced to transportation for the term of their natural lives and Yates was told he would be transported for a term of fifteen years.

Needless to say there was little chance of them ever bothering the sheep or shepherds of Walsall again.

On the 13th of April, 1840, Slater and Yates were placed aboard the 'Warrior' and Cattell went onto the 'Justicia' hulk moored at Woolwich.

Slater sailed on the 'Eden' on the 8th of July, 1840 and arrived in Australia on the 18th of November, 1840. He did not receive a pardon until he reached the age of 74 years on the 19th of February, 1852.

Yates sailed on the 'Duncan' on the 10th of December, 1840 and arrived in Van Diemen's Land on the 18th of April, 1841.

Cattell sailed on the 'Lady Raffles' on the 30th of November, 1840 and arrived at Van Diemen's Land on 17th of March, 1841.

As they say in the trade, the criminal has to be lucky every time, the police only have to be lucky once. [95] [96] [97] [98] [99] [100] [101]

23. Bloxwich Breakers Win Five Bob Trip - November 1839

At half-past five on the morning of Saturday the 23rd of November, 1839, John Reynolds a labourer living in Bloxwich, left his home to do the milking. While he was away at work, two men Joseph Broadhurst, twenty years and John Willis, nineteen years broke into his house. Inside the premises they forced open a cupboard and stole a wallet containing about five bob in copper.

Edward Boddeley, who was Reynold's neighbour knew Broadhurst and Willis. He saw them both near the house on their knees, dividing up some money and then discarding the wallet which belonged to Mr.

Reynolds. Boddeley reported what he had seen to Superintendent Foxall, who quickly arrested them both.

Joseph Broadhurst and John Willis, appeared at Stafford Assizes charged with housebreaking, on Thursday the 12th of March, 1840.

Willis brought two alibi witnesses to court, Phoebe Jasper, his mother's servant and a washerwoman named Ann Minors.

After the Judge's summing up, the jury only needed a short time to find them both guilty. The Judge expressed his complete contempt for Willis, who brought two false alibi witnesses in an attempt to defeat justice. He also noted that Broadhurst and Willis both had some previous minor convictions recorded against them. Burglary was considered a very serious offence at this time and the Judge sentenced them both be transported to Australia for a period of twelve years each.

On the 8th of July, 1840, Joseph Broadhurst sailed on the 'Eden' and arrived at Australia on the 18th of November, 1840.

On the 13th of April, 1840 John Willis was placed on the 'Warrior' hulk at Chatham to await transportation. He boarded the 'Lady Raffles' on the 30th of November, 1840 and arrived at Van Diemen's Land on the 17th of March, 1841. Irrespective of sentence, it was very rare that anyone ever returned from Australia, so for five bob, both of them had a one way ticket to the other side of the world! [102] [103] [104] [105] [106] [107]

24. Sleight of Hand, Costs Liberty for Life - November 1839

Thomas Clements was a plasterer by trade who lived with his wife Sarah in Garden Walk. Clements received a five pound note from the South Staffordshire and Walsall Bank in payment for some plastering work he did for a lady named Ann Brewer.

On the 2nd of November, 1839, Sarah Clements needed some change, so she took the five pound note to the butchers shop and asked thirty year old James Gregory if he could help. He said he hadn't got the change himself, but if she gave him the note, he would ask another shop keeper for her. He then slipped out the back and disappeared for a short time. When he came back, he said he couldn't get it changed, but underhandedly switched the genuine note for a forged five pound note from the Bank of England. Sarah Clements instantly noticed the note had been changed and asked for her own note back. James Gregory denied all knowledge, and said he didn't know what she was talking about and must be mistaken. She informed her husband about what had happened and they realised the note was a forgery. Thomas Clements went to sort the matter out with Gregory, but he refused to make any concessions. Unhappy at being ripped off, Thomas Clements took the note to Police Constable John Raymond for his help. Constable Raymond took one look at the forgery and went around to the butchers, where accepting no nonsense he took Gregory into his custody. In the cells at Walsall, Constable Raymond overheard Gregory telling someone that the note came from a man named Tom Butler.

It soon became clear that the police had the right man. Mrs. Brookes reported Gregory for passing her a forged note after he killed a pig for her on the 29th of October, 1839. George Rowley who worked at the New Inn in Park Street, found another forged note in the toilets after Gregory had visited.

Gregory appeared at the Stafford Assizes on the 10th of March, 1840, for uttering a forged five pound Bank of England note to Sarah Clements.

Joshua Freeman from the Bank of England, proved that all three of the notes connected to Gregory were counterfeit and were all made from the same printing plate with sequential numbers.

The jury found Gregory guilty and the Judge called the case an aggravated one, insofar as Gregory was not a poor man and had the means at his disposal to make an honest living. He reminded Gregory, that this was once a capital offence, where he could have been hung for such behaviour. Although that option was no longer available, Gregory was sentenced to be transported to Australia for the rest of his natural life.

He was taken to the hulk 'Warrior' at Chatham on the 13th of April, 1840, to await transportation. He was collected by the 'Eden' on the 8th of July, 1840 and arrived in Australia on the 18th of November, 1840.

Gregory received a conditional pardon in 1851, on the understanding that he never returned to England from Australia. [108] [109] [110] [111]

25. Two Days In Gaol for Girl of Fifteen - February 1840

William and Moses Eyland were owners of an iron and brass foundry, making spectacle frames for their opticians business. They employed twenty young girls and five men, one of whom was Caroline Archer who was fifteen years old. At some point early in 1840, the Eyland brothers suspected that small amounts of metal and swarf were being pilfered by a member of staff. They notified the police and William Foxall was brought in to investigate. Foxall knew all the dealers in Walsall and on the 14th of February, 1840, he visited the premises of a tinman and brazier William Tulley in George Street, who bought scrap metal and swarf to melt down. Anne Tulley, his daughter, told Foxall that Caroline Archer had been paid seven pence that day for some metal, but she had visited previously as well. Foxall recovered two pounds in weight of brass and swarf, which was later identified by Eyland.

Caroline Archer appeared before Recorder Clarke at the Guildhall Borough Quarter Sessions on the 24th of March, 1840. It must have been a terrifyingly daunting thing for her, but several respectable Walsall people gave her excellent character references. The jury found Archer 'guilty' and was sentenced to two days in the Borough Gaol.

Caroline Archer married in 1845 and had nine children before her death from heart failure on the 20th of March, 1877. At fifty-two she lived a short hard life, but probably has lots of descendants about. [112] [113]

26. Taking Stock - March 1840

There was a scuffle in the market place on Saturday the 29th of February, 1840, between two Walsall butchers, Joseph Cooper and Richard Meeson. It resulted in them both appearing at the Guildhall on 2nd of March, 1840, having been charged by William Foxall with committing a breach of the peace. Cooper, who was twenty-seven from New Street was fined five shillings and costs for being found drunk. His attitude upset the magistrates so much, they told him that if he didn't pay the fine, they would force him to sit in the borough stocks for three hours on market day.

For anyone who is unsure, the stocks were a method of securing someone's head, hands or feet, so that people could throw rotten food or scorn at them, especially on market days. The Walsall stocks were positioned at the foot of St. Matthew's church steps until 1847, when they were repositioned outside the Guildhall. They were rarely used as a means of punishment and finally removed altogether in 1854. [114]

27. Drink Induced Drunken Fit - May 1840

At between four and five o'clock on the afternoon of Sunday the 17th of May, 1840, forty year old Sarah Bradley suffered a fit at her Park Brook home. Her seventeen year old son George Bradley, quickly summoned forty-five year old Mary Peach and her thirty-five year old lodger, Rupert Brindley both neighbours to help.

After Sarah Bradley recovered from her fit, she complained to the police that someone had stolen four half crowns from her pocket while she was indisposed. Police Constable John Raymond spoke to Rupert Brindley the lodger, who alleged that Mary Peach gave him four half crowns for no apparent reason to keep. The coins were handed over and Peach was arrested.

Mary Peach was committed by Walsall magistrates to appear before Borough Quarter Sessions.

When Mary Peach attended court on the 27th of June, 1840, she was defended by Mr. Meteyard. During cross examination, Mr. Meteyard established that Sarah Bradley's alleged fit was totally drink induced. Rupert Brindley, the man who alleged Mary Peach gave him the stolen coins was totally discredited. He admitted to drinking with Sarah Bradley and others on the day in question, where they collectively consumed roughly four quarts of rum. When Mr. Meteyard addressed the jury on behalf of Mary Peach, he pointed out that Brindley was clearly a drunk and unreliable and that other than him there was no evidence against her. The Jury immediately returned a verdict of 'not guilty.' Looks like a case of Yo Ho Ho and a bottle of rum! [115] [116] [117]

28. Silent Victim with Something to Hide? - May 1840

On the night of Saturday the 16th of May, 1840, John Turner walked along High Street and turned into George Street, where he was knocked down to the ground and attacked by three men, who rifled through his pockets. He screamed out "Watch," attracting the attention of Police Constable William Foxall, who was on duty outside the Guildhall. He sprang into action and chased down two of the suspects, James Stringer and Thomas Moore who were arrested.

At court, Turner rather oddly refused to swear that the prisoners were the ones that struck him or attempted to pick his pockets. He was obviously hiding something and his cagey behaviour was not impressing the Bench.

Constable Foxall told the magistrates that on the night, Turner reported being robbed and he recovered two shillings and sixpence in silver and some coppers on the ground where he was. He identified the two suspects in court as the men he saw running away.

The magistrates, decided to 'skin the cat' in a different way and fined them all five shillings each for being drunk, saying if they didn't pay the fine, they would find themselves sitting in the stocks for four hours each. You can only guess what the unsavoury reason was for all the mystery. [118]

29. Kill A Nag to Escape the Nagging - June 1840

Only in Walsall! At just before midnight on Friday the 5th of June, 1840, Police Constable William Foxall was on duty at the police station, when a strange visitor named Samuel Partridge walked in. Partridge who had never been arrested before, asked if he could stay the night in the cells. Foxall found his request very strange and said that they were normally reserved to hold felons. Partridge then admitted he stabbed a horse in a field on the way to see him, so it should be all right. Foxall was quite perplexed by Partridge's behaviour, so asked him if he was being serious or if he was a lunatic. Partridge pulled out a knife, in a none threatening manner and told Foxall that he had used the weapon to stab the beast. There seemed to be no getting rid of the bizarre Partridge, who offered to show Foxall where the horse was. He took him to the poor stricken animal in a field off the Birmingham turnpike. Curious as to why anyone would do such an awful thing, Foxall asked him what the hell was going on. Partridge then told him all about his matrimonial woes and how his awful wife never stopped nagging, so he did it to get locked up to escape her.

The next day the nag belonging to a man named Westley died. Partridge was committed to the Borough Quarter Sessions, but I can find no record of what happened to him after this, but what ever it was it was probably bizarre. [119]

30. Wild Cat Lady Breaker in Little Bloxwich - June 1840

Overnight on Tuesday the 9th of June, 1840, there was a break in at the home of William Peadie at Little Bloxwich. The burglar removed a pane of glass from the back casement window and entered the house during the hours of darkness. The following day when the servant got up, the front door was found open and a bonnet, two silk handkerchiefs, a gown and a pair of female's leather boots had been stolen.

Mr. Peadie had his suspicions about a seventeen year old girl named Elizabeth Bullock, who he had seen loitering about and lived nearby. Peadie informed Police Constable Foxall about his inkling and on the evening of Wednesday the 10th of June, 1840, he went to bring her in for questioning. Although Constable Foxall was a big powerful man, the young Bullock girl was no pushover and he ended up having a considerable violent struggle with the little wild cat, before he made the arrest.

Bullock appeared at the Guildhall on Friday the 12th of June, 1840, where she was committed to the Borough Sessions.

On Saturday the 27th of June, 1840, at the Borough Quarter Sessions, Elizabeth Bullock pleaded guilty. The prosecutor recommended her to the mercy of the court, as the girl was of previous good character. Bullock received the merciful sentence for her housebreaking of being imprisoned in the House of Correction for three calendar months with hard labour. [120] [121] [122]

31. The Unlucky 7 Till Snatch - June 1840

On Tuesday the 16th of June, 1840, thirty-six year old Joseph Reynolds, entered Mary Barker's provision shop and asked Catherine Unett the young shop girl, for some bacon. He told Catherine the story that he was on his way to Sheffield from Birmingham and was in a hurry. The bacon slicer was upstairs, so she ran to slice the meat for him, momentarily leaving him alone in the shop. While she was distracted upstairs doing the bacon, Mrs. Barker thought she heard someone at the till. Reynolds was given the bobs worth of sliced bacon and he handed over half a crown in payment, receiving one shilling and sixpence in change.

Mary Barker was concerned about what she heard and decided to check the till, which had fourteen shillings in the drawer prior to Reynolds going into the shop. She found eight shillings were missing, one of them cleverly stamped on the head by Mrs. Barker with a figure seven.

Constable Foxall was given Reynolds description and caught him, before he had chance to leave town. He was searched and in his pocket was the distinctive shilling with the number '7' on it. He was arrested and appeared before court the next day.

The Magistrates committed Reynolds for trial at the next Borough Quarter Sessions, where he appeared on the 27th of June, 1840, before the Recorder, N. R. Clarke. He was found guilty and imprisoned in the

House of Correction for three months. This time there was nobody to 'save his bacon.' [123] [124]

32. Six Months 'Bird' for Fowl Play - September 1840

John Baker was the landlord of the Green Man at 38, George Street, where in addition to selling beer, he also kept chickens in his rear yard. In the early hours of Saturday the 19th of September, 1840, a night watchman named George Bullock, saw two suspicious looking characters carrying a bundle under their arm in the shadows. Concerned that something was amiss, he got word to Superintendent Raymond. It wasn't too long afterwards that enquiries led the police to a house in Temple Street, where they found twenty year old William Whitehouse and twenty-one year old Benjamin Faultless. Whitehouse had two warm freshly dispatched fowls in his pocket. Both men were taken into custody and later John Baker identified the fowls, as two of the four stolen from his yard that night.

Whitehouse and Faultless were both found guilty at the Walsall Borough Quarter Sessions on the 15th of October, 1840 and imprisoned for six calendar months each with hard labour, the last week to be served in solitary confinement. [125] [126]

33. Flight of the Harden Duck Snatcher - November 1840

Between eight and nine o'clock on Monday the 16th of November, 1840, Constable William Foxall was on his way back to Bloxwich, when he saw a very suspicious character on the opposite side of the road. Never one to miss an opportunity to check things out, he crossed over to get a better look at the mystery man. Immediately the dodgy man began to run away, dropping a duck from under his coat. Foxall caught up with him and recognised the person as a notorious crook named Lunn. A considerable violent struggle took place, where Lunn managed to wriggle free and run away, abandoning a sack full of nine fowls stolen from Mr. Carrington at Harden. Despite great efforts made to find him, Lunn disappeared without trace from the area, no doubt not fancying his chances with Foxall if they ever met again. [127]

34. More Tea Vicar? - February 1841

Constable William Foxall could spot a wrong'un from a mile away and very few ever evaded his attention. At about eleven o'clock on the morning of Sunday the 14th of February, 1841, Foxall saw a stranger walking the road to Bloxwich carrying a heavy suspicious looking bag on his back. He approached, to find out what his business was in the area and instantly got a feeling that something was wrong. The thirty-eight year old man Samuel Garner, was very nervous and when asked a few simple questions, he became very evasive and changed his story several times. Unhappy with his general demeanour, Foxall decided to search his heavy bag. He found that it contained, eight two pound and three one pound packets of the finest tea available. This was no ordinary load for a man in Bloxwich to be carrying, so Foxall asked him how he came by the tea. Garner originally said he found it, but then came up with the elaborate story that he was delivering it to two men in Rugeley. Garner was apprehended and placed into the cells, while Foxall rode to Rugeley to check out the spurious story. Making all the necessary enquiries, Foxall found that not surprisingly, the men did not exist.

On Monday the 15th of February, 1841, it was discovered that the tea was stolen from the cargo of a narrow boat moored on the cut at Wolverhampton. The barge belonging to Pickford and Co., arrived at Wolverhampton captained by Thomas Herrick on Friday, the 29th of January, 1841, with a cargo from London. On the Saturday, whilst moored at Wolverhampton, someone entered the hold and forced open a chest and stole twenty-two pounds of hand packed tea. The beverage sent from the company of Antrobus, of 446, West Strand, London was destined for the Reverend G. R. Downward at Whitchurch.

The Wolverhampton Magistrates committed Garner for trial and he appeared at the Staffordshire County Sessions on Tuesday the 9th of

March, 1841. James Craddock from the firm of Antrobus in London identified the tea, saying that he personally hand packed it. Samuel Garner was inevitably found guilty and sentenced to be transported to Australia for fourteen years. William Foxall was given five pounds for his vigilance in apprehending the prisoner.

Garner left England on the ship 'David Clarke' on the 3rd of June, 1841 and landed in Van Diemen's Land on the 4th of October, 1841. It didn't turn out to be quite the tea party he was expecting after all. [128] [129] [130] [131] [132] [133]

35. Severity and Mercy - August 1841

Superintendent John Raymond had two cases at the Walsall Quarter Sessions held on the 3rd August, 1841.

The first involved thirty-seven year old John Taylor, charged with stabbing John Shaw at Walsall on Saturday the 13th of February, 1841. He was initially granted bail by the magistrates, but failed to appear and they issued a warrant for his arrest. John Raymond found him drinking in a pub on the Birmingham Road and he was arrested.

Skipping bail annoyed the Recorder at court and he told Taylor he would be given the most severe punishment possible, as they needed to bring the number of stabbings down in the town. Taylor was sentenced to be transported for ten years.

On the 3rd of September, 1841, Taylor was taken to the 'Warrior' hulk at Woolwich and sailed on the 'Duchess of Northumberland' on the 1st of October, 1842 reaching Van Diemen's land on the 18th of January, 1843. [134] [135] [136]

The second case involved John Raymond being assaulted by thirty-eight year old John Potts, while in the execution of his duty. Potts pleaded guilty and was given six months imprisonment with hard labour. John Raymond made a compassionate plea to the Recorder to exercise some mercy and as a result his sentence was reduced to three months. [137]

36. Tracking Down the Gailey Lee Burglars - August 1841

At three o'clock on the morning of Friday the 6th of August, 1841, four travelling burglars broke in Thomas Storer's farmhouse at Gailey Lee, Penkridge. The quartet of criminals responsible were, Richard Mincher, twenty-one from Kinver, Henry Shirley, thirty-five from Penkridge, William Walker, seventeen and Joseph Blackham, nineteen, both from Wolverhampton. They broke a window and stole a large quantity of clothing, before making off towards Walsall.

At seven o'clock that morning, a witness spotted four dodgy characters loitering on the canal near Bloxwich flour mill at Pratt's Bridge about a mile from Walsall. They were conspicuously in the process of dividing up three large bundles of clothing between themselves. Realising they had been spotted they hastily packed up and made off towards Walsall town centre.

Constable William Foxall at Bloxwich was informed of the mens furtive activities, so he saddled up his horse and galloped towards Walsall. This was no ordinary blue light run, he was a man with a mission to find the villains. He rode at speed into Ablewell Street, where he caught sight of the four tearaways. The vision of the mounted lawman charging in, struck fear into their veins, they dropped their swag and star burst to get away. Members of the general public were so impressed, they eagerly helped Foxall to round up the scattering villains before they got away. By eight o'clock that morning they were all languishing in the cells at Walsall gaol. The property they abandoned was all subsequently identified as coming from the burglary at Thomas Storer's farmhouse in Gailey Lee.

Constable Tuft from Wolverhampton knew William Walker and Joseph Blackham very well and identified them both from their previous court appearances.

When they appeared at the magistrates court, Constable Foxall was highly commended for his enthusiasm in pursuing and capturing the prisoners so speedily.

All four men appeared at the Stafford Assizes on Tuesday the 19th of October, 1841, where on the clearest of evidence they were all found guilty. Two of them had previous convictions, so it was no surprise when the Judge sentenced them all to be transported for fifteen years each.

On the 6th of December, 1841, they went to the 'Justicia' hulk at Woolwich. The convict ship 'Isabella' picked them up on the 15th of January, 1842 and docked at Van Diemen's land, Tasmania on the 19th of May, 1842. [138] [139] [140] [141] [142]

37. The Murderous Hatherton Burglary - October 1841

On the night of Sunday the 10th of October, 1841, John Lovatt, twenty-six years and John Spencer, twenty-two years, were drinking at William Edgerton's beer house in Great Wyrley. Edgerton knew them both well and he overheard a man named John Whitehouse say to Spencer, "isn't your name John Spencer?" Lovatt replied, "no, he comes from Sheffield, and has been working on the railroad there." He thought this was very strange, but they both left together and walked off towards the general direction of Cannock.

In the dead of night during the early hours of Tuesday the 12th October, 1841, Weston Turner, aged sixty-five years and his wife Mary were asleep in their beds in the Red Lion public house at Hatherton. Weston usually slept with the bedroom door open, because he liked to hear the clock and could listen out for the girls. On this fateful night he was suddenly disturbed by a noise outside his room and called out "what are you girls getting up so soon for?" Unknown to him the parlour window downstairs was open and two dangerous men had entered into his house with evil intent. He got no answer from the girls, but was startled by the sight of a man's hand holding a lit match. He called out "who are you, what do you do there?" A gruff voice replied, "down your bloody eyes. I'll let you know what I want, if you make any resistance I'll blow your bloody brains out."

Weston Turner immediately recognised the voice as that of John Lovatt, who he had known from a child. Turner began to get out of bed, but the light went out and the door burst open. He was suddenly belted over the head with a sharp blow, that cut straight through his night cap. He heard the same threatening voice, "down your bloody eyes, I'll knock your bloody head off." His attacker then called to an accomplice, "Jack, bring up the pistols and balls." From out of the darkness he was struck again on the back of the head, which knocked him down to the floor. As he contemplated getting up, a third blow sent him flying across the floor towards the window. At this point he knew these men might kill him and fearing for his life, he jumped out of the window, falling fifteen feet to the ground below. From his cold and helpless position, he heard his wife shriek, as she was also beaten by the robbers. They stole various articles, including six silver teaspoons and a gun, before finally leaving.

Weston Turner was so badly injured that a surgeon, Thomas Holmes from Cannock was called to examine him. He found two deep lacerated wounds, which had bled profusely completely soaking his bed clothes and bruising the top of his head. He considered the injuries to be very serious, leaving him in a dangerous and precarious state of health. Turner told the police that the man responsible was John Lovatt.

At just after seven o'clock on the morning of the robbery, John Lockley saw both Lovatt and Spencer together at Churchbridge. He noticed that Lovatt was carrying a gun and his pockets looked full.

William Parker a neighbour, followed the offenders muddy footprints from the parlour window for about a mile along the Cannock road. The trail ran cold on the lane that led to Spencer's father's house.

These two sightings obviously suggested that Spencer might be the other suspect the police were looking for.

On Wednesday the 13th of October, 1841, Humphrey Williams saw Lovatt and Spencer, near a bank somewhere between Rushall and Pelsall. After they left, his son, Thomas Williams investigated and found six tablespoons concealed inside a handkerchief.

Lovatt realised he was the prime suspect and went on the run to evade arrest. On the 17th October, 1841, Isaac Webb recognised Lovatt at The Erdington Arms, but he was using the alias of Holland. Lovatt knew he had been rumbled, when Webb asked if he had a brother in the Cannock police, which was true. Lovatt warned Webb not to try capturing him, as he knew there was a ten pound reward on his head. Webb didn't do anything, but told him that Raymond and Foxall from Walsall were searching for him. Lovatt threatened to stab the relentless Foxall if ever he came for him, because he knew he would hunt him by day and by night otherwise. After departing, Webb contacted the police and Lovatt was arrested at a lodging house in Sutton Coldfield by Police Constables Thomas Hutler and John Pearson.

On Wednesday the 20th of October, 1841, Jane Bradbury, a house servant at John Spencer's house, overheard him say to his sister Anne, "I am afraid they are going to take me for the robbery, they suspect me and Jack Lovatt, and I will be dead if I must not be off, or they will hang or transport me, for I've got such a hell of a character." Spencer was later taken prisoner by Constable William Foxall.

On Wednesday the 9th of March, 1842, both men appeared before Mr. Justice Cresswell at the Stafford Assizes.

Lovatt's solicitor, Mr. Yardley claimed the only evidence against him was the recognition of his voice and a conversation with Webb. Spencer's solicitor, Mr. Allen said there was no direct evidence against his client at all, only that they had been seen together before and after the event.

The Judge when summing up reminded the jury that this was a serious capital offence, but they should not shrink from performing their duty. The jury consulted for half an hour in their box, but then retired into their room with a sworn officer and remained there for another hour in consultation. They returned into court finding Lovatt guilty, but without intent to murder and acquitted Spencer. The Judge deferred sentence for a day to make his own review of the evidence, but reminded Lovatt that it was a capital offence carrying the death penalty.

On Thursday the 10th of March, Lovatt came back into court and was asked whether he had anything to say why the death penalty should not be given, to which he said, "I am innocent."

The Judge said, "I have not the least doubt of your guilt, and my impression at first was, that it would have been my painful duty to have passed upon you the awful sentence of death, and left you for execution. But I have most anxiously reconsidered your case, and as the jury negatived that part of the indictment which charged you with an intention to murder, I shall recommend that your life may be spared, and probably that recommendation may be attended to, but it can only be expected on the condition that you be transported for life." He was then sentenced to be transported to Australia for the rest of his natural life. William Foxall received a signed letter of commendation from several local dignitaries in the area around the Red Lion, for his success in apprehending John Spencer and his conduct in the case, including Mr. and Mrs. Hawkes from Norton Hall.

Weston Turner died a couple of weeks after Lovatt was sentenced and was buried at St. Luke's Church, Cannock on the 29th of March, 1842.

John Lovatt was sent to the prison hulk 'Warrior' where he was picked up by the 'Waterloo' on the 20th of May, 1842, destined for Van Diemen's Land. What became of Lovatt will be described in our next story. [143] [144] [145] [146] [147] [148]

38. The Dastardly Delves Bank Murder - December 1841

This dreadful story is a real measure of the state of society and justice in the early 1840s. It graphically illustrates, how low some people were prepared to stoop to get money and how they could expect to be punished if they got caught for outrageous violent crimes.

This villainous and awful act was perpetrated at Delves Bank, a run down near god forsaken neighbourhood comprising of only a few homes. The place could be reached by an old and seldom trod track, between Walsall and the old church at West Bromwich.

Seventy-four year old Matthew Adams, built four small cottages at Delves Bank after he retired, he lived in one and rented out the other three. Adams lived alone, but had a comfortable and respectable life with his own independent income. His cottage was a simple dwelling consisting of one bedroom upstairs and one room downstairs with a rear pantry. The pantry at the back of the house had a low sloping roof, almost down to the ground. [149]

Old man Adams was a family man, his son James ran the Bull's Head public house just a short walk away at Tame Bridge. On the approach to Christmas 1841, there was a family wedding on the horizon, Sarah Adams, James daughter and Matthew's granddaughter was getting married in February. Matthew Adams promised to give his granddaughter a significant wedding present of one hundred pounds to start her married life. How could Adams have known that his kind and generous gesture would have been his downfall. Unfortunately there were men living in the district who would risk everything for the chance of getting £100, which in 1841 was a small fortune (about £12K in 2023). When the size of the gift reached the ears of the wrong kind, it was a recipe for disaster. [150]

One such unscrupulous character was Thomas Boswell, a twenty-one year old awl blade maker, who lived with his mother and stepfather at Town End Bank. [151] Boswell was already off the rails, he committed a burglary at a house in Longdon, Staffordshire on the 24th of November, 1841, with James Wilkes senior and his son, James junior. The stolen property from that burglary ended up in the hands of two Walsall handlers, John and Mary Lingard at Short Acre. The Wilkes family were newcomers to the area, James Wilkes senior was a disgraced former gamekeeper for Lord Hatherton, dismissed for dishonesty and his two sons, James junior, twenty-five and Joseph, seventeen were chips off the old block and involved in poaching.

When Boswell got wind of Matthew Adams £100 he started to look for people to help him steal the money and take a share of the risk. He enlisted the help of the Wilkes brothers, James and Joseph and another man named George Giles a stirrup maker from Fullbrook, who was twenty-one.

On the 28th of November, 1841, Boswell met another disreputable character Joseph Smith from Shaw's Alley in Wolverhampton Lane and asked if he wanted to be in on the robbery. Boswell told him they had "goose pops," meaning pistols and the rest of the gang were set to go. Smith said he had moved away from crime, but if he did change his mind he would meet them at Boswell's.

The night of the job was set for Tuesday the 30th of November, 1841, Smith never showed up, but Boswell, the Wilkes brothers and George Giles were ready. The gang were armed with pistols and ready to 'do for the old man' if he got in their way. On that moonlit evening, Matthew Adams went out socialising at Bell Green, but returned home at about half past ten and retired to bed. The four thieves of the night crept to Adams cottage at Delves Bank in silence, then watched and waited for the dim candle light in his bedroom to go out, before making a move.

About one o'clock on Wednesday morning, still mindful of the neighbours, they began removing tiles from the low pantry roof at the rear of Matthew Adams house. Having gained access to the pantry, they encountered a secure internal door to the main house. Slowly, in the confined space and with only a candle for light they started the process of silently breaking in. They picked away at the door, which proved painstakingly difficult. At one point they heard the old man cough and quickly blew out the candle to avoid being detected. For nearly half an hour they sat still in complete darkness, before they thought it was safe to start again.

At just before two o'clock, Matthew Adams heard a noise and woke up. He got out of bed and armed himself by picking up a pikel, a small forked weapon then began to creep down stairs. He heard a shuffling from the pantry as the burglars realised they had been sussed and began hurriedly climbing back out through the roof. In the panic to get out, Boswell left his loaded pistol on the pantry floor.

Matthew Adams ran to his front door to get a look at the crooks before they fled. As he opened the door, to his surprise he was met by the presence of Joseph Wilkes at the threshold, who had armed himself with a hammer from the pantry. In that split second Wilkes saw the spikes of Matthew Adams pikel in his hand. He was too quick for the old man, lashing out viciously and violently he smashed the hammer down on to the old mans head. Two savage blows rained down in murderous quick succession, with a sickening thudding sound. The impact instantly stupefied Adams who slumped against the door frame totally stunned with his skull cracked open. By the time the others ran around to see what was going on, the game was up as Job and Sarah Rollason from next door had been woken. Sarah looked out of the bedroom window and saw three men coming from the back of Matthew Adams house and a fourth man near the front door, who was wearing a distinctive smock frock.

She shouted, "what are you doing there?" One of them threw a stone up narrowly missing Sarah Rollason who cried out, "Murder" and screamed to her husband, "they are breaking into old granddad's house." They banged the party wall to alert all the other neighbours.

Wilkes shouted, "Come out, or we shall be seen." Hearing the cry of murder, Alexander Brown, a labourer, who lived in one of the other cottages, jumped out of bed and immediately ran down the stairs semi-naked, followed by four other lodgers. Brown climbed through the hole in the pantry roof and found Matthew Adams still leaning against the front door. Blood was streaming profusely down his face from the wicked hammer wounds on his head. Sarah Rollason helped Matthew Adams to a chair in her house, where he flopped down, but he had no idea who his attackers were. Several of the neighbours went off in pursuit of the villains across the fields, but they escaped into the dark.

Job Rollason went immediately to tell his son James Adams, the awful news that his father had nearly been killed. Twenty minutes later James Adams was with his father at the Rollason's cottage and a doctor had been called. Matthew Adams was seriously ill and fading fast, having lost a lot of blood from the head wounds.

James Adams and George Watson, who was one of the lodgers from next door searched the cottage and found the loaded pistol on the pantry floor. Watson withdrew the charge from the weapon to make it safe and gave it back to James Adams.

At about eight o'clock that morning, Samuel Hatherley the baker from Little London arrived with his cart doing his rounds. Hatherley agreed to take the pistol to Superintendent John Raymond and tell him what had happened as soon as he got back to town.

The surgeon Thomas Pitt from Walsall arrived about nine o'clock that morning. Matthew Adams was in a serious life threatening condition, insensible and totally exhausted by the incident. Pitt found two serious contused wounds on the left side of his head, one just above the frontal bone and the other above the ear, both extensively fracturing the skull. The reality was nothing could be done for him and although he lingered for a while, he died at about seven o'clock surrounded by his son, the doctor and Sarah Rollason.

Samuel Hatherley gave the pistol and bullet to Superintendent Raymond at Walsall, where it soon became apparent he was dealing with a murder investigation. Superintendent Raymond was a clever and resourceful officer and he immediately initiated enquiries to gather information from his sources.

Walsall Borough Police force only consisted of four men at the time, Superintendent Raymond and his three constables, Richard Humphries and Thomas Osbourne worked at Walsall and his old friend William Foxall at Bloxwich.

Later that morning, Joseph Smith, the man who never turned up to do the job, bumped into Boswell at the top of Park Street. Boswell told him they had, "cracked the crib" (broke into the house) and "settled the old taw" (killed Adams), but they never got any of the cash. Boswell accused Smith of being fainthearted, but asked him to keep quiet about the matter. There was no keeping it quiet, the word of the terrible murder soon spread around the town and whether it was Smith or someone else, Thomas Boswell's name was given to the superintendent.

On Thursday morning at seven o'clock, Superintendent Raymond went to Boswell's house, posting Constable Humphries at the back to prevent any one escaping. Raymond was let in by Boswell's mother and he saw Boswell cooly coming down the stairs. He showed Boswell the pistol found at the murder scene and asked him if he knew any thing about it. Boswell denied all knowledge and fetched another pistol, saying that this was his gun. Looking for any sign of guilt, Superintendent Raymond told Boswell that old man Adams was murdered at Delves Bank and this pistol was left by the murderer. It was a mind game, where Superintendent Raymond was slowly sinking his investigative teeth into Boswell. Superintendent Raymond was unconvinced by Boswell's denials and he was arrested on suspicion of Matthew Adams murder, then conveyed him to the borough gaol.

That same day, Superintendent Raymond took the pistol to a lock maker and asked him to examine it for clues. It was taken apart revealing that a new main spring had been fitted fairly recently.

The Coroner, Mr. H. Smith commenced an inquest by summoning a jury. Their first duty was to file past the lifeless pale corpse of Matthew Adams, paying particular attention to the three wounds inflicted upon the dead mans head. It was then adjourned for a week, to facilitate a formal post mortem examination and for the police to conduct some outstanding urgent enquires.

Boswell was placed before the county magistrate, Charles Smith Forster from Great Barr Hall, who remanded him in custody, while the police gathered further evidence. Superintendent Raymond carried on with his enquiries very discreetly, hoping to arrest the outstanding offenders, before they had chance to go on the run.

On Friday at Walsall gaol, Boswell asked to speak to Superintendent Raymond. Raymond took the baker Samuel Hatherley, with him to corroborate what was said. Boswell confessed to being one of the four, but grassed up Joseph and James Wilkes laying it on thick that the Wilkes brothers were the violent ones. Boswell gave Superintendent Raymond an accurate description of the Wilkes's, but warned that if he went to their house in Long Acre, he should be very careful, because they wouldn't hesitate to use guns if cornered. Why he decided to confess is unknown, most likely he wanted to minimise his involvement at the expense of the others, either way the net was now closing in.

Earlier that morning, John Pearson from New Street spoke to James Wilkes. Wilkes predicted that Boswell would confess, because it was his pistol left at the murder scene. Wilkes also told Pearson, that it was his brother Joseph, who actually struck the fatal blows which killed Adams.

Thomas Pitt the surgeon conducted the post mortem on behalf of the Coroner that day. He concluded that the two extensive fractures to his head made with a blunt instrument had depressed Matthew Adams brain and caused his death.

Early on the morning of Saturday 4th of December, Superintendent Raymond with two constables, Humphries and Osborne, went to Wilkes's house in Long Acre. Taking no chances, they used the element of surprise to burst through the door, where James Wilkes was sitting by the fire. He was quickly secured in handcuffs and taken to the borough prison.

After regrouping the officers went out again looking for Joseph Wilkes. Old fashioned police work led them to John Lingard's house in Short Acre a known associate. Lingard was a local fence (receiver of stolen property). Joseph Wilkes was taken prisoner with several blood splashes clearly visible on his coat. In his pockets, was a jemmy, a brace and a bunch of skeleton keys, all tools of his housebreaking trade.

Lingard proved the old adage 'there is no honour amongst thieves,' and tried to distance himself from the murder. Lingard said he had spoken to Boswell under the cell door at the gaol and been told "Little Joe," meaning Joseph Wilkes, had murdered Matthew Adams. Lingard also told the superintendent that Joseph Wilkes confessed to the murder when he confronted him, but said he never intended to kill Adams and only struck out when he saw the pikel. He said Joseph Wilkes told him the others were Thomas Boswell, George Giles and James Wilkes. Boswell confirmed the fourth man was Giles when he was asked by Constable Foxall at the borough prison.

On Sunday, Constable Foxall went to George Giles house, but unfortunately it became very confusing when he found out that Giles had an identical twin brother named John. Finding it impossible to work out for sure, who was who, he arrested them both until he could establish which one was which. John, who was less than helpful told Foxall, "I'll be dead if I care."

Constable Osborne returned to Wilkes father's house in Long Acre to conduct a further search. This time he found a distinctive smock frock, like the one described by Sarah Rollason and there was blood down the sleeve. At the borough gaol, James Wilkes admitted the smock frock was his, but said the blood was from a pig he killed.

Boswell was proving to be a real grass, he informed Constable Osborne that Joseph Wilkes struck the killer blows at the front door with George Giles. Boswell put himself at the back of the house with James Wilkes, until he left him to assist his brother incase the old man overpowered him. Conveniently, the rat Boswell seemed determined to put himself the furthest away from what happened, while placing his friends at the mercy of the police. Boswell's Plan A was to blame the others, masking the facts that he set the whole thing up and messed it up by leaving his gun at the scene. Boswell also had a Plan B up his sleeve, that night he scratched away the mortar from the wall of the prison and removed three bricks with an awl blade in an attempt to make his escape. Superintendent Raymond foiled his plan when he discovered what he was up to and had him transferred from the gaol to the station house, where they could keep a closer eye on him.

On Monday morning, Walter Baggott a gun lock filer from Park Street came forward to see Superintendent Raymond. Baggott told him that on Saturday the 13th of November, 1841, a fifteen year old boy named William Johns brought in a pistol for him to repair. He replaced the main spring, but Thomas Boswell collected it and paid the sixpence, not the lad who took it in. William Johns, who was Boswell's stepbrother admitted taking the gun to Baggott for repair.

Matthew Adams was buried at St. Bartholomew's Church, Wednesbury on the 6th of December, 1841. [152]

The Government sometimes provided reward money in high profile murders cases and Superintendent Raymond secured one hundred pounds for information leading to the arrest and conviction of Matthew Adams murderer.

This Reward bill read: -

ONE HUNDRED POUND REWARD
BURGLARY AND MURDER

WHEREAS on the night of Friday, the 30th of November last, the dwelling-house of Matthew Adams, of Delves Bank, in the parish of Wednesbury, in the county of Stafford was feloniously and burglariously broken into and entered by several men, who most violently and barbarously beat and wounded the said Matthew Adams upon the head, with some blunt instrument (supposed to be a Life Preserver) and thereby fractured his skull. He was found insensible, and lingered until the following evening, when he died. The deceased was 74 years of age, at the time of the outrage, the only inmate of the house.

The circumstances of the murder having been represented to the Secretary of State for the Home Department, a reward of ONE HUNDRED POUNDS will be paid by Government to any person who shall give such information and evidence as shall lead to the discovery and conviction of the person or persons concerned in the said Murder. And the Secretary of State will recommend the grant of her Majesty's gracious pardon to an accomplice, not being the person who actually committed the Murder, who shall give such information as shall lead to the same result."

The last part of the reward notice seemed to suggest a way out for Boswell, a pardon from the Queen in return for giving evidence against his friends. Boswell specifically asked Superintendent Raymond for a copy of the printed notice, which he was given on Wednesday the 8th of December, 1841.

The Coroner, Mr. Smith continued the inquest on Thursday the 9th of December, 1841 at the Bull's Head, Tame Bridge. This was the home of James Adams, the deceased son, which may appear cruel, but it was customary to hold inquests at the nearest pub in those days. After the jury were given preliminary details, the inquest was adjourned until Monday 13th of December, 1841. The Coroner took the decision that it would be in everyone's interest to reconvene the inquest at a new venue, instead of adding to James Adams grief. The Coroner made a point of personally thanking Superintendent Raymond and the rest of Walsall police, for their indefatigable endeavours to find the perpetrators and making early arrests.

Later that day, Superintendent Raymond was doing his security checks at the gaol, when Boswell asked to speak to him in private. Constable Humphries was called to corroborate any conversation that took place. Boswell told them he had no intention of suffering for the crime committed by another man, he had read the reward notice and wanted to avail himself of the free pardon on offer, before any of the others had chance to. The unscrupulous snake said he didn't strike the fatal blow, it was Joseph Wilkes who picked up the hammer in Matthew Adams pantry and smashed the old man over the head with it.

The inquest reconvened on Monday 13th of December, at the Red Lion in Wednesbury. Boswell was on the verge of publicly turning in the others and eagerly intimated that he wanted to address the Coroner directly. Boswell was brought forward to speak, but before he could the Coroner sternly cautioned him, reminding him that anything he did say would be taken down in writing and could be used in evidence at any future hearing to satisfy the ends of justice. After this warning Boswell hesitated, then declined to say anything further and was taken back to sit with his codefendants.

The jury, at the conclusion of the evidence returned a verdict of "Wilful Murder" against Joseph Wilkes, as principal in the first degree, and found James Wilkes, Thomas Boswell and George Giles, principals in the second degree. All of the prisoners were committed with the Coroner's warrant to stand trial at the Stafford Assizes.

After the inquest, the four defendants were loaded onto a cart to be returned to Walsall. The escort comprised of Superintendent Raymond, Charlotte Raymond his wife, the two constables Humphries and

Osborne and Samuel Hatherley the baker. It was during this journey that several conversations were noted.

Hatherley overheard a conversation between Joseph Wilkes and Mrs. Raymond, where she said to Joseph Wilkes "How came you to strike the poor old man?" He replied, "I dunna know, I should not have gone there but for one in the cart, but it dunna matter now, it was me that killed him." Hatherley also overheard Joseph Wilkes say that he had thrown the murder weapon into a field when they fled that night.

Superintendent Raymond heard Joseph Wilkes say to someone, "I could not tell whether he was an old'un or a young'un, he jabbed at me with a pikel, but I was too quick for him, and then I struck him." Raymond also heard Joseph Wilkes, say "I flung it into one of the leasows as I went along," talking about the murder weapon.

Charlotte Raymond, said she heard James and Joseph Wilkes, blaming their father's influence for their demise. Joseph Wilkes insinuated to her that Boswell's fine tales had talked him into doing the job. George Giles told Mrs. Raymond that he only sat watching the others from the bank that night, as it was his very first robbery, adding "if you had not come as you did, I should have sold the cow, and been on the road to America before this."

Constable Osborne heard Joseph Wilkes admit to striking the old man and throwing the weapon away into the fields. He heard Mrs. Raymond say, "It was wonder he did not hurt you with the fork," on which Wilkes said, "I was too quick for him."

Constable Humphries heard James Wilkes say, he would have rather broken his neck than gone out that night. Wilkes squarely blamed Boswell for talking him into doing the robbery and for telling him to go round to the front door, where everything went wrong.

The following day, all four defendants were taken to Stafford Gaol to await trial on remand, where they were allocated consecutive prison numbers, 1095, 1096, 1097 and 1098. [153]

On Monday the 1st of January, 1842, a blacksmith named Eli Sheldon who lived near to the deceased house, found a one pound hammer. It was found discarded in the field about one hundred yards from Matthew

Adams cottage and still had traces of blood stained grey hair stuck to it. Sheldon gave the hammer to Superintendent Raymond who showed it to Thomas Pitt the surgeon on the 3rd of January. Pitt believed the hammer was very likely to be the weapon used to cause the fatal injuries.

The trial started before Judge Mr. Justice Cresswell at Stafford Assizes on Wednesday the 9th of March, 1842. The case attracted massive interest from all over the county, especially from Walsall. On the day vast crowds travelled to Stafford and gathered outside the court building hoping to get in. When the doors did open there was a frenzy to get into the courtroom in the hope of securing a place in the public gallery. There was uproar when all the seats were gone and the doors were firmly closed, shutting the unlucky ones out. One man refused entry played up by trying to force his way in, only to be detained and kept in custody all day by orders of the Judge.

Mr. F. V. Lee, assisted by Mr. Whitmore, appeared for the prosecution, Mr. Yardley defended Boswell and Giles, but neither of the Wilkes brothers were defended.

Before the case commenced, Mr. Yardley mounted a legal challenge in respect of Boswell, arguing that his confession was obtained under the misapprehension that he would be eligible for a free pardon and as that didn't happen, his admission should not be allowed. Despite his objections, the Judge ruled the trial must continue.

When it came out during the presentation of the prosecution case, that Boswell had been given a copy of the wanted bill by Superintendent Raymond on the 8th of December, 1841, the Judge ruled that any conversations or admissions made after that date should be struck from the evidence.

After all the witnesses had given their evidence there was a break in proceedings.

Mr. Yardley then addressed the jury for Boswell and Giles. He told them there was little or no direct evidence against Giles, except for an alleged conversation in a cart on the way back from the inquest. He contested that the prosecution had failed to present any evidence at all to show a common purpose of 'resisting to the death,' other than the word of Joseph Smith, who was a compulsive liar and a man of bad character. Yardley's compassionate address to the jury lasted a considerable time.

The Judge then commenced his summing up, expressing he was most anxious for the jury to take great care and attention, as this was a case of the greatest magnitude. He instructed the jury on the relevant points of law in relation to murder. Basically, if they all went out armed with intent to "resist unto the death," it would only take one of them to commit murder, for them all to be found guilty. It was however, for the prosecution to show they were all of the same mind. At the conclusion of his speech, the jury were sent out to deliberate.

After just ten minutes they returned with a guilty verdict against Joseph Wilkes, but they acquitted the other three prisoners of murder.

Joseph Wilkes was asked if he had anything to say, as to why the sentence of death should not be passed, but he remained silent. The Judge then donned his fatal coif and said, "Joseph Wilkes, you have been convicted upon evidence, which could leave no doubt upon the minds of either judge or jury that you are guilty of the heinous crime, for which you have been tried and for which you will have to forfeit your life. Amongst the first laws that man received from God was this, that whoso sheddeth man's blood, by man shall his blood be shed and the institutions of this Country have adopted that law, and you must die. Your earthly trail is over. Prepare for a more fearful tribunal beyond the grave. It only remains for me to pass upon you the awful sentence, of the law, which is, that you be taken to the place from whence you came and from thence to the place of execution and that you be there hanged by the neck until you are dead, that your body be buried within the precincts of the prison and may Almighty God have mercy on your soul!"

Wilkes stared into the courtroom unmoved by the words, the Judge by contrast leaned back in his chair with his head in his hands, evidently feeling the weight of his considerable responsibility. Joseph Wilkes, turned to his friends and said, "I'm to be hung" and weirdly twitched his neck. He then walked away from the bar with an unfaltering step, letting out a peculiar nervous chuckle.

It certainly wasn't the end of the matter for the other three men acquitted of the murder, the Judge ordered them to be brought back to the bar of the Assizes on the following day, to face the charge of burglariously breaking and entering into the house of the said Matthew Adams at Delves Bank, with intent to commit a felony.

The next day, Mr. Lee and Mr. Whitmore, conducted the prosecution, Mr. Yardley appeared for Giles and this time Boswell had decided to conduct his own defence. The same witnesses gave their evidence again, but this time Boswell cross examined them all, including the constables. Boswell was given more than enough rope to hang himself, he came over as cocky and it was clear to everyone present that he was the leader of the group.

At the end of the prosecution and defence speeches, the Judge summed up, reminding the jury that the burden of proof was with the prosecution to show guilt beyond all reasonable doubt. If they had any doubt whatsoever, they must give the defendants the benefit of it, but if there was none, they must find them guilty.

After a very short consultation the jury returned a verdict of guilty against all three prisoners, recommending only Giles for mercy.

The Judge said Boswell was undoubtably the ringleader of the dreadful business. The crime they committed was a frightful offence that resulted in the murder of Matthew Adams. Boswell and James Wilkes would be transported to Australia for the whole term of their natural lives and George Giles would be transported for a term of fifteen years

Mr. Lee made a special request for the Judge to compensate Superintendent Raymond who was five pounds out of pocket as a result of the enquiry. Mr. Justice Cresswell said, he was not aware that he possessed any such power and no payment was ever made.

Boswell and James Wilkes also pleaded guilty to the other burglary at Longdon in Staffordshire, mentioned earlier. James Wilkes senior, was also charged with burglary and John and Mary Lingard appeared for handling stolen property. The Judge decided that there was insufficient evidence to proceed against James Wilkes senior and the two Lingard's and it was pointless to proceed against Boswell and Wilkes, in view of the fact he had already sentenced them to transportation for life.

On the 24th of March, 1842, the prison chaplain the Reverend Buckeridge wrote to the trial judge, begging him to reconsider Joseph Wilkes death sentence, with some mitigating circumstances. Buckeridge described Boswell as the trainer and tutor of thieves, who planned the whole job and dragged the young Joseph Wilkes along with him. He said Joseph Wilkes never intended to kill Matthew Adams and only struck out in self defence, when he saw the pikel. Joseph Wilkes didn't take the hammer to the scene as a weapon, but picked it up while he was there. The letter was countersigned by the Prison Governor Thomas Brutton, four magistrates named, Clarke, Chetwynd, Beech and Keen and the Undersheriff Mr. Hand.

The Judge forwarded the chaplain's letter with a copy of his trial notes to the Home Office for consideration, but Joseph Wilkes was never told about the appeal, so as not to give him unrealistic hope.

It was just as well, Sir. James Graham at the Home Office, wrote to the Judge on the 29th of March, 1842, saying "Having considered all the circumstances of the case which appears to me to be an aggravated one of murder, I am deeply concerned to be under the necessity of informing your Lordship that I can not perceive any sufficient ground to justify me in recommending the prisoner to the mercy of the Crown."

Joseph Wilkes received his last family visit from his mother on Thursday the 31st of March, 1842. His sister did intend to go and see him, but she was overcome by repeated fainting fits. Joseph Wilkes met his heartbroken mother who sobbed throughout in the condemned cell, she uttered in broken sentences, while he remained apparently unmoved never shedding a tear or showing any emotion. When his mother gave him her last kiss as she left, he calmly said, "Good bye mother, good bye."

Joseph Wilkes made a final declaration on Friday the 1st of April, 1842, which he signed with an 'X'. He said he never intended to kill old man Adams and would not have done, if he had known what the outcome was going to be. Later that day there was a 'condemned sermon' held in the prison chapel for prisoners and staff. It was conducted by the Reverend Buckeridge, who preached on a theme of 'Repent and be converted.' The Reverend concluded by saying to Wilkes, "Many a prisoner, has been removed from prison to Paradise, and so may you, if you seek, through the merits of Christ, the pardoning and supporting grace of God."

On the morning of Saturday the 2nd of April, 1842, Wilkes got up at an early hour and was silently engaged in mental prayer when the Under-Sheriff arrived to signal the start of the mournful proceedings. The hangman George 'Throttler' Smith from Rowley Regis, entered the cell to pinion his arms. His final journey began, with the Reverend Buckeridge reading the burial service as they walked to the lodge, where Wilkes shook hands with the Chaplain and the Governor.

Outside of the prison there was some commotion, as the half past seven train from Walsall to Stafford had arrived late at five to eight. Short of time and not wanting to be disappointed, the distinctly rough looking Walsall contingent ran through the town to the public assembly point outside the County Gaol. Most of them turned up to witness the melancholy spectacle, sweaty and out of breath and not a pleasant sight.

Joseph Wilkes calmly ascended the drop, giving a fleeting glance at the crowd below, before the rope was wrapped firmly around his neck. His last view of the world was just before the sack was adjusted over his head. At just a few minutes past eight, after the clock had chimed, the drop fell, leaving Wilkes dangling and dancing at the end of his tight rope. After a handful of grim seconds watching him struggling in vain, Wilkes world closed upon him forever. The macabre show was over, the rope was still and the smelly crowd started to disperse, scurrying away back to the railway station at a much slower pace than they arrived. [154] [155]

On Monday the 28th of March, 1842, Thomas Boswell and James Wilkes were taken to the hulk ship 'Warrior' moored at Chatham dock, where they were joined by George Giles on the 12th of April, 1842. On the 20th of May, 1842, it was time to go, the convict ship 'Waterloo' came alongside the 'Warrior' to collect its cargo of prisoners for the long voyage ahead. The ship was manned by a crew of sailers and a detachment of the 99th Regiment of Foot, including some wives and fourteen children. The 'Waterloo' sailed off into the English Channel on the 1st of June, 1842, destined for Van Diemen's Land on Tasmania.
156

As Joseph Wilkes lay cold in his unmarked prison grave, Thomas Boswell, James Wilkes and George Giles must have thanked their lucky stars they escaped the noose. After all, even though incarcerated the three remaining amigo's were off to start a new chapter of their lives.

At Cape Town the 'Waterloo' sailed into Table Bay to stock up with provisions for the rest of the journey. On the night of the 27th of August, 1842, a terrible storm of biblical proportions whipped up on the Cape Town coast, with loud claps of thunder and bright forks of lightning. The Gods certainly weren't happy on that pitch black night as the rain lashed down in torrents and the winds blew at hurricane speeds.

The troop carrier 'Abercrombie Robinson' got into terrible trouble and was blown perilously towards the shore. Large crowds gathered on the beach to help everyone to get ashore, miraculously without the loss of life, but the ship itself was smashed to pieces, by the fury of the weather.

The 'Waterloo' also drifted precariously close to the breakers, but the crew decided to hold out praying for the weather to pass. The fact was it never did and at about ten o'clock the anchor moorings snapped, when the stress on them proved too great. The vessel was suddenly swept broadside by the waves, smashing it into the breakers, the force of which stripped all three masts from the deck. The beleaguered ship was doomed and in frantic desperation all the hatches were opened to release the prisoners. It was every man for himself, there were no lifeboats and the swim to shore was like taking a dance with the devil. Horrified spectators on the shore watched in dread, as the terrified souls jumped one by one into the raging sea with little hope of getting to land. Haunting screams echoed from the soldiers wives clinging on to their children, as the decks beneath their feet were slowly becoming less tenable.

Almost unbelievably, a shoreline of witnesses watched aghast, as victims vanished beneath the waves only seconds after making the leap. The ghostly screams rang out from the deck for what seemed like an eternity and in almost perfect synchronisation, with the thunder claps and lightning strikes that flashed in the sky. That was until half past eleven, when the ship finally split in two, removing any last hope of life for the petrified women and children. When the two halves of the 'Waterloo' were shredded to matchwood by the immense power of the sea, the last few shrieks were drowned out by the sound of the waves as the occupants fell silent dragged down to a watery grave.

Of the three hundred and thirty men, women and children onboard, two hundred and fifty never set foot on terra firma alive.

Unknown to the Adams family back in Walsall, Karma was restored that night when Thomas Boswell and George Giles visited the eternity of Davy Jones locker. Only James Wilkes survived and he was locked up in Cape Town prison on the 2nd of September. He was eventually delivered to Van Diemen's Land on the 22nd of November, 1842 on the 'Cape Packet.' Wilkes behaviour was classed as very good and he received a conditional pardon on the 7th of February, 1854. [157] [158] [159] [160] [161] [162] [163] [164] [165] [166]

John Lovatt the offender from our previous tale (story 37), was also on the 'Waterloo' and he too went down to a watery grave off the coast of South Africa with his Walsall shipmates.

39. A Long Time for Watch Shop Heist - March 1842

At quarter to eight on the evening of Wednesday the 23rd of March, 1842, Joseph Gent's, watch and clockmaker's shop in the High Street became the target of a daring burglary. The two young offenders, Benjamin Whitehouse (alias Whittle) aged sixteen and John Hodson aged nineteen, smashed the display window, reached inside and removed two gold watches with engine turned gold dials, one plain gold watch, a silver watch and three sets of reading glasses. The smash and grab crime only took a few seconds and then they made off, slipping through an adjoining court and into the next street to avoid the coppers. In their determination to escape they dropped a valuable silver watch from their haul of swag. Such a crime attracted the attention of Superintendent John Rofe of Walsall Borough Police, who quickly managed to apprehend the suspects and recover Mr. Gent's property.

The magistrates went as far as to describe Superintendent Rofe's endeavours as 'indefatigable' to trace the perpetrators and recover the property.

Whitehouse and Hodson appeared at Walsall Quarter Sessions on Friday the 1st of April, 1842, before the Recorder N. R. Clarke. The evidence was plain enough for them both to be found guilty. Whitehouse, although only sixteen already had previous convictions recorded against him and paid the very heavy price of being transported to Australia for ten years. Hodson on the other hand was sentenced to be imprisoned for six months with hard labour.

Whitehouse was dispatched down to the prison hulk 'Justicia' at Woolwich on the 5th of July, 1842. Thomas Oerton, a Walsall Councillor and Justice of the Peace, raised a petition for mercy on the grounds of his young age, but ultimately this failed to get him any reduction in sentence.

On the 4th of October, 1842, the convict ship 'Earl Grey' collected Whitehouse from the 'Justicia' and delivered him to Van Diemen's Land on the 14th of January, 1843. [167] [168] [169] [170] [171] [172] [173]

40. Boney Jack and the Rioters - September 1842

On Wednesday the 31st of August, 1842, there was industrial unrest outside Mr. Dudley's works premises, where some damage and disruption was caused during a riot. The magistrates issued an arrest warrant for the main suspect and on the following day, John Edwards, commonly known by his nickname of 'Boney Jack' was arrested by Constable William Foxall.

That afternoon 'Boney Jack' appeared before the magistrates at the Guildhall, while outside over two hundred disgruntled colliers gathered in his support.

A man named James Fowler, swore he knew 'Boney Jack' very well and claimed he saw him at the scene of the destruction, smashing a wheelbarrow and some tools. Fowler said he also saw 'Boney Jack' throwing stones at Mr. Dudley, while shouting and threatening to cut his "bloody brains out."

Boney Jack called three alibi witnesses, Thomas Andrews, Daniel Baggott and John Hollowood, all who swore he was more than a mile from Mr. Dudley's works at the time of the alleged incident.

The case dragged on for over three hours, where it looked like truth would never be reached. Eventually 'Boney Jack' was discharged by the magistrates, probably to avoid another riot outside the Guildhall. [174]

41. The Burntwood 'Ménage à trois' Murder - November 1843

The quiet little village of Burntwood, near Lichfield was thrown into the national spotlight in late 1843, when it was stunned by the notorious case of the Burntwood Poisoner.

Forty year old, John Westwood, lived in the village and ran his own nail making business from a workshop at the rear of his cottage. Living with him was his forty-two year old wife, Sarah and their seven children. John Westwood married Sarah Parker, at St. Michael's Church, Lichfield on the 22nd of December, 1823 and their children ranged from nineteen down to five years of age. [175]

This whole story revolves around an ungodly 'ménage à trois' between, John Westwood, his wife Sarah and their twenty-seven year old lodger named Samuel Phillips, who had lived with the family for about eight years. For some time leading up to late 1843, rumours and accusations had started to circulate around Burntwood, implying that Sarah was having an extra marital relationship with Samuel Phillips. Everything was becoming extremely toxic as John Westwood got more and more jealous about his wife and their lodger.

On the 19th of October, 1843, Robert Westwood, John's brother was present when they argued about Sarah and Phillips being seen out together. On that occasion Sarah defiantly told her husband, that she would go out with Phillips whenever she felt like it.

On the morning of Thursday the 9th of November, 1843, John Westwood started working with his teenage son Charles, in his workshop as usual. Although John Westwood complained of having a headache and an inexplicable ravenous hunger, he appeared otherwise in good health. Several people who saw him that morning could confirm he seemed fine.

At about twelve o'clock, John went in for dinner with his wife, son and three young daughters. He ate some gruel, prepared by his wife as did the young children. Sarah and Charles had something different altogether. He sat in his chair after dinner and asked one of the young children to fetch him his bible. He read for a short time, but quickly started to look very unwell and was forced to retire to his bed, complaining of feeling really cold and chilly. During the evening he was sick several times, but no doctor was called to see him.

Sometime between eight and nine o'clock that night, the next door neighbour Mary Dawson looked in on him. She saw him earlier in the day when he appeared fine, but now John Westwood was lying on the bed in what appeared to be a dying state. Mary Dawson was so concerned she sent the lodger, Samuel Phillips to fetch his brother Robert Westwood, who lived nearby. Robert arrived at about half past eight, by which time John was speechless and fading fast, but he never rallied and died about ten past nine that night. John Westwood's sudden death was a great shock, had nobody expected the unfortunate man's swift and untimely demise.

The following day, Sarah Westwood went to Lichfield, hoping that the Registrar would give her a death certificate to allow burial, but this was refused due to the circumstances. Sarah returned empty handed, but asked Mary Dawson if she would ask William Stretton, the parish clerk, to issue a certificate for a burial that Sunday. Although it was customary for working class people to bury their dead relatives on a Sunday, this would have meant bypassing the coroners involvement in the death.

In the little communities like Ranter Row, Sarah Westwood's behaviour caused great suspicion amongst her Burntwood neighbours. Gossip and rumour was rife, people were saying that Sarah Westwood murdered her husband by poisoning. The grapevine tittle tattle soon spread to Coroner Thomas Moss Phillips who became aware of the whispers. He was duty bound to determine why an otherwise fit and healthy man died suddenly from unknown causes. Under the suspicious circumstances, Phillips ordered an inquest to commence at the Star Inn, Burntwood Green on Monday the 13th of November, 1843. After the jury were sworn in, the inquest entourage vacated with the Coroner to visit the deceased cottage. The Coroner and jury members shuffled past John Westwood's four day old corpse to complete their morbid duty of inspecting the body. After this was done they returned to the Star Inn where the witness depositions were taken.

Two men named Charles Bailey and Thomas Hall, both confirmed they saw John Westwood in good health and spirits on the morning of the day he died. Both of them suspected Sarah Westwood was having an improper intimacy with Samuel Phillips and alleged she quarrelled with John Westwood about it. Hall said he also lodged with the Westwood's and there was no mention of any illness prior to that fateful day.

Charles Westwood said on the day his father died, they worked together all morning, until they went in for dinner at about twelve o'clock. After dinner, his father became very unwell, but only his mother attended him in the afternoon as no surgeon was called. He recalled that his father was sick a few times in the afternoon, because he saw his mother bring the vomit down to throw it away.

The neighbour Mary Dawson, corroborated Hall's testimony about John Westwood being well earlier in the day. She visited him again later that evening, but by then he was lying uncovered in a darkened room, wearing nothing whatsoever except for his night clothes. She described him as being in a dying state, while his wife was down stairs by the fire.

Samuel Phillips said that he had lodged with the Westwood's for eight years. Phillips believed John Westwood often complained of being ill and to his knowledge the couple were on good terms with each other. He knew nothing about them ever quarrelling about him, but he had heard the rumour that the deceased was poisoned. On the day John Westwood died, Phillips stated he was at work until quite late and when he returned, Mary Dawson asked him to fetch Robert Westwood, his brother. Not long after they got back to the cottage, John Westwood was dead.

The Coroner adjourned the inquest after this initial evidence was given, to enable the police to make further enquiries and for a post mortem examination to take place on the body.

The inquest recommenced at the Star Inn on Monday the 20th of November, 1843.

Robert Westwood, said his brother John was definitely jealous of Samuel Phillips and he knew for certain they sometimes quarrelled about it.

The next witness was tiny ten year old Eliza Westwood, daughter of the deceased. The Coroner satisfied himself that the young girl was intelligent enough to understand the nature of an oath, before asking any questions. Eliza said that her father was quite well when he came in for dinner on the day he died. She recalled hearing her father ask, "What's this that's white like flour in my gruel?" Her mother replied, "I don't know," but she did not see anything like that in her own, or her sister's food. Eliza Westwood said she normally did the washing up, but on that day her mother did it instead. Her father went to bed after dinner and by four o'clock he was very sick as she saw her mother bringing vomit down stairs to throw it away.

Lichfield surgeon Charles Allen Chavasse from Bore Street, said he conducted the mortem examination on Tuesday the 14th of November, 1843. He found the body of the deceased was a healthy specimen, still in a perfect state of preservation and with no external bruises or marks of violence. When he looked at his stomach however, he became very suspicious as there were obvious signs of severe and recent inflammation. In amongst the contents of the stomach, he discovered some small grains, which he removed and subjected to six separate tests in the presence of Dr. Rowley. The analysis performed on the samples, all proved the presence of arsenic, strongly indicating foul play. He estimated there was between a quarter and a half an ounce of arsenic present, which was a significant quantity, sufficient enough to have acted quickly on the nervous system to produce narcotic coldness. Charles Allen Chavasse concluded that the only possible way that amount of arsenic poison could have entered the deceased stomach was by ingestion and there was no doubt it caused his death.

Mary Dawson was recalled in relation to when Sarah Westwood asked her to visit Mr. Stretton, the parish clerk and talk him into granting her a certificate. Mary Dawson said Sarah Westwood seemed anxious and agitated about the possibility of an inquest delaying matters by a week, because she wanted the burial as soon as possible.

Sarah Westwood was present throughout the proceedings and at the end was asked if she wished to say anything about what had been said. She made a long and rambling statement, which was reduced into writing and signed by her.

While the Coroner summed up the evidence, Sarah Westwood was taken into another room. The jury only required a few minutes of deliberation to return a verdict of 'Wilful murder' against her. She was brought back into the room and informed of the decision, but remained remarkably unmoved saying merely, "I'm innocent, but I reckon, sir, you'll take bail." She was sadly mistaken, bail was not an option for a suspected murderess and she was committed for trial at the Stafford Assizes. [176]

Listening intensely to the proceedings was John Raymond, who had recently transferred from Walsall Borough Police to join the County Police Force as an inspector at Shenstone. In December, 1841, John Raymond's excellent detective work was instrumental in solving the Delves Bank murder (Story 38).

Inspector Raymond was charged with Sarah Westwood's custody after the inquest and her conveyance to Stafford gaol. During the journey to Stafford gaol, Sarah Westwood told Inspector Raymond that it was a shame they could not have given her bail. He replied, "How could you expect it in a case like this? You are charged with poisoning your husband." She replied, "no person could prove I did poison him." Sarah Westwood had unwittingly set Inspector Raymond a challenge, but if anyone could find where the arsenic came from it would be him.

Inspector Raymond told Sarah Westwood in an authoritative and confident way, that it would be his personal duty to find out where she purchased the poison. He recalled that during her rambling to the coroner, she mentioned being in Walsall with a woman named Hannah Mason. This made him highly suspicious and intrigued to find out more, she denied going to any chemist's or druggist's in Walsall and said she had never purchased poison in her life. The challenge given to Inspector Raymond was a mistake on her part and would ultimately lead to her downfall. [177]

Inspector Raymond concentrated his efforts on finding the identity of the woman named Hannah Mason. He soon discovered she was a woman in her seventies, a native of Hammerwich who now lived in Taylors Yard, Hill Street, Walsall. She was what people commonly called a 'wise woman,' someone who mixed up healing potions and treatments for various ailments. These people were unregulated quacks who messed about doing experiments on human guinea pigs and would probably have been considered witches a few years earlier. It is also almost certain that Hannah Mason was the mother of the questionable lodger, Samuel Phillips. Inspector Raymond discovered that Hannah

Mason frequented Henry Heighway's chemist shop in High Street, Walsall, to purchase the ingredients for her healing potions and ointments. More importantly he found out that on Wednesday the 1st of November, 1843, Mason went to Heighway's with another woman to buy the ingredients for what she said was a cure for the 'itch.' She ordered a quarter of a pound of hellebore powder, two pennyworth each of white and red precipitate and some arsenic. On this occasion, Mason mixed the components up in front of Heighway and the other woman paid for them.

The other woman returned to Heighway's chemist shop alone on Wednesday the 8th of November, 1843, the day before John Westwood's death. She asked the shop assistant Francis Richards, for the same ingredients, purchased the week before, but this time separately. Richards refused to supply the arsenic on its own, but she appealed directly to Mr. Heighway on the grounds it was for the 'itch' like before. He agreed to let her have the ingredients, but Francis Richards was told to clearly mark it, 'Arsenic poison.' She had half an ounce, fourpenny worth, the same amount used to kill John Westwood.

Inspector Raymond went to see Hannah Mason and the chilling reality of what happened was revealed, of course the other woman was Sarah Westwood the suspected poisoner. Raymond had cracked the case, all the elements of the crime were present, motive, means and opportunity. Sarah Westwood had underestimated Inspector Raymond he had found the missing final piece of the jigsaw. Hannah Mason was not beyond suspicion herself considering her relationship to Phillips, but despite her advancing years, she would now be obliged to give evidence against Sarah Westwood at the Assizes.

Three days before Christmas, on Friday the 22nd of December, 1843, John Westwood's funeral took place at Christ Church, Burntwood. The poor children had neither parent present, one was in the coffin and the other in a cell at Stafford. They stood in the little churchyard around the grave like orphans, it really was going to be a cold and lonely Christmas. [178] [179]

Sarah Westwood's trial took place at Stafford Assizes on Thursday the 28th of December, 1843, before Judge Baron Rolfe. Sarah Westwood turned up plainly dressed in a cotton shawl and black bonnet and in a low voice at the bar, she pleaded not guilty. She was allowed to sit whilst listening to the proceedings, but was constantly fidgeting and frequently moving a handkerchief up to her face.

Mr. Corbett appeared for the prosecution and Mr. Yardley for the defence. Mr. Corbett briefly outlined the circumstances of the case, before calling in each witness to give evidence in turn. Painfully for Sarah Westwood, many of the witnesses against her were her own children.

The first was Charles Westwood, her seventeen year old son, who said that on the 9th of November, 1843, he was working with his father in the workshop. In the morning he appeared alright, except that he complained of a headache and being famished. They went in for dinner with his mother and young sisters, Eliza, Keziah and Harriet about twelve o'clock. His father had gruel, the same as his sisters followed by some meat and bread. After dinner John Westwood asked the children to fetch him the bible, which he had done for the last two or three days. He went back to work at twelve thirty, but his father did not return with him. At one o'clock, he went to see where his father was, but he had retired to bed ill. At five o'clock his father said he felt cold and chilly and at some point had been sick, because his mother had disposed of the waste at the front of the house. The last time he saw his father alive was with his mother at about nine o'clock, shortly before he died. Charles Westwood told Mr. Yardley that his parents lived on good terms and that he heard his mother ask if she should send for the doctor, but his father refused.

The next witness was ten year old, Eliza Westwood her daughter, who the Judge asked some questions before proceeding, to ensure she knew the difference between telling the truth and lies. Eliza Westwood said she ate gruel the same as her father that her mother made for dinner on the day he died. She did see her mother put some butter and sugar into the mix, but was sure hers did not have the butter in it. She remembered her father asking what the white stuff was, but her mother did not know. Eliza thought her mother took him some more gruel up at tea time, but then threw what was left out at the front of the house.

Mary Dawson saw John Westwood in good health between eleven and twelve o'clock at his workshop. The next time she saw him was sometime between eight and nine o'clock that night, by which time he was in a dying state and couldn't speak. Mary Dawson was present when John Westwood died, but his wife didn't say anything. The next day, Sarah Westwood asked her to get a burial certificate from William Stretton, the parish clerk, to bury him on that coming Sunday. Mary Dawson said it was customary for the working people to bury their dead relatives on a Sunday.

Robert Westwood, John's brother also from Burntwood, said the lodger Phillips asked him to come quick on the day he died. He got to his brothers at about half past eight, but he was unable to speak and died a short time later. He witnessed his brother arguing with his wife about her relationship with Phillip's, most recently on the 19th of October.

William Dawson another Burntwood resident, said he knew both the Westwood's and Phillips their lodger. On the 2nd of November, 1843, he witnessed a fight where John Westwood knocked Phillips to the ground after accusing him of having an affair with his wife. Sarah Westwood was present at the time and she said, she'd rather beg her bread, door to door, than live with her husband.

Charles Dawson, husband of Mary, said he witnessed the couple arguing in a lane near their house during harvest. Sarah Westwood was violent towards her husband and wished him dead.

Chemist assistant Francis Richards, from Mr. Heighway's said he only ever saw Sarah Westwood twice, the first time with Hannah Mason and the second time when she returned alone. The last time he served her with arsenic after permission was given by Mr. Heighway, but he clearly labelled it 'Poison.' Henry Heighway corroborated his assistant Richards evidence.

Hannah Mason 'the wise woman' was called to give evidence and due to her age and infirmity was allowed to sit. Hannah Mason said she had known Sarah Westwood for years when she asked for a cure for the 'itch.' The ingredients for the 'itch' cure were never discussed with Sarah Westwood, she only told her the treatment would cure the rankest outbursts of the contagion. They went to Heighway's chemists together and Sarah Westwood was present when she ordered the ingredients, but they were all mixed up before leaving. Hannah Mason said she wasn't asked to give any evidence at the Coroners inquest.

Mary Westwood the couples elder daughter, said she had not lived with her parents for the last two years, but she knew they lived very uncomfortably with Phillip's being in the house. Many times, she heard her father say he wanted him gone, but her mother said she'd leave if he did. Two weeks ago she visited her mother in prison and asked her outright where she went on the 1st of November. Her mother confessed to visiting Hannah Mason in Walsall, who recommended some poison to cure the 'itch' for herself and her father.

Inspector John Raymond was asked about the conversation on the way to Stafford, where Sarah Westwood categorically denied ever having purchased poison. Mr. Yardley strongly objected to this evidence because his client was never properly cautioned, but this was overruled.

Charles Allen Chavasse, the surgeon who conducted the post mortem, gave evidence of finding the ingested arsenic in the stomach of John Westwood. Mr. Yardley questioned him intensely about how the arsenic could have got into Westwood's system, but he very firmly and positively said it could have only occurred through eating.

The Coroner Thomas Moss Phillips, then read the statement made by Sarah Westwood at the inquest, which concluded with her denying ever having poison at their house.

Mr. Yardley addressed the jury for more than two hours, expressing the vast importance of the verdict, which might consign Sarah Westwood to her grave.

The Judge summed the evidence up for an hour and twenty minutes, during which time he impressed on the jury, that the fate of this unfortunate woman was one of true life and death, completely resting in their hands.

The jury consulted for around a quarter of an hour, before the foreman said, "Guilty, but we recommend her to mercy, my lord." The Judge asked on what grounds they recommended mercy. There was an awkward silence and then the foreman replied, "We wish to recommend her to your mercy, my lord, that is all." When asked again, the foreman confirmed there were no other grounds for their request.

Sarah Westwood was heard to say, "Oh dear, oh dear, I'm innocent!"

The Judge placed on the notorious black cap, before proceeding to pass sentence, "Sarah Westwood, the result of this long investigation has been to satisfy a very attentive jury that you have been guilty of the crime of murder, perpetrated by the foulest means and against him whom it was your duty to protect instead of attack. I can hardly conceive a case of greater aggravation or enormity. In cases of murder perpetrated by violence there are at hand comparatively easy means of detection, but it is only by the advance of science and greater knowledge on scientific subjects that guilt like yours can be investigated, and when investigated and discovered it is pre-eminently that case in which the law is bound to interfere with its severest vengeance. I speak not these words in order to reproach or upbraid you, but in order that, by pointing out to you the extent and enormity of your guilt, I may influence you as far I can to employ the few hours of life which yet remain to you in endeavouring to do all you can in this world to prepare for another. The sentence of the Court upon you is that you be taken from the place from whence you came, from thence to the place of execution, and that you be there hanged by the neck until you be dead, and that your body, when dead, be buried within the precincts of the prison, according the forms of the statute in such case made and provided."

Sarah Westwood, began trembling violently and seemed to be on the verge of a fainting fit, but the Clerk, Mr. Bellamy, asked her if she had anything to say to the judgment that had been made. She starred with the look of imminent speech for what seemed like an eternity, but without a single word coming out of her mouth. Just as those present had given up all expectation and to everyone's amazement, Sarah

Westwood uttered the words "I'm pregnant." No one in the courtroom and especially the Judge was expecting or could have anticipated there would be a literal, 'pregnant pause.'

The Judge ordered the doors of the court to be closed and summoned a Jury of Matrons, from amongst the married women present in the courtroom. He ordered them to retire into the grand jury room with Sarah Westwood to consider what, if any, medical evidence existed to prove her alleged condition.

Three quarters of an hour went by before the Jury of Matrons returned and Sarah Westwood sat back on a chair in the dock, still visibly shaking. The forewoman of the matrons was asked, "is the prisoner with child or not" and she replied, "she is not." Sarah Westwood collapsed and had to be carried unceremoniously down the steps.

It emerged after the trial that Sarah Westwood was born in Chorley, near Burntwood, the daughter of Charles Parker and his wife, Elizabeth. She was a difficult teenager and had an illegitimate child eighteen months prior to her marriage to Westwood. She was estranged from both her parents who had basically washed their hands of her and neither of them took any interest in her court case or visited her in gaol.

On Tuesday the 9th of January, 1844, Hannah Smith, John Westwood's sister, visited Sarah at Stafford gaol in company with a man who claimed to be her husband. The Governor suspected this man was lying about his identity so questioned him, only to find out he was really Samuel Phillips the paramour. He was refused admission and ordered to leave the prison forthwith. Hannah Smith told Sarah Westwood that the ruse to get Phillips into the prison had been sussed and she was very disappointed as it was the last chance to see him.

On the 9th of January, Mr. Hand from the Sheriff's office wrote to the Home Secretary asking for advice about postponing the execution. His dilemma was that Sarah Westwood was having to be carried everywhere around the gaol like an invalid and if the execution took place on time, she would have to be positioned with difficulty on the scaffold to be executed. The reply from Sir. James Graham arrived the following day, to say the Home Secretary could not give any further instructions with regard to the case of Sarah Westwood. This answer was basically saying get on and hang her.

On Thursday the 11th of January, 1844, her son Charles and thirteen year old daughter Harriet visited for the very last time. They had been expecting a last minute reprieve to arrive sparing her life, but this was not to be. Sarah Westwood spoke affectionately about her husband and asked Charles to take care of all his father's belongings. Sarah was apparently convinced that her daughter Mary, was her most bitter enemy, after giving such evidence against her. The visit lasted about an hour and ended with a heartbreaking separation, when Sarah Westwood begged Charles to look after his five year old sibling, which he promised to do.

On Friday, the prison chaplain George Norman conducted the condemned sermon. For an hour and a half during the sacrament of the Lord's supper, Sarah Westwood remained sat in a chair as she continued having fainting fits. Eventually she became insensible and drifted into a state of delirium, wailing for Amy her youngest child to come to her. The chaplain tried to comfort her, but she kept mithering about being innocent of poisoning her husband, right into the late night hours.

She only slept for about three hours during the night and woke up just after six o'clock on the morning of Saturday the 13th of January, 1844. After two cups of tea and some bread and butter, the chaplain arrived, but she was still traumatised by the whole situation and tormented by the impending doom. Sarah Westwood was still adamant about her innocence, but now resigned to her fate. After a brief period of prayer the Under Sheriff arrived with George 'Throttler' Smith in his long white coat the hangman, from Rowley Regis. With her arms pinioned and supported by two prison officers, the procession set off to the drop. She followed the Under Sheriff, the Chaplain and the Governor to the drop, but had to be carried up the steps where she was placed on a stool under the beam. Her last view of the outside world, was to see a huge crowd assembled. The morbid onlookers were served up with a cocktail of ungodly and haunting groans from Sarah

Westwood as she was placed in position on the scaffold. It was relatively rare to see a woman publicly hanged, so this grotesque show attracted numerous curious women amongst the audience. The county police were out in force, keeping order amongst the attendees at the show of final demise. Sarah Westwood was the last woman to be publicly executed in the county town of Stafford and she did not disappoint those looking for a distressing and disturbing spectacle. The almost silent audience listened to the screaming from the stool while hundreds of wide eyes looked up at the figure of Sarah Westwood as George Smith, wearing his distinctive regalia passed the fatal noose of the rope over her head. The cries and groans stopped for a few seconds as she uttered her last words, "It's hard to die for a thing that one's innocent of." Smith pulled the rope tight and while she was still seated, there was a sudden drop followed by a thud, launching the poor woman into eternity. After the regulation time, the body was cut down and taken to be interred in an unmarked grave within the precincts of the prison. [180] [181] [182] [183] [184] [185]

Incidentally, George 'Throttler' Smith, got to publicly dispatch another famous Staffordshire poisoner twelve years later, the notorious, Rugeley or Prince of Poisoners, Doctor William Palmer. He used strychnine to murder his friend John Cook and was found guilty of murder at the Old Bailey. George 'Throttler' Smith and William Palmer pulled an audience of around 30,000 at Stafford on the 14th of June, 1856, for his final show.

42. The Sabbath Day Bloxwich Brawlers - March 1845

Sunday afternoons in 1845, became an excuse to let off steam in Bloxwich, with regular sabbath day drunken street brawls with anyone who fancied it. The Borough Police closely monitored licensed premises and clamped down on landlords who allowed drunkenness, but Bloxwich was on the border. The problem was drinking took place across the Staffordshire boundary where the County force had jurisdiction and things were less strictly controlled. The pubs over the county line were within easy distance, so on Sundays the Bloxwich men crossed the line, in more ways than one and then returned blind drunk to cause trouble.

On Sunday the 30th of March, 1845, Police Constable Jennings was called to attend one such disturbance at Bloxwich. Things were in full swing when he arrived, but he was the only policeman to deal with the large number of men already brawling. When he tried to intervene, a man named John Hawkins pulled out a knife and tried to stab him. Luckily Constable Jennings drew his staff and managed to disarm him by knocking it out of his hand. Despite the knife being gone, a considerable violent struggle took place before Hawkins was finally arrested.

At the Guildhall on Monday the 31st of March, 1845, John Hawkins appeared at court charged with assaulting Constable Jennings. The officer informed the magistrates that this was a regular occurrence in Bloxwich, because the men were getting drunk on the County on a Sunday afternoon, then returning to Bloxwich.

Hawkins was fined three pounds or in default of payment to serve two months with hard labour in the House of Correction.

Superintendent John Rofe from Walsall Borough Police was instructed to communicate on the subject with Mr. Hatton the Staffordshire Chief Constable, to prevent this nuisance coming to the borough in future. [186]

Some would say that this problem continued for several more years and well into the following century, if it stopped at all.

43. The Mayor's Melancholy and Murky End - July 1845

In November, 1844, thirty-seven year old John Hyatt Harvey an attorney by profession was elected as Mayor of Walsall.

In his official capacity, John Harvey was a member of the Watch Committee and attended a meeting at Walsall Guildhall on the evening of Tuesday the 8th of July, 1845, where he appeared both in good spirits and good health. On his way home he decided to dine at the Stork Inn on Bridge Street, where he ate some anchovy toast, swilled down with a glass of ale and a brandy and lemonade chaser, before leaving cheerful and sober at just after nine o'clock.

At a quarter to ten he saw a colleague, Thomas Wilkins near the gate to the pool in Lichfield Street. He told him he would be back shortly and headed off towards the water.

He never returned that evening and at five o'clock on Wednesday morning, two boys saw a neatly stacked pile of clothes near to the waters edge. They were concerned enough to alert a man named Nathaniel Mallam who worked in Lichfield Street. He followed the boys back to the water to investigate and discovered a whole outfit comprising, a hat, a coat, a shirt, a waistcoat, drawers, stockings, boots, a pair of gloves, a gold watch, a black stock and a walking stick. There was no sign of any owner nearby so fearing the worst, Mallam sent for the police. A short time later three constables, Thomas Smith, Charles Welch and Etheridge arrived at the scene. They discovered the shirt had a sewn in laundry label, with the name 'J. H. Harvey,' which they immediately recognised as belonging to the Mayor. Constable Welch took some paper bills, sovereigns, silver, copper and keys from the pockets of the clothes for safekeeping, before going to the Mayor's home to make enquiries. It was bad news for his family when they confirmed that the Mayor had not returned home.

Superintendent John Rofe was appraised of the situation and attended the scene with several drag ropes to supervise the proceedings. The obvious thought was that the Mayor had somehow tragically drowned, whilst taking an evening dip, which he was known to do. Talk of the tragedy soon circulated around the town, resulting in several hundred people making their way to the lake in order to observe the police at work. Victorian society seemed to have a morbid obsession with seeing death, up close and personal. Superintendent Rofe recruited several local men to help find the unfortunate gentleman's body, but their initial efforts were fruitless. As the operation went on, Superintendent Rofe decided to try a different tactic and secured the use of a boat, nine foot long and four foot seven inches wide. With him as the captain, he put together a crew of three volunteers, Thomas Stanton, Edward James Oakley and George Dutton. They rowed out with drag ropes and began to search the water, near to where they thought the body might be. The rope was thrown out several times, but unfortunately the line got tangled in between some weeds and a rock. The men stood up in the boat and began to yank at it as hard as they could, in an attempt to tug the rope free. Their exertion paid off when the rope suddenly broke free, but it took them by complete surprise and causing them to lose balance and fall backwards. The boat became very unstable when it rocked and half filled with water almost to the point of capsizing. Superintendent Rofe did his best to steady the craft, but he realised it was in imminent danger of sinking. He told the crew to sit tight and wait to be rescued and he would swim back to give them all a better chance without his weight. Rofe then jumped out and swam slowly to the bank as the crowds looked on. Regrettably, Thomas Stanton panicked he saw the superintendent make it back and he also decided to jump into the water to save himself. Disastrously his actions caused the boat to rock and capsize, dunking the last two occupants into the water. Edward Oakley couldn't swim and began flailing and splashing in the water, until he frantically grabbed onto George Dutton for dear life, shouting "George, help me." The crowds of people who congregated around the lake watched the spectacle in horror, powerless to help as poor Edward Oakley struggled for his life. Oakley clung onto his crew mate so forcefully that Dutton's head sank under the water. Dutton realised that he was in grave danger of drowning, Oakley was taking him down with him. Believing he was going to die, Dutton forcibly broke free of Oakley's grasp allowing him to come up gasping for air. The unfortunate young Oakley was not so lucky, as the two separated he disappeared to the murky depths of the lake, chilling the mesmerised audience to the bone. Dutton was considerably weakened by the exertion and was desperately trying to get back, when Police Constable Matthew Jennings saw him ailing and jumped into save him and heroically helped drag him to safety. With Dutton safe, Jennings returned to the water in a last ditch attempt to save Oakley, but all was in vain, he was gone.

The lake had now claimed the bodies of two men in as many days and despite continued attempts to recover them throughout the day, it refused to give them back.

On Saturday a diving rig was brought up from London to assist with the search, but by the end of Sunday neither body was found. It seemed clear at this point, that time and the interaction of the sciences would ultimately need to play their part in returning the men to the surface.

On Monday, John Harvey's naked body floated back up to the top. Nathaniel Mallam pulled the lifeless corpse of the mayor from the lake and took it to the Butts Inn, owned by Mr. Sayer. Later the family sent a private hearse to convey the body to the home of Charles Foster Cotterill a member of his family.

The deputy coroner J. G. James opened an inquest that Monday evening. The coroner William Cotterill (see story 15) was unable to act in the matter, as he was a member of the deceased family and a partner at the same firm of solicitors. Several witnesses confirmed that Mr. Harvey frequently swam in the lake on his own. The Town Crier, Henry Wainwright said a fortnight previously, Mr. Harvey had mentioned swimming across the lake, but said he thought he could swim all around the circumference as well. After hearing the evidence, the jury returned a verdict of 'accidentally drowned whilst bathing.'

Searching for the body of Edward Oakley continued until Saturday the 19th of July, 1845, when a man named Stevens managed to succeed where others had failed, in recovering the body using his homemade drag device.

That same evening William Cotterill opened an inquest into his death at the Stork Inn. The jury immediately returned a verdict of accidental death. The foreman of the jury, Mr. Edwards praised the efforts of Superintendent Rofe and thanked him for the mental and physical strength he showed during the whole melancholy occurrence. He mentioned that in his youth, John Rofe had been a merchant seaman and was a clever sailor.

John Hyatt Harvey's funeral took place on Wednesday the 16th of July, 1845. Hundreds turned out to line the route and many town shops stayed closed as a mark of respect. The Walsall magistrates, members of the legal profession and a number of the clergy were present. The muffled bells of St. Matthew's rang as the procession moved off at twelve o'clock from his home in Bradford Street, along the length of Digbeth and up High Street to the church. Police Superintendent Rofe and his constables wore black crape rosettes on their arms as a mark of respect. The funeral service was conducted by the Reverend Sharwood who recited the 21st verse as the coffin was lowered into the vault, which had not been opened for over half a century. There is a memorial on the wall inside the church to the life of John Hyatt Harvey. [187] [188] [189] [190] [191]

44. Discreditable Deceit - August 1847

On the 20th of August, 1847, Superintendent John Rofe was out patrolling the town when he noticed a suspicious young girl of about seventeen years of age carrying bundles in and out of Mrs. Matthew's pawnbrokers in Rushall Street. Due to the strange behaviour he followed her to the Woolpack Inn in High Street, where she met up with a much older man. Superintendent Rofe observed money changing hands between them, so instructed Constable Welch to follow and detain her when she left. The girl walked out again, towards Bridge Street where Constable Welch apprehended her. The Superintendent then made some enquiries at the Woolpack Inn and found out she had stayed the night before. Due to his suspicions, he searched her room and found various items of clothing with labels displaying the names 'Yates' and 'King.'

The girls behaviour became very suspicious, when she gave a false name adding to the mystery and was evasive about her movements, failing to give any consistent or credible account.

Superintendent Rofe decided that he had no choice, but to lay all the facts before the magistrates, to review the evidence against her. At court, a man in his forties named Francis Morgan King from Eastgate Street, Stafford appeared to represent her. He gave her true identity as Sarah Gittins, who he personally employed as a young servant girl. He said the clothing all belonged to him and his wife, whose maiden name was Yates. It then transpired that while his wife was away visiting family, King had seduced Gittins into a night of passion at the Woolpack Inn. Mrs. Barlow, the landlady of the Woolpack was called into court. She confirmed they both stopped the night together, but King had assured her that the girl was his sister and had to stay in his room, because she was afraid to sleep on her own.

King pointed the finger of blame at Superintendent Rofe and complained about his conduct in arresting the girl when no crime had been committed. The magistrates stopped King in his tracks, telling him they thought Superintendent Rofe had acted in a praiseworthy and proper manner. They told King that it was his behaviour that was questionable. The Magistrates decided to release the girl from custody under the circumstances, but described King's behaviour as disgraceful. They said for a man to brazenly put such a young girl at least twenty years younger in a disreputable situation was reprehensible. The couple then left court together to conclude the delicate affair, before the wife got back! [192]

45. The Bilston Bacon Burglars - June 1848

On the early morning of Sunday of the 18th of June, 1848, John Mann's Cleat Hill farmhouse at Lichfield, became the target of a burglary. Stolen during the break in were, four hams, a piece of bacon, some butter, honey, an old snaffle bridle, a new curb bridle, three men's drabbet frocks and a bay mare from the field near the house.

Sergeant Charles Welch at Walsall received some information that a thirty-two year old puddler named John Buffy from Bilston was responsible for the crime. At noon on Monday the 19th of June, 1848, armed only with a name, Sergeant Welch and Constable Joseph Scott travelled to Bilston in an attempt to locate their suspect. After making determined enquiries they acquired Buffy's address and made a search of the premises. Buffy was absent, but they found three hams and the piece of bacon belonging to the farmer. Joseph Whitmore, a forty-five year old miner was arrested for knowingly receiving the stolen property and Buffy was also arrested a short time later.

At the Guildhall on Wednesday the 11th of June, 1848, Superintendent Rofe requested that the prisoners be remanded in custody. He said the crime occurred outside the jurisdiction of Walsall Borough and the County Police would have to collect them.

When the case was heard at Stafford Assizes on the 22nd of July, 1848, John Buffy, George Bentley (26) and Thomas Mitchell (23) were jointly charged with the burglary at the farm and Joseph Whitmore was charged with handling stolen property.

Bentley pleaded guilty to the burglary and it was disclosed during the evidence that Buffy and Whitmore lodged together in Bilston. The jury found them all guilty with the exception of Buffy who was acquitted.

The Judge declared that Whitmore being the handler of stolen goods was the greatest offender as 'one receiver made fifty thieves.' He sentenced Whitmore to fourteen years transportation and Bentley and Mitchell to ten years transportation each.

James Loxdale a barrister of Oxford Street, Bilston wrote to the Secretary of State on the 26th of August, 1848, after being approached by Elizabeth Austin, Whitmore's common-law-wife. She claimed there had been a miscarriage of justice and several people were prepared to stand up for Whitmore. One of the people spoken to was Sergeant Welch, who said he did not think Whitmore knew anything about the burglary itself. The decision of the petition went in Joseph Whitmore's favour, he received a free pardon from the Queen and was set free on the 12th of September, 1848.

Millbank Prison was the holding facility in London for all convicts sentenced to be transported to Australia, where prisoners were kept in solitary confinement and restricted to silence for part of their stay.

George Bentley never went to Australia, he died from asthma at Millbank on the 3rd of January, 1849, which the inquest determined was natural causes.

Mitchell's transportation was delayed for some reason until the 16th of April, 1852. He arrived at Van Diemen's Land on the 'Pestonjee Bomanjee' on the 31st of July, 1852.

As for John Buffy, the man the police originally believed had committed the crime, he died from cholera aged thirty-seven at Bilston on the 20th of August, 1849. [193] [194] [195] [196] [197] [198] [199] [200] [201] [202] [203]

46. *Confidence Tricksters on the Hop - July 1848*

In July 1848, Thomas Morris, his wife, three children and a female servant moved into a respectable property in Lichfield Street. This was the affluent part of town, the Morris's all seemed to be genuinely representative of a typical middle class family. Thomas Morris supposedly traded as a successful hop merchant and the whole family dressed respectably with an air of believable decency. On the face of it everything seemed to be credible and within a fortnight of their arrival, the Morris family had ingratiated themselves with several local traders who offered convenient credit terms in return for their appreciated patronage.

Mr. Brettell the grocer from Lichfield Street supplied three pounds and five shillings worth of goods, while Mr. Amphlett the provision dealer also from Lichfield Street, supplied two pounds worth. Mr. Lynex the butcher from Rushall Street, sent two pound and five shillings worth of lamb. Morris confidently introduced himself to Barrett the foreman of Mrs. Oakley's tailoring firm in Digbeth. He got measured up for a new 'first rate cut' suit and ordered lots of children's clothing, which Barrett was more than happy to supply. Next on the list was Mr. H. Fletcher, a wine and spirits merchant in Ablewell Street, who provided two pounds and ten shillings worth of orders.

It all appeared that the Morris family were big spenders who were making a splash with the local businesses. Morris then took a pair of boots into Mr. Shelley's in High Street for repair and ordered a new waistcoat from Mr. Perkins in the same street, but oddly did not collect either when payment was immediately required. The warning signs were there, something just wasn't right with the Morris family.

The ironmonger, Mr. Oerton in Digbeth was next to receive Morris's custom on Friday the 4th of August, 1848, when he ordered six pounds worth of the very best cutlery. This was a considerable amount of credit and potentially risky for Mr. Oerton who felt uneasy about the transaction. Before he dispatched the goods Oerton decided to seek the advice of Superintendent John Rofe. He listened carefully to the story and 'smelt a rat,' his astute and finely tuned senses suspected the work of a pack of swindlers.

Superintendent Rofe began making immediate enquiries with several local traders to firm up his suspicions and it soon became very apparent that Morris had already racked up considerable debts. Many other traders had been approached in the same way, one for furniture valued at fifteen pounds, but luckily he was just in time to prevent several businesses from making serious losses or even going under.

The Superintendent decided not to delay, at nine o'clock that night he went with two sergeants and a constable straight to Morris's house. Rofe went into the premises and found the only occupant was the woman servant in the back parlour. The Superintendent demanded all the items from Mrs. Oakley's tailors to be brought to him immediately. The servant refused to help until he threatened to empty the entire house, 'sans cérémonie,' which forced the woman to reluctantly produce the goods. The police recovered some of the fraudulently obtained property and left the house intending to return later.

None of the Morris family ever did return to the house in Lichfield Street, the game was up and they vanished from town into thin air. A hue and cry went out describing the suspects involved.

Thomas Morris was in his early to mid forties, about five feet ten inches tall, fair complexion and a full face beard. He was last seen in a dark shooting jacket, black hat and striped fashionable trousers. His wife was about twenty-seven years old with a babe in arms. She was slightly built with a Worcestershire accent and was wearing a crimson shawl and a straw bonnet. The servant had a dark complexion, also about twenty-seven years of age with smallpox pitted skin. One of the children, a little girl was dark skinned aged about seven years and the other a boy aged five who wore trendy apparel. Superintendent Rofe's quick actions brought him into great esteem amongst the town traders, who were spared from some terrible losses. [204]

47. Blue Lane Beer House Burglary - December 1849

Overnight on Wednesday the 12th of December, 1849, the rear door at Henry Gnosill's beer house in Blue Lane was forced open and burglars got away with a substantial haul, a gun, thirty shillings in silver, three pound of tobacco, several hams, five cheeses and various items of clothing.

Twenty year old Henry Russell was the prime suspect as he committed a very similar burglary at the same premises on the 16th of October, 1848, where he received two months imprisonment. His accomplice was believed to be Samuel Smith (alias Humphries), who he had been seen associating with.

On Saturday the 15th of December, 1849, Superintendent Rofe and Sergeant Welch went searching for the suspects and tracked the two villains down to the Malt Shovel public house in Birmingham Road. Russell and Smith saw the officers walk in and decided they were not going quietly, the table went up and they were only arrested after a violent fight, where the sergeant was badly assaulted.

The gun, two cheeses and nearly all the clothing were found at Smith's lodgings and the rest in the house of a man named John Beebee, who said he innocently bought the items in good faith from Henry Russell.

At the Guildhall court, Russell and Smith were committed for trial at the Assizes and both officers were commended for their capture of the prisoners.

They appeared at Stafford Assizes on the 12th of March, 1850, where Smith was found guilty and sentenced to eighteen months imprisonment, but Russell was somehow acquitted.

Within no time at all the bad'n Russell was at it again. On the 15th of June, 1850, he was seen making off with property from a burglary at Ryecroft Hill, Rushall at half past two in the morning. Constable Price, spotted him and another man going across fields. He arrested Russell, but the unknown man managed to get away, after he produced a knife to threaten the officer.

Russell's luck finally ran out when he appeared at Stafford Assizes on the 1st of July, 1850, where he was convicted of the Rushall burglary and transported to Australia for seven years. [205] [206] [207] [208] [209] [210] [211] [212]

48. A Poultry Family Arrangement - December 1849

In late 1849, a Walsall gang of thieves were targeting farmers and residents throughout the area, stealing chickens, ducks and geese. Nothing with feathers seemed to be safe from these relentless villains and the police were bombarded with complaints almost daily. Despite the combined efforts of Walsall Borough and Staffordshire County Police, no significant detections or arrests were made.

In the week before Christmas, things were becoming silly, there was a ready market for a cheap seasonal bird for the festivities and demand was high. On the 16th of December, 1849, John Smith, lost forty-one fowls and a cock from his farm at Norton Canes. Three days later, during the night of the 19th of December, Thomas Forster from Bloxwich Hall had his farm attacked at Black Leas, near Shareshill and lost fourteen fowls and six fat geese. At the second burglary, the resourceful scoundrels had managed to get into his poultry house through the roof, but they hadn't noticed most of the birds had a peculiar marking on their feet.

Everyone knew the offenders lived somewhere in Walsall and Superintendent John Rofe was determined to bring this crime spree to a swift end. Sergeant Welch and Police Constable George Woolley were dispatched to Black Leas Farm, to look for evidence at the crime scene. Although the farm was outside the jurisdiction of Walsall, the officers discovered two distinct sets of footprints and tracked them for six miles back towards Walsall, where the trail went cold in the town.

The officers untiringly visited every nearby house, one by one, determined to get to the bottom of things. Eventually the residents got tired of the police activity and gave the names of twenty-six year old Joseph Tomlinson and Alexander Jameson (alias Henry Smith).

It transpired that both these men were seen in the vicinity of Black Leas Farm on the afternoon of the break in. Tomlinson and Jameson were both arrested in a house at Short Acre, with freshly blooded feathers in their pockets and more significantly wearing footwear that identically matched the prints left at the crime scene.

Superintendent John Rofe discovered that Tomlinson's brother-in-law, a man named William Matthews, had fairly recently opened a small provision shop in Ablewell Street, which unsurprisingly sold fowl and geese. The shop was visited by police officers on Saturday the 22nd of December, 1849. Twenty-four year old Ellen Matthews, William's wife and Tomlinson's sister, did everything she could to prevent the search being made in the absence of her husband, but ultimately the police ended up seizing nearly a hundred head of poultry, consisting fowls, ducks and geese. Some of the birds recovered were between twelve and fourteen pounds in weight each. The distinctive feet from the Black Leas Farm birds were found discarded at the back of the premises.

Twenty-six year old William Matthews was eventually found drinking in the Bull's Head Inn in Rushall Street and he and his wife were taken into custody. Matthews admitted purchasing many of the fowl, including the ones identified as stolen from his wife's brother, Joseph Tomlinson.

All prisoners appeared before the magistrates at Shenstone on Monday, Christmas Eve. Tomlinson and Jameson were committed to Stafford County Quarter Sessions for theft and the prisoner Matthews and his wife, for knowingly receiving feloniously stolen poultry. The court highly commended the work of the officers in bringing the suspects to justice and ending their reign of terror over local farms.

At Stafford Epiphany Quarter Sessions in January, 1850, before Mr. Hill the Black Leas Farm case was heard. Mr. Vaughan prosecuted and Mr. Kettle appeared for the defence. Mr. Kettle said that Mrs. Matthews was not being obstructive during the search, she was merely asking the officers to wait until her husband was present. He also said it was not unusual for a poulterer to have a large amount of stock in the week before Christmas. Defence witnesses were called to give the Matthews family a good character. The hearing lasted almost five hours and at the conclusion the jury remained in consultation for another half an hour. They eventually found the prisoners Jameson and Tomlinson guilty and acquitted the Matthew's couple.

The same four prisoners, were ordered to be brought up again the next morning for trial in the Norton Canes job. In that trial they were all found guilty, Jameson and Tomlinson were sentenced to be imprisoned for twelve months each. The two Matthews were given bail and judgement was deferred. The case against Ellen Matthews was eventually dropped, but on the 1st of July, 1850, William Matthews was sentenced to nine months imprisonment at Stafford Assizes. It turned out not so paltry for the poultry thieves. [213] [214] [215] [216] [217]

49. Highwaymen In Violent Attack - April 1850

Approaching Walsall at night could be a dangerous game if you were travelling alone, especially in the outlying areas. At ten o'clock on the night of Tuesday the 23rd of April, 1850, John Bishop Rutter a saddler from Dudley Port was travelling in the darkness towards Walsall through some fields near Bescot Hall. Suddenly to his complete surprise four unknown bandits jumped out of the shadows and violently attacked him with a life preserver. Rutter was knocked to the ground, where he was beaten senseless about the head and face. As he lay semiconscious and totally defenceless on the ground the bandits rifled through his pockets and stole two half sovereigns, a silk handkerchief and other personal items. A passerby stumbled across him in a dreadful state and covered in blood and took him to a nearby public house for help.

A message was sent to Superintendent Burton of Walsall Borough Police, who soon arrived at Bescot together with Constable James Newman. The officers conducted a comprehensive area search for the ruffians, but they were well gone.

Burton returned to the public house and arranged for the severely injured Rutter to be transported back home in a cart. The following day he was seen by a surgeon named Whittaker, who noted five severe wounds to his scalp, two of them over an inch in length and exposing the bone.

In February, 1851 a man named James Parton was arrested at a public house in Portobello for a burglary in Wolverhampton. Whilst in custody, Parton confessed to robbing Rutter on the proviso he would get a pardon, but implicated John Yates, Thomas Knight and John Hall as his accomplices. Yates, Knight and Hall appeared at Stafford Assizes on the 11th of March, 1851 and were found guilty. Yates who inflicted the injuries was sentenced to death and the other two got twelve months with hard labour. Yates was recommended for mercy and his sentence was commuted to seven years transportation. Yates never went to Australia and was released on licence on the 17th of August, 1854 (see story 58). [218] [219] [220] [221]

50. *Justice for Turnips and Handkerchiefs - September 1850*

Justice in the 1850s could be brutal for those who got caught as these two cases will show. On Monday the 16th of September, 1850, two particular cases were brought before Walsall magistrates, Major James and S. Stephens.

James Whittaker, was a twelve year old boy who was caught stealing turnips from Mr. Carrington's field at Harden. The saying "Spare the rod spoil the child" (which originates from Proverbs 13:24) was certainly adopted with this boy. Whittaker was severely sentenced to a whole month in the Borough gaol and ordered to be whipped.

Our second case that day revolves around the 1850 Walsall Races which was a big social occasion. The main event was the horse racing, but there was also a fair to draw in the crowds from near and far. The races attracted chancers and petty criminals hoping to take advantage of the revellers, while their guard was down. Inevitably the police were on the lookout and Superintendent Burton clocked John Wood, Richard Dawson and William Lake practicing their artful skills as pickpockets at the racecourse fair. Acting as a team they eventually stole a silk handkerchief from the pocket of Mr. G. Gilbert and were arrested.

The magistrates committed them for trial at the Walsall Quarter Sessions in October, where they were found guilty before the Recorder Mr. Clarke and sentenced to twelve months imprisonment each, with hard labour. The magistrates must have thought that crimes involving handkerchiefs were not to be sniffed at! [222] [223] [224]

51. Enlisting Embezzler - September 1850

James Douglas employed William Rae as a travelling salesman, but between the 2nd of September and the 30th of September, 1850, he embezzled ten shillings from him.

Realising his crime would be found out Rae ran to avoid being arrested and enlisted with the 4th Dragoon Guards at Birmingham. Superintendent Burton found out about his plan to escape justice and brought Rae back to Walsall from the Birmingham barracks.

The magistrates committed him to appear at the Borough Quarter Sessions on Thursday the 5th of December, 1850. The ten shillings he nicked earned him a sentence of three months imprisonment for each of the two counts. [225] [226] [227]

52. Crime Cutting Police Cutlass - March 1851

Over the winter and into the spring of 1851, Walsall town centre was plagued by a spate of commercial burglaries. The police suspected a professional gang of villains were at work, but so far had no luck with any arrests. Cheap goods with 'no questions asked' were in great demand, especially amongst the poor people, so there was a ready market waiting for more.

On Wednesday the 19th of March, 1851, Superintendent John Armishaw received some reliable information that there was going to be a burglary at the premises of Joseph Stackhouse's grocery shop in Park Street. Could this be the lucky break the police had been waiting for? The Superintendent decided to stake the premises out, lying in wait with Sergeant James Smith, Constable George Wood and his eldest son Joseph Armishaw, who was nineteen.

At about two o'clock on the morning of Thursday the 20th March, 1851, the information proved right when two notorious characters turned up on plot. Arthur Key, alias George Wood, was a thirty-five year old bricklayer and thirty-two year old Mark Smith, was a locksmith. Using the moonlight to aid their crime, the pair unsuspectingly picked away at the lock on the rear door of the premises in St. Paul's Row. They persisted until eventually the lock was cracked and the door was opened. Almost as soon as they got in, they must have got wind that something was wrong and began to scarper. Unfortunately for them, they were cornered like rats, so like two pesky rodents they produced a bludgeon and life preserver to fight their way to freedom. In the battle to get away, Key was overpowered by Superintendent Armishaw and Sergeant Smith, while Mark Smith made a run for it down the yard. Constable Wood and Joseph Armishaw chased after Smith, with Sergeant Smith following. Mark Smith turned and ran at the sergeant striking him twice with a large staff. Sergeant Smith drew his police cutlass in self defence and delivered a swift blow to Mark Smith's head, knocking him down to the ground. Both men were then taken to the station house, where Mark Smith's wound was dressed by the police surgeon, Mr. Whymper. The police recovered thirty discarded lock picks at Stackhouse's premises and another thirty-seven at Wood's home address.

Key and Smith appeared before the magistrates at the Guildhall on the 31st of March, 1851, charged with assaulting police officers and resisting lawful capture. Magistrates praised the police officers intrepidity in capturing the suspects who they understood to be part of a much bigger band of organised thieves. Key and Smith were committed for trial at the next Borough Quarter Sessions.

While at Stafford gaol awaiting trial, Smith's medical condition gradually deteriorated and on the 17th of April he died from the head injury inflicted by the police cutlass.

Arthur Key was tried at Walsall Quarter Sessions alone, before the Recorder N. Clarke on Thursday the 24th of April, 1851. Key was found guilty of assaulting the officers and sentenced to ten years transportation.

An inquest was opened at Stafford gaol on Saturday the 26th of April, 1851 by Mr. W. Ward the coroner. The surgeon Mr. Hughes had conducted a post mortem and concluded that death was caused by a fractured skull as a result of being struck with the cutlass. The inquest was then adjourned until Friday the 2nd of May, 1851, where the jury returned a verdict of 'justifiable homicide.'

Arthur Key was a nasty piece of work, who had been in court several times for various offences, including assaulting a police officer on the 2nd of July, 1839, where he received four months imprisonment. For some reason, it would appear that Key was not transported, but served his sentence firstly at Millbank Prison in London, before being transferred to Portsmouth. He was released on licence as a 'Ticket of Leave Man' (or on parole) from Portsmouth on the 27th of July, 1855. On the 4th of December, 1857, his licence was revoked when he committed a common assault at Armitage in Staffordshire. For that he was sentenced to another nine months imprisonment and returned to Portsmouth to serve out the rest of his original sentence. [228] [229] [230] [231] [232] [233] [234] [235] [236] [237]

53. Irishmen's 'Mayor of a Mistake' - June 1851

Somewhere between three and four hundred Irishmen gathered in Lower Rushall Street on the evening of Sunday the 8th of June, 1851. By about eight thirty they could be described as a typical rowdy bunch of drunken lower class people, swearing, brawling and creating a general disturbance to residents or anyone else passing by. One of those people verbally abused was the Mayor John Shannon, who was returning from chapel when he was subjected to menacing and annoying behaviour by the mob in the street.

Two police officers, Constables Eggington and Simons found themselves the target of the ruffians riotous conduct very quickly after arriving in the Rushall Street area. Constable Eggington received a vicious blow with a poker to the head and both officers were knocked to the ground where they were kicked and stamped on. Fearing for their lives and grossly outnumbered, the two officers were forced to retreat back to the police station.

Superintendent Armishaw, Sergeant James Smith, and several other officers, bravely returned to the scene. In a battle of brute strength and determination, the men of Walsall Police took nine of the violent drunken Irishmen into custody.

On Monday the 9th June, 1851, the Irishmen appearing before the Mayor at the Guildhall were, John Flanagan, John Cullen, Matthew Conroy, Mark Finnon, John Mannin, John Downing, Dennis Downing, Thomas McCarty and James Welch.

The Mayor said he was tired of the all too common drunken Irish outrages and he intended to deliver the severest of sentences to remind them of the consequences of such behaviour. All men were found guilty and given fines of between twenty and forty shillings. It was very unlikely they could pay and in default they had to serve either twenty-one days, one month, or two months with hard labour. The Mayor said that the police deserved the greatest of praise for their actions on the night.

The moral of the story is, if you are going to get drunk and abuse people in the street, it's best you don't pick on the Mayor, especially if he is the chairman of the Bench. There was a general clampdown on licensed premises, where the laws were enforced rigidly. [238] [239]

54. The Indecent 'Wise Man of Walsall' - March 1852

Thomas Butler the 'Wise Man of Walsall,' was earning a small fortune by making extraordinary mystical claims to be able to foretell the future. His money spinning business was an offence under the Vagrancy Act of 1824, as anyone who professed to be able to see into the future, could be classed as a rogue and vagabond under that law.

Superintendent Armishaw saw through Butler's little scam and was determined to put an end to his undesirable practice of obtaining money from vulnerable punters, taken in by the deception. Superintendent Armishaw enlisted the assistance of a Birmingham Detective named William Manton and together they formulated a plan of action. Detective Manton arranged the services of a Birmingham woman named Apolonia Ford, who was to visit Butler posing as a prospective client and find out exactly what was going on.

With a marked half crown to use in payment, Apolonia Ford visited the 'Wise Man' on Tuesday the 17th of February, 1852. She was taken into to an elaborately decorated parlour with various mystical emblems and symbolic signs decorating the walls. Butler went through his creepy and unnerving performance, while she sat in a high backed chair. At the end of the fortune telling, Apolonia handed over the marked half crown in payment for his services. It was an uncomfortable encounter, with a dubious man, then when she got up to leave he slimily slipped his business card into her hand requesting that she return again soon. Holding on to her hand, he caressed it and insisted on a kiss to finalise the meeting. When she refused, he scarily grabbed her wrist by force and planted a kiss upon her 'nolens volens.' The frightened Apolonia Ford left the lecherous predators lair and immediately told Superintendent Armishaw and Detective Manton what had occurred.

They decided to pay Butler an immediate personal visit, which unfortunately for him he failed to foresee. It was obvious that Butler was making a small fortune from his illicit trade, they found on his person thirty-eight pounds in gold, two pounds in silver, the marked half crown and fourpence in copper. There was a disturbing element of indecency evidently thrown in for his lady clients.

On the 18th of February, 1852, Butler appeared before the magistrates at the Guildhall, charged with being a rogue and vagabond under the Vagrancy Act. He was found guilty and sentenced to three months with hard labour at the County gaol in Stafford. His solicitor, Mr. Wilkinson gave immediate notice of an appeal and Butler was granted bail for fifty pounds with two sureties of twenty-five pounds, all paid that same day.

Superintendent Armishaw formed an instant professional dislike to Butler, so determined to see justice done he took a complaint of indecent assault from Apolonia Ford. Butler was summoned back to the Magistrates Court on the 3rd of March, 1852, for indecent assault. Butler was represented by Mr. G. Edmonds of Birmingham, but this time he was fined five shillings, which he paid immediately.

On Thursday the 8th of April, 1852, Thomas Butler appeared for his appeal at the Walsall Quarter Sessions, before John Leigh. His appeal against conviction was dismissed and his original sentence confirmed, so he was sent forthwith to Stafford Gaol for three months. [240] [241] [242] [243]

55. Return of the Irish Shenanigans - April 1852

All Sunday afternoon on the 18th April, 1852, a large group of Irish men and women were heavily drinking at the Victoria Inn in Lower Rushall Street. This was an all too regular venue for the Irish contingent to flock together and at about six o'clock the inevitable brawling began. The landlady who lost control of her clientele was forced to send for a constable to clear the house.

Police Constable Frazer was the first officer on the scene and bravely made his way into the premises. It was a hopeless situation, John Burn violently struck him over the head with a heavy metal poker as soon as he entered the door. They began violently struggling together, but luckily Constable George Reay arrived to assist. Together they attempted to drag Burn out of the public house, but several other Irishmen surrounded them and before long a crowd of about one hundred made the situation dangerous. Constable Reay was battered to the ground with a weapon and kicked and punched unmercifully, almost to death. His police staff was taken and used to beat Constable Frazer, until it was broken in two. It is near certain that both officers would have been killed, had it not been for the timely arrival of Superintendent Armishaw. He and several other officers waded in determinedly, dispersing the crowd and taking some prisoners.

On Monday the 19th of April, 1852, John Burn, Barney Kelly, Thomas Kelly, Patrick Rosby, Michael Gunning, Thomas Gateley, Patrick Moylet, Martin Boyle and Mary Gunning appeared before the Mayor Henry Highway at the Guildhall. They were charged with riot and assaulting the police officers.

Police Constable Smith said he had been to see Constable Reay that morning, but he was still confined to his bed and so physically disfigured that he could hardly recognise him. The only good news was that the police surgeon now considered that his life was no longer in danger.

Constable Frazer attended as one of the walking wounded, with his head tied up in bandages. All defendants were remanded in custody until the following Wednesday.

When they reappeared, all but one was committed for trial at the Borough Quarter Sessions.

On the 5th of July, 1852, eight of them appeared at the Borough Sessions. John Burn, Patrick Rosby, Barnard Kelly, Michael Gunning, and Thomas Gateley, all received three calendar months each. Anthony Glen, got one days imprisonment, Thomas Kelly was acquitted and Mary Gunning was discharged. [244] [245] [246]

Sadly, Constable Reay who had two years police service was so badly injured that he was forced to resign. This is a grim reminder of the dangers faced by police officers every day they go to work and something that has changed very little with the passing of time.

56. *An Epitome of Misery the Old Pit Murder - May 1853*

This is a very sad and miserable case, highlighting the tragic consequences of extreme poverty and sheer desperation. Unfortunately in the 1850s, there was very little in the way of welfare provision and when you reached rock bottom, it was a very dark and gloomy place to be.

Sarah Baker can only be described as one of life's poor unfortunates, who as a young girl was dragged up from birth in a life of poverty by her mother at Wyrley Bank. Her father was alive, but he had abandoned them both to extreme deprivation, with Sarah scraping out a meagre existence as a pit bank girl.

At the age of twenty-two in 1850, Sarah Baker fell pregnant, but Charles Whitaker the child's father abandoned her, leaving the country to avoid having to support them. He did return the following year, but decided to marry another woman instead of facing his responsibilities for the child. Sarah Baker gave birth to her illegitimate son, Charles Baker in the harsh and austere environment of Brewood workhouse at the end of 1850, almost certainly condemned to a life of extreme poverty, just as her mother had been. At this vital and vulnerable time in her life she was completely alone, without any friends or relations and with no help or support. At the end of her confinement at the workhouse she was chucked out homeless and destitute, but now with a babe in arms. To make things even worse the birth had been a very difficult one medically and now she was suffering from the complications.

Sarah Baker's pauper mother was of no help to her, she after years of poverty slowly descended into complete madness and eventually was admitted to a lunatic asylum out of her mind. Her maternal grandmother was in a similar state and although not in the asylum, by all accounts she should have been.

The only place Sarah Baker could possibly think to go, was to stay with her widowed aunt Rebecca Whitehouse, herself in receipt of the parish allowance back at Wyrley Bank. Rebecca Whitehouse was the widowed wife of Sarah Baker's mother's brother. Out of desperation Rebecca allowed her to stay there with the child. Sarah managed to get some work at Pelsall pit washing brays for a shilling a day. Brays were mules or pit ponies used to move the coal around the colliery. In a world of adversity and with all the odds stacked against her, she somehow managed to keep the child fed and thriving, by daily sacrificing her own food for him. She spent her life short of money, with little food and desperately struggling, but worst of all there was no light at the end of the very dark tunnel.

Inevitably her health began to suffer, the hard work and poor diet made her physically weak and the complications from the birth brought her to her knees. Sarah Baker was plagued by illness with severe bouts of extreme pain, she was tired and fatigued. Eventually at the beginning of 1853, she was physically no longer capable of carrying on and was forced to stop. No work meant no money, she had nothing to fall back on and the crust to survive was gone.

Starving and without a soul in the world to rely on, she was forced to take the child and seek refuse at the workhouse in Walsall. Wyrley Bank was outside the Borough, so they refused to help her, directing the wretched girl to the parish of Brewood, who were supposedly responsible for her welfare. She was now too weak to get to Brewood Workhouse under her own steam, but her aunt sent a message and they sent a cart to pick her up from Wyrley Bank. By the time it arrived, the pain and agony was so intense she appeared on the verge of death.

It took three long months of constant care for her to recover enough to get to her feet. On Thursday the 26th of May, 1853, at the age of twenty-four, Sarah Baker left Brewood Workhouse with her two year old child, having barely recovered from her illness. She only had the clothes on her back, not a penny in her pocket and no roof to shelter under. Desperate for any crumbs of sustenance, she walked like a vagrant with her ragamuffin child visiting anyone who might give her the slightest of help. Trudging along the dirty horse shite filled tracks in all weathers, she went from Bloxwich to Walsall to Hill Top and Wednesbury dragging the little toddler tied on to her apron strings.

Eventually on Thursday the 9th of June, 1853, she returned on the doorstep of her widow aunt, Rebecca Whitehouse at Wyrley Bank, who allowed her to stop for the night due to her sheer desperation. Sarah Baker certainly hadn't fully recovered from her old illness, it had made another appearance and she spent the night sitting up in agony in the kitchen. At eleven o'clock the following morning, she left her aunt's house very unwell with the child, saying she would try to get into the hospital. The reality was Sarah Baker had reached the end of her tether, she was running on empty.

This is where the story turns ugly, the poor girl was starving without the basic support to sustain her own life, let alone the child and her mind and body was failing. Desperate and alone, you can only imagine what thoughts ran through her troubled mind as she lost all hope of better things to come. She wandered off from Wyrley Bank bewildered and probably petrified at what might happen to them both whilst slowly losing the will to live.

Where she spent the night or what they ate doesn't bare thinking about, but at six o'clock on the evening of Sunday the 12th of June, 1853, she visited her aunt Jane Whitehouse at Bloxwich with the child. Sarah Baker told her aunt a story, about how she had visited Mr. Harrison at Norton Hall to ask him for a dispensary ticket for the poor. While she was there, she met a young lady visitor from Derbyshire, who saw her child crying. The lady enquired about her situation and suggested she could adopt the boy, assuring her that the child would be well cared for. Out of desperation and to relieve the child's state of distress she'd agreed to hand him over at ten o'clock in the morning back at Norton Hall. At about nine o'clock, she left her aunts house very low-spirited and met a woman named Caroline Westwood on the main road shortly after. Westwood could see they were destitute, so out of sheer pity gave the child some bread and butter. They walked together for just over a mile until they reached Little Bloxwich Bridge, where Sarah told Caroline Westwood she intended going to see her aunt Mary at Pelsall. They parted company at about half past nine, Sarah Baker continued along the road towards Pelsall.

Sarah Baker's apparent normality was nothing but a sham, the real truth was she had given up and was unable to cope any longer. Out under the stars, she roamed aimlessly along the horse road without any purpose or destination, whilst starved half to death. It never rains but it pours, it started to belt it down and soon they were soaked through, with nowhere to shelter from the storm. This was probably the final straw that broke the camels back, she had finally lost it. Out of her mind and probably totally unaware of where she was, she drifted off the track looking for whatever sanctuary she could find. Instead of finding any safe place to rest darkness descended and she stumbled across an old abandoned worked out mine on Pelsall Wood Common. Rummaging around, she found where random planks of wood had been nailed across the entrance to the old mine shaft. As the rain fell down on her little son's face, despondency overcame her when she spotted a one foot gap in between the planks to the shaft. In that split second of time, she imagined that her son could be spared the cruel death of starvation by seeking salvation of the next world. Charles was asleep, so she carefully pinned the hood up over his face and slowly lowered him into the void. In a breath, she let go and his little body silently plummeted down into the dark, terminating with a thump and a splash, there were no cries his suffering was over. Her only wish was to end it for herself, but the planks were too close even for her emaciated frame to get through. Everything was gone with the exception of her life and she desperately wanted to end that too. Soaking wet Sarah Baker made her way from the scene of heartache, not knowing where on earth she could find refuge.

At about half past twelve in the early hours of Monday the 13th June, 1853, she arrived back up at her aunt Rebecca's house in Wyrley Bank, which was just over three miles from the Pelsall mine shaft. She arrived soaking wet and alone, Rebecca was obviously suspicious and asked where the child was, so she told her the same story about the adoption that she told her other aunt. She stayed that night, but rumours soon began to circulate about the missing child and a neighbour John Pearson from next door, asked her outright if she had killed the child. She told him the same adoption story, adding that she loved the child. She said that she was going to tell Mr. Buck the receiving officer at Cannock and give him all the necessary details. At about one o'clock that afternoon she left her aunts, supposedly intending to see Mr. Buck.

Instead at eight o'clock she turned back up at the home of her aunt, Jane Whitehouse in Bloxwich. She told her aunt that the sleeping child was delivered to the nice lady at Norton Hall as planned at half past ten that morning. She slept at her aunt's house that night, but left at seven o'clock on Tuesday morning.

Later that morning she arrived at Hannah Longmore's house in Ablewell Street, Walsall and told her the story about how the woman at Norton Hall had adopted the child. Sarah Baker was not a good liar, nobody seemed to believe her story and soon Constable Thomas Walters at Bloxwich got wind of the rumours. Due to the gravity of the allegations Constable Walters sought the advice of Superintendent Edward Bilson at Walsall, who made urgent enquiries at Norton Hall. It was quickly ascertained that the whole tale was a fabrication, there was no mystery benefactor who picked up the child. Constable Walters was tasked to commence enquiries to find the whereabouts of Sarah Baker to locate the missing child. He visited the aunt at Bloxwich and another relative at Hill Top without any success, then at about nine o'clock he discovered her at Hannah Longmore's house. Constable Walters informed Sarah Baker that they suspected her of killing her child, but she calmly stuck to the story that the child had been adopted. The constable sensed all was not right and knew this story was false, so he asked her to show him exactly where she met the woman who took the child. She agreed to show him, so they got in the cart and she directed him towards Pelsall. As they travelled together, darkness once again began to fall and the closer they got to the fateful mine her mood visibly changed. Constable Walters asked her once again, if she had killed the child. This time Sarah Baker broke down and began to cry, she realised the game was up and decided to confess, "I have made away with my child, and if you will come with me, I will show you where my child lies, but I hope the Lord will have mercy on me."

The dreadful truth was out, Constable Walters said, "Then I charge you with the wilful murder of your own son."

She replied, "Do you think they'll hang me?"

Sarah Baker led the officer along the main road until she stopped about a mile from Little Bloxwich Bridge. They made their way to the old worked out pit shaft in Fryer's field on Pelsall Wood Common. It was on the Walsall side of the forge, south of the Wyrley and Essington canal. Fryers field is probably a reference to Richard Fryer, a Wolverhampton banker who opened Pelsall Ironworks in 1832, next to the canal. A nearby canal bridge bears his name and he also opened several of the coal pits in the area. When they finally arrived at the old pit head it was dark, but Constable Walters could see a gap between the wooden planks just wide enough to fit a child's body through. Chillingly, Sarah Baker told Constable Walters, that she had pinned the boys frock over his face and then dropped him down the shaft, describing the child's clothing as a blue frock with a white stripe, a straw hat, stockings and shoes. She confessed to killing her baby boy out of sheer desperation, sometime between nine and ten o'clock on Sunday night.

Constable Walters took her to the cells at Walsall and handed her into the charge of Superintendent Bilson. Whilst at Walsall, Sarah Baker made the following statement, "I have been destitute in the world these three weeks. When I made away my baby I intended to make away with myself, but was prevented from doing so by the timber across the pit. I came out of the workhouse three weeks yesterday. I was in the workhouse four months, and I applied to the gentlemen to send me to the infirmary, or to let me leave my baby until I got stout, but they told me I must take out, and work for it myself. I have been destitute. I was from Thursday morning nine o'clock until between one and two on Saturday, when I went to my aunt's, and never had anything. I don't think I have anything further to state."

Sarah Baker was charged with murdering her child based on her own confession, which she made most likely to ease her troubled mind. The police now had the unenviable task of finding and recovering the child's body. On Wednesday the 15th of June, 1853, two miners, Francis Bradbury and Thomas Dale were employed to descend the eighty-one yards deep pit shaft to search for a body. At the bottom, they found a pool of murky water a few feet deep, which after dragging for a short time, gave up the boy's dead body, dressed exactly as the mother had described. Constable Walters took the lifeless wet body of Charles Baker to the Swan Inn at Pelsall.

Later that day Sarah Baker was taken before the borough magistrates and was remanded in custody.

The inquest at the Swan Inn was opened on Friday, before Mr. T. M. Phillip's the coroner. Charles Baker's little body lay in the bar room and was identified by his aunt, Jane Whitehouse. He had a conspicuous and severe wound on his head, together with several other bruises on his body. The main question the coroner wanted answered was if there was anything in the pit shaft, that could have possibly caused such an injury as he fell. After three hours the proceedings were adjourned, for enquiries to be made down the shaft and for a surgeon to complete a post mortem examination on the body.

Francis Bradbury from Catshill, one of the miners who found the body was employed to return down the shaft again, this time looking for any additional evidence relating to the death. He discovered a wooden plank protruding out into the shaft, with an iron pin sticking out and pointing up. He noted that the pin had what looked like human hair and blood stuck to it.

When the inquests resumed the following day the jury returned a verdict of "Wilful Murder" against Sarah Baker and she was committed for trial.

The trial at Stafford Assizes commenced on Thursday the 21st of July, 1853, before Judge Justice Crompton, with Mr. Scotland prosecuting and Mr. Huddleston defending Sarah Baker who pleaded not guilty.

The prosecutor opened the case and advised the jury not to be led away from their duty by any pity or sympathy for the woman. He outlined the prisoners lifestyle and her movements after leaving the workhouse at Brewood.

All of the prosecution witnesses were called in one by one. The first witness was Rebecca Whitehouse, followed by John Pearson the next door neighbour. They both gave evidence about Sarah Baker's adoption story. The next witness was the aunt Jane Whitehouse, who spoke about the visits to her home and then Caroline Westwood related the events of walking with her to Little Bloxwich. Hannah Longmore said Sarah Baker arrived at her house without the child and later a police officer came. Ex-Police Constable Thomas Walters gave evidence about the confession and being led to the disused pit shaft, where the child was found. Francis Bradbury, the miner said he found the body of the child at the bottom of the shaft and noted the iron pin sticking out at an angle with human hair stuck to it. Superintendent Bilson gave evidence of Sarah Baker's detention and confession at the police office. Finally Mr. Scotland read out the statement Sarah Baker made before the Coroner and that concluded the evidence for the prosecution.

Mr. Huddleston addressed the jury for Sarah Baker, pleading that she was a poor creature, who had suffered more worldly trouble than most could ever imagine and deserved some sympathy and compassion for her desperate plight. He asked the jury to consider their own everyday luxuries, family, friends, food and a roof over their head of which she had none. She wandered the earth in wretchedness and misery, starving and helpless. At the age of just seventeen, she was without a father, her mother was insane and her grandmother raving mad. Alone she became pregnant, only to be cast off by the father who married another. Desperately poor and in ill health, she kept the child safe and well for two years, sacrificing everything she had to keep him alive. At the end she was starving, walking the streets by day and by night and now she faced the scaffold. He asked them to consider what could have motivated her to do such a thing, could it be that in a moment of madness she lost her mind and self control. Alone and despondent, she let the child fall to its death, but she had no motive to cause the child any harm. Mr. Huddleston explained that she had reached the brink of a human precipice, with an almost ungovernable impulse of self destruction. The very foundations of her mind were agitated by desperate thoughts, allowing her to lose full possession of reason. On that wet night, Sarah Baker had no friends at her side and no means to support herself. Without a farthing in her pocket Sarah Baker was abandoned in this world, overwhelmed with misery and suffering the heavy weight of the severe complication of disease. Who could say that for a second she did not glimpse some happiness in the next world. In her lowest moment of despair, she had the misfortune of stumbling across the fateful abandoned pit and in a breath the child was gone. If she had also fallen to her death that night, the verdict would have certainly been one of suicide, whilst in a temporary state of insanity. It has been shown that madness did run in the family and had in fact stricken the two previous generations. Mr. Huddleston said that if the jury thought Sarah Baker was insane, it would not mean she would not be let off scot free, she would be confined indefinitely at her Majesty's pleasure. He said that Sarah Baker must to be given the benefit of the slightest doubt about her mental state of mind at the crucial moment.

The Judge summed up, but after only a short period of consultation the jury returned a guilty verdict. For murder the Judge could only administer the sentence prescribed by law, which at that time was death.

The Judge positioned the black cap before he spoke, "Sarah Baker, you have been convicted, and I think most properly, by the jury and their verdict does them credit, of the murder of your child. There can be no doubt that this was intentional act on your part, and also that you were in such a state of mind at the time as to render you responsible for your acts. I think the jury have returned a most proper verdict, and although your case is a very distressing one, it has been proved in such a manner that they would not have done their duty if they had not found a verdict of wilful murder against you. They have deemed it right to repel the argument of your not being in a right state of mind, there being no evidence before them to lead to such a conclusion, and as such defence is dangerous to adopt, the jury have acted properly. They have, however, humanely recommended you to mercy. Yours is a distressing and painful case, and I hope it will be warning to all young people likely to be led away in a moment of weakness by men who will betray them with false promises. It is not in my power to hold out to you any hope, but I shall forward the recommendation of the jury to the proper quarter, and I trust may be attended with success. I can say no more. You must prepare yourself for the worst, and it only remains for me to pass upon you the sentence of the law, namely, that you be taken to the place from whence you came, that you be thence taken to the place of execution, that you be hanged by the neck until you are dead, and that your body be buried within the precincts of the prison. And may the Lord have mercy upon your soul."

Sarah Baker cried bitterly as she listened to those words and had to be removed from the dock in an hysterical state at the end of an almost four hour trial.

The Jury submitted a letter to the Judge, signed by every member asking for mercy. It said Sarah Baker committed the crime at a time of great misery, due to want and distress and while suffering the great pressure of friendlessness and total despondency. All twelve men begged the Judge to recommend her poor soul for mercy as until then she had only shown the greatest kindness and affection for the child. It was signed by them all, Joseph Cartwright, John Townsend, George Dixon, William Reeves, John Benton, Abraham Clarke, John Machin, James Mitchell, George Onions, John Earp, John Roberts and William Dodd.

True to his word, Judge Charles Crompton wrote to Lord Palmerston at the Home Office on the 24th of July, 1853, recommending the prisoner for mercy. He sent Lord Palmerston a copy of his trial notes with the letter signed by the jury asking for mercy. Crompton's letter outlined the terrible circumstances of Sarah Baker's case and her possible state of mind when the crime was committed. He finishes by saying, "I thought it by no means a case in which it would be at all right, that the sentence should be carried out....I quite agree with the jury in their strong recommendations for mercy and that this is a case in which the sentence ought to be commuted to transportation."

Viscount Palmerston reviewed the appeal for mercy based on the pitiable circumstances of her case and on the 28th of July, 1853, he sent a communication to the High Sheriff of Staffordshire, declaring that the sentence of death had been respited to one of being detained at Her Majesty's Pleasure. The prison Governor acknowledged receipt of the order on the 30th of July, 1853.

Judge Justice Crompton did not receive the decision and was so concerned that Sarah Baker might be executed, he sent another letter on the 31st of July, 1853. In it he said, "I have a very strong opinion that it is a case in which execution is quite out of the question." On the 2nd of August, 1853, several of the Walsall and Bloxwich clergy sent a further letter to Lord Palmerston, begging for leniency and asking for mercy and clemency for Sarah Baker. Judge Justice Crompton officially commuted the sentence of death to one of transportation for life on the 13th of August, 1853.

Sarah Baker was imprisoned at Fulham Refuge until the 30th of October, 1862, when she was sent to Millbank Prison. Her final move was to Brixton on 2nd of April, 1863. The Superintendent of Brixton Prison sent a letter to the Home Office in reference to Prisoner 708 Baker on the 9th of September, 1863, recommending her release on licence. Her uncle, Mr. Whitehouse of Bell Lane, Bloxwich had agreed with the Staffordshire Chief Constable, to look after her when released.

On the 22nd of March, 1864, Sir George Grey, the Home Secretary reported that Sarah Baker's conduct at Brixton Prison was very good and he signed the official licence to release her on the 30th of March, 1864, effectively ordering her discharge from prison within the next thirty days. [247] [248] [249] [250] [251] [252] [253] [254] [255]

57. Moore's Tailor Made Trouble - 1853 & 1854

Joseph Moore owned a successful drapers shop in Upper Rushall Street, Walsall, but 1853 turned out to be the start of his unlucky run.

At the end of October 1853, Moore employed Richard Bainbridge as a new shopman at his business. Not too long afterwards he noticed that his stock was unexpectedly down and suspected the new man Bainbridge might be responsible. Moore started to secretly mark certain items and didn't have too long to wait, until some of them disappeared.

Due to his suspicions Moore visited a magistrates to obtain a search warrant for Bainbridge's address. The warrant was personally delivered to Superintendent Bilson who executed it resulting in the recovery of six of the covertly marked silk handkerchiefs. Bainbridge was arrested, but he assured Superintendent Bilson there was nothing more to find. During the search however, evidence was found to suggest that other stolen property had gone to the premises of Thomas Scott a draper in Halifax.

Superintendent Bilson visited Scott's premises and he openly admitted to having property from Bainbridge. Upon request, Scott produced twenty-three silk handkerchiefs, three fans, seven and a half yards of satin, eight yards of Persian silk, fourteen yards of striped silk, three mufflers, seven and a half yards of velvet, twelve ladies neckties, two shawls, and seven yards of merino. The total value of this property was about twenty pounds and it was all identified by Mr. Moore. As a result Scott was apprehended for receiving stolen property.

On Wednesday the 28th December, 1853, Bainbridge and Scott appeared at Walsall Court. Mr. Mitchell a Halifax lawyer represented Scott and informed the Bench that his client was a highly respected business man in Halifax. Mr. Mitchell said that Bainbridge falsely purported that these were genuine business transactions to Mr. Scott.

Mr. Duignan who was prosecuting, said he was happy with the explanation and had no desire to pursue the charge against Mr. Scott for handling stolen property. The magistrates allowed Scott to leave the dock, stating that there was not the slightest stain on his character.

Bainbridge was tried on the 20th of January, 1854, where he was found guilty and sentenced to nine calendar months imprisonment. [256] [257] [258]

Mr. Moore must have been an incredibly bad judge of character or a very unlucky man, because not too long after this unfortunate event he went on to employ twenty-four year old, William John Briddon. When Briddon first applied for the position, he stated his employer was H. Williams and Company in Deansgate, Manchester. In reality the firm did not exist, so when Moore sent them a postal enquiry, it obviously could not be delivered. Briddon however sent Mr. Moore a reply which he had written himself, which not surprisingly contained a glowing reference. This convinced Mr. Moore to take him on, but Briddon was no shopman he was a travelling fraudster, who moved from draper to draper stripping out their stock.

Briddon started his employment as a shopman on the 21st of January, 1854, the day after Bainbridge was sent to prison. To Moore's disbelief and horror, soon after his arrival, history repeated itself when property began to disappear again. This time, before he had chance to take any action, Briddon gave notice that he intended to emigrate to South Africa and would be leaving Walsall on Sunday the 5th of February, 1854. After he left, ninety-nine yards of valuable silk was found to be missing.

Superintendent Bilson discovered that on the morning Briddon left, he went to Bescot railway station and arranged for two brown parcels to be delivered to William Briddon, at 88, Leaf Street, Manchester. Superintendent Bilson planned with his counterpart, Inspector John Neaves at Manchester Police to wait for the delivery to arrive at Leaf Street. Briddon signed for the parcels when they arrived and then the two police pounced on the address. A search of the premises was made and the parcels were found to contain valuable silk stolen from Moore. Also found were several items belonging to Mr. C. M. Cox, draper at Hanley, where he had previously worked the same scam. No less than twenty-nine concealed pawn tickets were found, pledging stolen goods from other places. William Briddon was arrested for theft and his wife, Ann Briddon for receiving stolen property.

On Monday the 20th of February, 1854 the Briddon's appeared at Walsall Court, where they were committed for trial at the next Borough Quarter Sessions. [259] [260]

On the 7th of March, 1854, both Briddon's appeared at court in Staffordshire for the theft from Mr. Cox at Hanley. William Briddon was sentenced to six years imprisonment, his wife was acquitted.

The Briddon's appeared together again at Walsall Quarter Sessions on Monday the 3rd of April, 1854. William Briddon pleaded guilty to the charge of stealing sixteen yards of silk and the case against Ann Briddon was withdrawn. Briddon had a previous conviction for a theft at Derby, so was sentenced to another four years penal servitude. [261] [262] [263] [264]

Altogether not the best year for the unfortunate Walsall draper Joseph Moore, hopefully he cut his cloth more carefully in the future and his shop staff measured up to the task!

58. Baby Body Stuck Up Turk's Head Chimney - 1854

On Thursday the 1st of June, 1854, Mrs. Payne the landlord's wife of the Turk's Head in Digbeth, was doing some cleaning work in one of her rooms when she discovered a strange looking package stuck up the chimney. She decided to investigate and with some difficulty, she eventually managed to pull the soot blackened bundle down. It was an old apron, which she cautiously unravelled to reveal the decaying grim dead body of a new born baby boy. Shockingly, a sinister garter was twisted twice around the baby's neck and tied very tightly on the left hand side.

The police immediately attended the scene to examine the body, which they suspected might have been there for at least a few months. Mrs. Payne told the story of a servant girl, who at around the right time worked at the Turk's Head and might have been pregnant. She thought it was suspicious when the girl who had been working there for five weeks, suddenly left without giving any notice. The girl initially gave her name as Heath, but later said it was Mary Ann Yates, the wife of a robber who had been transported (see story 49). This girl lodged at the pub occupying the room adjoining where the baby's body was found.

Superintendent Bilson launched a search for the mysterious woman and on Friday the 2nd of June, Thomas Heath, landlord of the Half Way House at Bentley attended the police station to say that he was the girls father. He told Police Constable Samuel Crombie that his daughter was living as the common law wife of Andrew Bullock, a pig dealer at the New Inn in Finchfield, Wolverhampton. Mary Ann Yates was located and taken into custody.

An inquest was opened that day by Mr. A. A. Fletcher the borough coroner, but adjourned for the police to gather more evidence.

On Monday the 5th of June, 1854, Mary Ann Yates appeared before the magistrates and was remanded in custody for a week.

The adjourned inquest was reopened on Friday the 9th of June, 1854 where Police Constable Crombie was called to give evidence. He alleged that when he first spoke to Thomas Heath, he said the dead child was his daughter's, but after her arrest, Heath told his daughter to say nothing to the police. Heath adamantly denied making any such comments and the inquest was adjourned for a second time.

On Monday the 12th of June 1854, Mary Ann Yates was brought up before the magistrates again, charged with being the murderess of the child. Superintendent Bilson, informed the Bench that he had found nothing to incriminate the woman and offered no evidence against her. The Mayor discharged Mary Ann Yates, telling her that her character had not been stained by the proceedings instituted against her.

At the inquest on Friday the 16th of June, 1854, Mr. Duignan represented Mary Ann Yates, who was allowed to sit at his side. Mr. Duignan demanded his constitutional right to put questions to any witness.

Mrs. Payne told the coroner that at about seven o'clock when Yates left for the last time, she appeared ill and there was blood on her bed.

The surgeon Herbert Procter, said he had conducted the post mortem, and it was impossible to tell if the child was born dead or alive due to the level of decomposition, but if it was born alive the ligature around its throat would have certainly killed it.

Superintendent Edward Bilson said Mary Ann Yates made a complete denial when she was arrested and nothing of note was found during the searches.

Constable Samuel Crombie said that on Friday night before the prisoner was apprehended, Thomas Heath, came to the station and said that the child was his daughter's and he hoped the matter would be looked into as soon as possible.

Thomas Heath denied saying anything to Constable Crombie about the dead child. He claimed his daughter had the appearance of being pregnant from the age of sixteen. The girls mother corroborated her husband's evidence and added that when Mary Ann returned from working at the Turk's Head she was fine and had certainly not been pregnant.

Two further witnesses, Richard Wood and Samuel Bailey both said they heard Mary Ann Yates give Mrs. Payne proper notice after a dispute at the Turk's Head. When the inquest was concluded, Mary Ann Yates was discharged. [265] [266]

On the 21st of June, 1854, Thomas Heath wrote a letter, which was published in the Staffordshire Advertiser, where he described Constable Crombie's statement as 'utterly destitute of truth' and a complete fabrication, disbelieved by both the coroner and his jury. Heath admitted he advised his daughter to stay quiet, but only after she had been charged and on the legal advice of Mr. Duignan his attorney. Heath alleged that Mrs. Payne concocted the whole dead baby story against his daughter and Superintendent Bilson attempted to make him look bad. Heath said Mrs. Payne was a complete liar who made the story up in revenge for his daughter having an ongoing claim in the County Court for unpaid wages against her. [267]

59. Riot and Tumult At The Pits - March 1855

During late March, 1855, several hundred disgruntled colliers defiantly marched in solidarity from pit to pit, disaffected with the terrible working conditions. They attacked every pit in their wake, wrecking enough of the workings to prevent them from operating, before they moved on to the next. They were causing total disruption to the whole mining industry in the local area.

On Friday the 23rd of March, 1855, a large mob descended on the town of Bilston, where not content with just attacking the mines, these troublemakers targeted several Bilston shopkeepers and then attacked the police officers when they came to break things up. The policemen initially struggled to bring the riotous band of stone throwing vandals under control, but the officers made cutlass charges and eventually the uncontrollable mob were driven back. Witnesses claimed that about a third of the rioting men were of Irish decent. Just after midnight, one hundred Essex Riflemen arrived in Bilston and were billeted in the police station. The soldiers presence had the desired effect, rioting subsided and when the Staffordshire Chief Constable arrived on horseback with his police reinforcements, the troublemakers decided it was time to move on.

A smaller group of about twenty to thirty drifted into Wolverhampton, attacking and breaking into shops to steal food. The Wolverhampton Chief Constable rode out with his men and smashed the group with a sabre charge in Horsley Fields.

The larger group decided to move away from Bilston on Saturday the 24th of March, 1885, and headed towards Willenhall. When the mob numbering about three hundred approached the town, they attacked Mr. Bagnell's colliery at Parkbrook. At around twelve o'clock they had reached the Birchills heading for the top end of Park Street. Marshalling the tumultuous group was a man named Patrick Coyle assisted by John Glynn. Carrying sticks and waving banners, the rabble marched down the street six to eight abreast. Their aggression was temporarily diverted to Mr. Jones colliery, opposite the forge belonging to Lancaster and Brayford in Pleck Road. Francis Evans, saw Coyle inciting violence, by throwing rails, sleepers and other things down into the pit shaft. Evans also identified John and Thomas Downey, who set fire to a hovel before they moved on.

By the time the mob reached Stafford Street, they were up for a riot and attacked the provision shop of John Luty, by smashing the windows and stealing his goods. Patrick Coyle and John Jones went to Highways shop, where the shopman Joseph Wright saw them smash the window and carry away looted property. John Golding saw another man named Anthony Higgins stealing cheese from Highways window.

The mob swarmed into Town End Bank, as the panicking shopkeepers rapidly tried to put the shutters up. Charles Newton and Joseph Kite, saw John Glynn with an armful of stolen property and decided to follow him with a view to taking him prisoner.

Before long they reached the High Street, where they freely raided and ransacked the market stalls of anything edible, helping themselves and filling their pockets on the way. John Walker's fruit stall was attacked by Thomas Connor and other men, who stole his oranges as he desperately tried to pack up his cart. In defence of his property, Walker thrashed Conner's hand with his whip, forcing him to drop the oranges all over the ground. In retaliation Patrick Coyle kicked Walker in the back as he attempted to make a hasty retreat and the mob pelted him with some of his own two-hundred and fifty oranges left behind.

Another fruiterer William Bishop and his son had their stall rifled by Connor and Coyle, who roughed them up and struck young Bishop with a hay fork handle.

Benjamin Jones was grabbed by the magistrate Mr. Highway, when he attacked widow Meeson's stall. Joseph Smallwood, saw them struggling, but then Jones escaped when Coyle and Higgins punched Mr. Highway several times.

Walsall Borough Police force only consisted of fifteen men, twelve constables, two sergeants and a superintendent. They wore a uniform consisting of a black shiny top hat, a swallow tailed blue coat and each man carried a cutlass. Superintendent Bilson determined to halt their advance towards the Guildhall, formed a brave police line across High Street with about eight or nine of his men. As the rioters approached the thin blue line the cutlasses were drawn and bravely they charged the rioters. It became a battle for the street, but the disciplined policemen although outnumbered had the determination to force the miners to scatter. As the rioters broke up, Sergeant Thomas Simpson saw Patrick Coyle distributing the oranges from Mr. Bishop's stall and after a struggle took him into custody. He also identified Anthony Higgins as being one of the men involved.

The intrepid policemen managed to drive the rioters back and they retreated towards Darlaston. The town magistrates immediately sent for the Walsall Yeomanry in case the rioters returned. They arrived later and remained at Walsall as reinforcements in readiness, but their services were not required in the end.

On Wednesday the 18th of April, 1855, at the Walsall Quarter Sessions, John Jones, Benjamin Jones, Patrick Coyle, Anthony Higgins, Thomas Conner, Martin Doyle, John Glynn, Thomas Murphy, John Downey and Thomas Downey appeared charged with riot and tumult. Mr. Kenealy conducted the case for the prosecution, but none of the prisoners were defended. Superintendent Bilson gave evidence of the riot itself and also the suffering caused to the inhabitants of the town. Not surprisingly all defendants were found guilty. In passing sentence, the Recorder Mr. Clarke remarked about the fact that all the leaders of the mob were Irish. He called it a disgrace for Irishmen to come to England in order to make a living, only to attack their masters and the nearest town after their first disagreement. He thought that such conduct deserved the severest punishment. Patrick Coyle, John Jones and Benjamin Jones were given twelve months imprisonment each. Thomas Connor, John Glynn, Anthony Higgins, John Downey and Dennis Downey were sentenced to nine months each. Martin Doyle who was a youth received three months imprisonment and Thomas Murphy, who pleaded guilty was sentenced to one month's imprisonment on account of his age. [268] [269] [270]

60. The Flawed Handling Case - September 1855

Small amounts of scrap metal started going missing from Highway's foundry at the Birchills in 1855. Mr. Langdon who worked there suspected a fifteen year old employee named Sarah Nicholls and on one occasion decided to follow her. Sarah Nicholls was seen to take some iron to John Smith, a marine store dealer in High Street, who was also a scrap metal dealer. After Sarah Nicholls left Smith's premises, Langdon visited and Smith admitted accepting the metal from her.

The police were informed and Constable Crombie arrested Sarah Nicholls for theft and John Smith for receiving stolen property. The defendants were put before the magistrates who committed them for trial at the Quarter Sessions.

On Monday the 29th of October, 1855, their case of theft and handling came up for trial at the Borough Quarter Sessions at the Guildhall. The Recorder, was Mr. Sergeant Clarke and the rest of the bench comprised of the Mayor Mr. Oerton and magistrates, Highway, Stephens, Whitgreave, Greatrex and Shannon. Mr. Kenealy appeared for the prosecution, Mr. Hill defended Smith and Mr. Duignan, defended Sarah Nicholls

The trial turned out to be full of twists and turns, with an allegation that the police had acted underhandedly in the matter. Langdon was called to give evidence for the prosecution and claimed that John Smith admitted to receiving about thirty-eight pounds of iron from the girl in total.

Mr. Hill who defended Smith, pointed to a woman sitting in court named Ann Hayden and asked Langdon if he had seen the lady in Smith's premises at the time he went in. Langdon denied ever seeing her.

Constable Crombie said that when he arrested Sarah Nicholls, she confessed to the theft. She took him to the marine shop where Smith admitted that she was the girl who brought in the stolen iron.

Mr. Hill then called Ann Hayden, who said she was present when Langdon went into Smith's shop. She overheard a conversation, where Smith was quite open about purchasing the iron from the girl and he even allowed Langdon to examine it in the corner. Smith told Langdon that he would have never bought the metal, if he had any idea of it being stolen.

Another witness for the defence named Adams, said he heard Smith tell Langdon, that if he could prove it was stolen, he would give it him back.

Michael Kendrick another Walsall scrap metal dealer said that Smith gave an honest price for the metal.

Mr. Hill called several other witnesses who were all prepared to give Smith a good character.

The trial ended when the jury found the girl Nicholls guilty, but acquitted Smith.

Before sentencing, Sarah Nicholls solicitor Mr. Duignan claimed that the police had promised his client immunity from prosecution, if she agreed to give evidence against Smith. She did agree, but afterwards the police reneged on the deal and he thought it was very unfair to have treated her in such a way.

Mr. Kenealy the prosecutor strongly denied knowing anything about it, but the Recorder said the suggestion would be most irregular. Superintendent John Wyatt Cater was called into court for clarity. He was only appointed in September, but he couldn't see how the case ever managed to get before a grand jury. The Recorder was not impressed about the allegation, but said he did not blame Superintendent Cater personally for it. Due to the suggestion from Mr. Duignan and the comments made by Superintendent Cater, Nicholls was discharged with one days imprisonment. [271] [272]

61. Lady 'Jack Sheppard' at Walsall - 1855

Sarah Jones was arrested on the 10th of October, 1855, after the police discovered she had taken stolen women's clothing into two pawnbroker shops in Walsall and Dudley.

Soon after arriving at the police station, Sarah Jones feigned illness by apparently giving the impression that she was suffering from some kind of epileptic fit. The police informed the magistrates of the situation and they gave their permission for her to be taken in a cab to the workhouse for medical treatment. After a couple of days of care at the workhouse, Sarah Jones wrapped only with a blanket, managed to escape out of the establishment and disappear.

Superintendent Cater circulated her description and later found out that Sarah Jones had fled to Stafford, where she was arrested for vagrancy and sentenced to one month's imprisonment. At the time of her release from gaol, Sarah Jones was gate arrested and brought back to Walsall to stand trial.

On the night before her trial set for Monday the 10th of December, 1855, the gaoler checked her cell, but it appeared empty. It was then discovered that Sarah Jones had managed to remove some masonry giving access to the chimney. She had stripped naked to prevent her clothes catching fire and scaled the chimney using a ripped up sheet. Unfortunately for her, twelve feet up the stack there was a bar built into the brickwork, which prevented her escape.

At court Superintendent Cater told the magistrates that after being coaxed to come back down the chimney, she refused to get dressed. Sarah Jones said nothing and was committed for theft to Walsall Borough Quarter Sessions.

She appeared there on the 16th of January, 1856 and was sentenced to three calendar months imprisonment.

Jack Sheppard, or 'Honest Jack', was a notorious English thief famous for his prison escapes during the early 18th century in London. His escapes became folklore amongst the working classes. [273] [274]

62. *Violent Bobby Bashings - 1856*

At quarter past midnight on the morning of Sunday the 27th of January, 1856, Police Constable 7 Conder was on duty near to the King's Arms in Caldmore, when he was approached by three drunken men. The three men were Thomas Bullers, a private in the Royal Artillery, Thomas Yardley, a well-known thief and Benjamin Russell. Whether anything was said is uncertain, but the men attacked Constable Conder, knocking him to the ground and giving him a brutal kicking. They then scarpered, but he bravely tried to follow them. They spotted him coming and lay in wait in Orlando Street, where they gave him another good pasting. This time he used his police rattle to summon help and luckily former policeman, Matthew Jennings who lived nearby heard it. Jennings went outside to the injured policeman and while he was rendering the officer some assistance, they both heard the moaning and the cries for help, from someone else further down the street.

The three brutes came across a young man named Henry Huddlestone in Vicarage Walk, who they attacked without any provocation, battering him half senseless and rifling his pockets to steal his money and belongings. Conder and Jennings found Huddlestone a short distance away lying in a pool of his own blood. Huddlestone described the distinctive blue artillery uniform worn by one of the men.

Later that morning, Police Constable Lockett saw three men fitting the description in Upper Rushall Street, so he asked them for their names. They made a run for it and he pursued them down into Intown Row, where he managed to capture and arrest Bullers. Police Constable Hughes apprehended Yardley a short distance away and Russell was found at two o'clock in a coffee shop in Bridge Street.

Constable Conder and Henry Huddlestone identified all three offenders at the police station as their attackers and they were charged with the assaults by Superintendent Cater.

At the magistrates court the prisoners denied the accusations against them, but were committed for trial.

Thomas Bullers, Thomas Yardley and Benjamin Russell appeared at the Borough Quarter Sessions on the 28th of April, 1856, where each was sentenced to twelve calendar months imprisonment. [275]

Due to a second incident on the night Constable Conder was assaulted, it turned out a particularly rough shift for Walsall policemen. Sergeant Dackus had earlier that evening been obliged to eject two navvies, John Phipps and James Hunt from the George Inn on The Bridge. They bore a grudge and waited for him, making him a target of a violent attack. He was knocked down, kicked, punched and they tore the skirts off his coat.

Phipps and Hunt appeared before the Borough Magistrates and were each fined £5, or in default two months imprisonment. [276]

63. The Leaping Darlaston Burglar - March 1856

At just after seven o'clock on the evening of Saturday the 8th of March, 1856, William Randall spotted two men breaking into the home of Nancy Stokes, a widow who lived in Foster Street, Darlaston. She was the elderly mother of his employer, John Stokes a gunlock manufacturer who lived just opposite. He quickly raised the alarm by fetching Mr. Stokes, but Mrs. Stokes had already been disturbed in her bedroom by John Wood and Job Dane, who stole eight and a half sovereigns.

John Stokes surrounded the house with several of his men, sending his biggest man John Rooker to keep watch at the back. John Wood saw the men surrounding the house from the window and realised the game was up. Wood jumped out of an upstairs window, grabbed hold of a plank of wood and without hesitation struck Rooker knocking him down, then cleared the hedge with a tremendous leap to get away. Job Dane was not so lucky, he tried hiding behind the cellar door, but was quickly found and taken into custody.

On Monday the 10th March, 1856, Superintendent John Cater and Sergeant Frederick Dackus were at Walsall Railway Station, when they saw a man fitting the description of John Wood. He was apprehended and found to have four sovereigns, fourteen and six shillings in silver and nine pence copper on his person. Two of the sovereigns were hidden in Wood's boots.

At Stafford Assizes on the 12th of March, 1856, Wood pleaded guilty, Dane had a previous conviction and both were sentenced to four years penal servitude. [277] [278]

64. The Cheese and the Pigeon - May 1856

Three blocks of best cheese were stolen from Mr. Rogers grocery and cheesemonger shop in Walsall town on the 15th of May, 1856 by person or persons unknown. Cheese was a valuable commodity in 1856 and when Rogers reported the theft to the police, they soon started sniffing around looking for clues.

Police Constable Michael O'Toole received some information that the cheese was at a beer house known as the Pigeon in Bullock Row. This was a well known den of iniquity, supposedly run by a dubious character named Daniel Keyte and frequented by all kinds of unsavoury types. Constable O'Toole spoke to Superintendent Cater and a search warrant was obtained from the magistrates.

Daniel Keyte was a Walsall man born in 1836, the son of a pump maker and well sinker. At only twenty years of age, he and his brothers were a thorn in the side of the local police, being involved in everything dishonest or immoral.

Officers raided the Pigeon and found a large piece of cheese wrapped up in an apron, hidden behind a mash tub in the brewhouse at the back of the premises. The cheese was distinctly marked and identified as coming from Mr. Rogers shop. As a result Daniel Keyte was arrested.

On Monday the 19th of May, 1856, Daniel Keyte appeared before Mr. Oerton the Mayor and other magistrates for handling stolen goods. Mr. Sill conducted the prosecution and Mr. Wilkinson represented Keyte. Superintendent Cater and Sergeant Dackus explained, that Keyte was the receiver of the stolen property, but as yet the thieves had not been caught, although they would be arrested soon. Mr. Cater requested that Keyte be remanded in custody, so that further enquiries could be made to arrest the others involved.

Mr. Wilkinson explained that the Pigeon beer house was situated within a very disreputable neighbourhood, full of indifferent characters. The brewhouse door where the cheese was found was unlocked and opened directly onto the street. Mr. Wilkinson argued that it was possible for literally anyone to have put it there, with a view to returning to retrieve it later. The Mayor agreed with him, saying there was insufficient evidence to justify remanding Keyte under the circumstances, as the cheese could have possibly been put there without him knowing. As a consequence Keyte was discharged, but this wasn't the end of the story. [279]

65. Walsall Wood Wrong'uns - September 1856

A spate of burglaries occurred overnight in Walsall Wood on Saturday the 27th of September, 1856. The first was discovered at the Boat Inn, Walsall Wood at about two o'clock in the morning by Isaiah Saunders. The offenders had gained entry to the premises through an open window and stolen a silver watch and guard, three pounds in cash and some alcohol. A second property belonging to a brickmaker named George Bullock was also broken into on the same night and a quantity of check linen was stolen.

Descriptions of the suspects who were seen making off from the premises and a list of the stolen property was circulated by Staffordshire County Police. Superintendent Cater briefed his Walsall Borough officers to keep a lookout for them on the 'qui vive.' It was fairly usual for criminal types to drift into Walsall, attempting to offload stolen goods from other parts of the area.

The Walsall Borough Force were always good at spotting a wrong'un and sure enough at between eleven and twelve o'clock that night, Sergeant Dackus apprehended a suspicious man in Digbeth and shortly after Superintendent Cater arrested another suspect at the Old Rodney public house in Park Street. The two strangers gave their names as twenty-two year old William Shorter and twenty-six year old John Sturmey.

From the enquiries they made, it was found that both men had been renting a room since the 21st of September from snaffle bit maker, Thomas Hartop in Dudley Street. Their room was searched and Sergeant Dackus found the stolen watch. Hartop said that when he came home at eleven o'clock on the night of Friday the 26th of

September he noticed that Sturmey was still out. At eight o'clock the following morning, when he got up, Sturmey was in bed and Shorter was standing in front of the fire downstairs. At breakfast Sturmey produced a watch and guard from his coat and handed it to Shorter, who took the watch and handed back the guard. Thomas Hartop confirmed that the watch found by Sergeant Dackus, was the same watch he saw them with at breakfast.

Both burglaries had been perpetrated outside the borough boundary and as a result the felons were handed over to Inspector Price from the County Constabulary. Two other men, John Holden and William Smith (alias Biddle) were later charged with handling some of the stolen goods.

On Friday the 10th of October, 1856, the four men all appeared before a County magistrate J. Bealey at Walsall. Sturmey and Shorter both entered guilty pleas for the two burglaries and were committed to Stafford Assizes. William Smith (alias Biddle) who was charged with handling stolen goods was released on bail to attend the Assizes, while the case against John Holden was discontinued.

Sturmey, Shorter and Smith appeared at Stafford Assizes before the Judge, Mr. Baron Watson on Friday the 5th of December, 1856. Sturmey and Shorter were sentenced to four years imprisment and Smith to twelve months.

Sturmey served his time at Stafford, Wakefield and finally Dartmoor before being released in 1859. Sturmey went on to be a career wrongdoer, even the harsh prison life could not deter him from reoffending. Shorter served his sentence at Stafford, Wakefield and Chatham before being finally released from Portland in 1860. [280] [281] [282] [283] [284]

66. *Judge Hacked Off with the Flour Case - December 1856*

This is the story of Henry Hack, a thirty-one year married man, who was a grocer made bankrupt in 1851. He was a chancer, who through his own inabilities drifted from one failed venture to the next. Over the

Christmas period of 1855, he opened up a small shop in Stafford Street with £72 inherited from his mother-in-law's will. Although he ran the shop, the name above the door was Sarah Hack, his wife, but that permanently closed in March, 1856. We know that Hack was then employed by James Mills a grocer in High Street, who caught him stealing. In April 1856, he got four months imprisonment with hard labour for that theft. When he was released from prison he obtained employment in Birmingham, but that ended in disaster when his employer accused him of embezzlement and he was dismissed. After this he struggled to find work and at one point was reduced to labouring for a paltry nine shillings a week.

His next attempt at business came in July 1856, when Hack rented a small shop in Ablewell Street, from fifty-one year old Samuel Hatherley, a respected Walsall baker. This is where the story begins.

In July 1856, Samuel Hatherley ordered fifty barrels of flour from John Bingham, a provisions dealer from Liverpool. Before the goods were delivered, Hatherley cancelled the order on the grounds that they had not arrived on time. However, the goods had already been despatched by Bingham in Liverpool and the first consignment of forty barrels were accepted by Hatherley in Ablewell Street on 29th of July. The remaining ten barrels arrived the following day, but he refused them and they were returned. Hatherley wrote to Bingham on the 8th of August, suggesting that he could sell the forty barrels of flour to a local trader, rather than returning them to Liverpool. Bingham agreed it was a good idea and on the 11th of August, Hatherley wrote to say that Hack would purchase the stock and that he was a respectable trader. On the 14th of August, Hack wrote to Bingham and agreed to pay thirty-two shillings a barrel with two months credit.

All seemed well, but before payment was due Bingham received an anonymous letter informing him that Hack was a dishonest man who had been to prison. Bingham asked Hatherley, who told him the bill would be paid.

Bingham was not happy and wanted his money, so on the 3rd of September he travelled to Walsall to establish what was going on. His first port of call was to see Superintendent Cater, who he told about his concerns saying that he would never have done business with Hack, had it not been for Hatherley's letters of recommendation.

Superintendent Cater and Bingham went to see Hatherley, who was initially very cagey with his answers, but categorically denied authorising any such letters. By the end of the conversation Hatherley described Hack as "a damn'd scoundrel." As a result of what Hatherley said about the letters, Hack was apprehended for obtaining goods by false pretences.

On Wednesday the 10th of September, 1856, the case against Hack was heard in a crowded magistrates court at the Guildhall, before the Mayor. Mr. Sill prosecuted and Mr. Wilkinson defended Hack.

Hatherley was the first witness called to give evidence, but appeared very excitable and agitated as if he didn't want to be there. Mr. Sill asked him whose handwriting was on the letters sent to Bingham and he seemed very reluctant to answer. The magistrates were very unhappy with Hatherley's hesitance and eventually threatened to commit him for being part of the fraud if he didn't answer the questions properly. The warning worked, Hatherley confirmed that the handwriting belonged to Hack, but then admitted he had written on his behalf as a kind of clerk with his authorisation.

Mr. Sill said this was a plain admission of guilt by Hatherley and asked for him to be jointly charged with Hack in a conspiracy. This was done and the case was adjourned for one week.

On Wednesday the 17th of September, 1856, the case resumed against Hack and Hatherley, before the Mayor Mr. Oerton. Mr. Sill prosecuted and this time Mr. Motteram a barrister defended Hack and Hatherley, who denied the charges.

Mr. Motteram gave Hack's background information and his current circumstances. The case continued for nine hours, with several legal arguments about mentioning previous convictions. The next day the magistrates ultimately decided to commit both men for trial at the Assizes, with bail available with two £50 sureties.

Judge Baron Watson, presided at Stafford Assizes when the trial started on Friday the 5th of December, 1856. Mr. Scotland was the prosecutor, Mr. Motteram represented Hatherley and Hack was undefended.

Mr. Scotland opened the case for the prosecution by producing a number of letters signed 'Hatherley.' He said that Hatherley gave Hack a good reference, which he knew to be false. It was explained that Hack wrote the letters himself, but with Hatherley's authority.

The Judge seemed displeased about the basis of the case and informed Mr. Scotland, that he did not have a 'leg to stand upon' if he was trying to prove false representation. He suggested that the injured party, Mr. Bingham should have pursued this matter through the Civil Court to get his money back. Mr. Scotland insisted that he would be able to make out the charge of conspiracy, so the Judge allowed the case to continue.

John Bingham was the first witness to be called, who said he knew Hatherley was a respectable baker in Walsall with a good and trustworthy reputation. He claimed that he was only prepared to do business with Hack on that understanding that Hatherley's good reference was true. When he was informed that Hack was a criminal, he became concerned and travelled to Walsall on the 3rd of September to see Superintendent Cater. Together they visited Hatherley, who denied writing or authorising any of the letters and as a consequence, Hack was apprehended for obtaining goods by false pretences.

The Judge, must have taken a dislike to John Bingham for the way he presented his evidence and was already unhappy that the case reached the Assizes.

Questioning Bingham directly he asked, "What did you have Hack apprehended for? Was it to get your money?"

Bingham replied, "No, my Lord, I knew I could not get my money in a criminal court."

The Judge almost in a disbelieving way said, "Why, don't you know that it's often done to coerce people to pay what they owe ?"

Bingham said, "I did it by the advice of my solicitors."

Baron Watson responded by saying, "Ah, you know nothing about the law."

It was fairly clear from what the Judge said, that he thought Bingham was using the criminal courts to settle a civil debt.

Bingham continued by saying Hatherley was evasive and hesitant about his authority to write the letters.

Everything about Bingham was obviously irritating the Judge who intervened again and asked him, "What do you mean by evasive answers, sir? You must not use such words here, sir."

Bingham cockily replied, "I give my evidence in my own plain way."

The Judge was furious with his reply and fiercely warned him, "But you must not give evidence in that way, sir. You must give it according to law."

John Bingham then sarcastically and somewhat foolishly said, "You just now told me I did not understand the law!"

Gasps circulated around the room in anticipation of how the Judge would respond to Bingham's insulting tone.

Baron Watson, placed his hands on the bench and rose up in an authoritative manner then with a raised voice he ordered, "Not another word, sir, I can tell you that you will not be allowed to reason with me, sir."

The prosecutor, Mr. Scotland knew instantly, that it would be very unwise for Bingham to continue with his evidence and risk the total wrath of the Judge, so decided not to annoy him any further and asked him to stand down.

The next witness was George Hill, a railway porter, who said Hatherley accepted the delivery of forty barrels of flour at his shop on the 29th July. The next day when he delivered ten more barrels, Hatherley refused to accept them and they were returned.

James Mills, a grocer from High Street, verified the handwriting was that of his former employee Hack, who got four months imprisonment with hard labour for stealing from him in April 1856.

Mr. Darwall, clerk to the Walsall Justices, confirmed that at the Magistrates Court, Hatherley said the letters were written with his authority.

Superintendent Cater said that when he originally spoke to Hatherley, he denied authorising the letters, suggesting that Hack was a "scoundrel," but then gave a conflicting account of things before the magistrates court.

The Registrar of Walsall County Court, Mr. Clark said that Hack filed for insolvency on the 19th of September with Hatherley as a named creditor.

The Judge said it seemed fairly clear to him, that by having Hack arrested on the 3rd of September and sending him to Stafford Gaol, they effectively prevented him from paying the bill due to Bingham on the 17th of October. At seven o'clock in the evening having dragged on all day the case was adjourned until the following morning.

The case continued on Saturday with James Lynex an inn keeper and collector of gas rates, who said he believed Hack was insolvent. He remembered him lodging at various places and being at a shop in Stafford Street over Christmas, 1855. The name above the door was Sarah Hack, but it closed in March, 1856. He knew Hatherley occupied a shop in Ablewell Street, that closed in September, but the gas rates were paid up to October.

Charles Holland, said he knew that Hack was connected to a shop in Stafford Street in his wife's name, but it only stayed open for four months.

Thomas Hartley had a grocery shop in Ablewell Street, next door to the shop Hatherley owned. During the last week of August, Hack occupied the premises selling, flour, bread, butter and cheese, but he was only in business for about two weeks in total. Hatherley continued his bakery business at the rear of the shop and remained in business after Hack left. Previously Hartley believed that Hatherley's daughter occupied the shop at the front, but she became a lunatic and was admitted to hospital.

A debt collector John Osbourne said he removed furniture from Hack's house in July, because he couldn't pay his rent. Hack disputed Osbourne's allegation and he then conceded that he actually only took the property to make sure the rent was paid. Osbourne's attitude annoyed the Judge and he was the second prosecution witness to do so. At the end of his evidence the Judge gave him some strong advice about his conduct, should he ever come to the witness box again.

The Town Crier Henry Griffin said Hack asked him to make an announcement on the 30th of August, as follows, "To be sold, on premises opposite the Nag's Head, Ablewell Street, a quantity of American flour, at half a crown per peck. By order of the poor mans friend. God Save the Queen." It was generally agreed that the price offered was a reasonable one for the flour and the Judge was very impressed that the announcement ended with, "God Save the Queen."

Mr. Motteram in his speech for the defence said the prosecution against Hatherley was cruel and unjust, as it was quite conceivable that Hack did add passages to letters without his knowledge. He noted that not one of the witnesses who gave evidence, had anything bad to say about Hatherley's character and he hoped the jury would find him not guilty.

When summing up, the Judge was critical of Mr. Bingham suggesting that cases of this nature were very often only brought to gratify a feeling of vengeance.

The Jury sympathised and returned a verdict of "Not Guilty," for both men obviously disliking Bingham's attitude as well. Hatherley was discharged at once, but Hack was detained in custody on another charge.

The Judge then gave his own opinion on the prosecution by saying the case should have been heard at the Borough Quarter Sessions at best. He criticised Walsall magistrates for wrongly sending the matter to the Assizes and ordered the prosecution to pay all the costs of the case.

Mr. Scotland felt compelled to apologise that Bingham had "excited his Lordship's displeasure," in giving his evidence.

The other matter for which Hack was remanded was heard at Walsall Quarter Sessions on Wednesday the 27th of January, 1857, before the Recorder Mr. Sergeant Clarke. He was charged with stealing a five pound note from Frederick Trussler a leather trader from Rushall Street. The circumstances were that on the 28th of October, 1856, Trussler asked Hack to write a letter for him and then send it to Manchester enclosing a five pound note. The letter never arrived, Hack admitted taking the money, but said he intended to replace it later. The jury didn't take long to find Hack guilty and he was sentenced to six months imprisonment. [285] [286] [287] [288] [289] [290] [291] [292]

67. Second Shot at the Pigeon - December 1856

The Pigeon beer house in Bullocks Row, was the roost of the nefarious Keyte brothers, who were a never ending menace to the local police (see story 64). The establishment was frequented by all kinds of unsavoury characters linked to almost every aspect of criminality.

One such crook was a man named George Reynolds, a twenty-six year old jeweller from Birmingham, who was involved in passing counterfeit bank notes. Reynolds devised his own devious way of conning local landlords out of beer and cash.

On the 29th of November, 1856, Reynolds went to the Alma Tavern in Paddock Lane, where he ordered five quarts of ale from the landlord William Bond. He told Bond his name was John Lloyd and he was fetching the beer for the workers of a local company. He passed over a forged £5 note in payment and took the beer with all the change. The note was later found to be a forgery, but his real identity at the time was unknown.

At about half past seven on Saturday the 6th of December, 1856, Reynolds practiced the same deception at the Green Man in Dudley Street, run by Joseph Archer. He ordered five pipes, six papers of tobacco and six quarts of ale, making out he worked for Mr. Murray a cabinet maker in Digbeth. Believing everything was genuine, Archer handed over the goods and unwittingly accepted another forged £5

Bank of England note in payment. Almost immediately after taking the fiver, Archer became suspicious and questioned himself, so he sent William Horton to follow the man. Reynolds walked up Dudley Street and met with Edward Keyte, whose brother Daniel kept the Pigeon beer house in Bullocks Row. At the Pigeon the goods were handed through the fence to Daniel Keyte. Joseph Keyte another of the brothers spotted Horton watching them, so they hastily took flight from the Pigeon and went off down Birmingham Road. Horton returned to the Green Man in Dudley Street where the £5 note was found to be a forgery.

Edward Keyte was arrested for his suspected involvement and was bailed for a week at court with a £20 surety. Attempts to identify the mystery note passer were fruitless, so when Edward Keyte appeared at court the following week, Superintendent Cater offered no evidence against him and the case was dismissed.

On the 19th of February, 1857 another forged £5 was passed under similar circumstances at a beer house in Birmingham.

All the crimes remained undetected and Reynolds real identity remained unknown. That was until Thursday the 16th of April, 1857, when Sergeant Dackus from Walsall Police received information that the offender for the Alma Tavern job was sleeping at the Pigeon. He went to the beer house and found George Reynolds, who perfectly fitted the offenders description. When arrested Reynolds said "What! Another eh."

At the police station, Agnes and Mary Ann Bond, the landlords two daughters identified Reynolds as the person responsible for passing the forgery at the Alma. At this point Reynolds had not been connected to the other two offences.

Reynolds appeared at Walsall Guildhall on Monday the 20th of April, 1857, defended by Mr. Sill. He challenged the validity of the identification procedure and said that even if Reynolds did pass the note, the prosecution had failed to provide any evidence of guilty knowledge. The magistrates decided to remand Reynolds in custody for a week.

When Reynolds appeared at court on Monday the 27th of April, 1857, the police further charged him with the crime at the Green Man. Mr. Blackburn from the bank said that both forged notes were made from the same printing plate. The following week the magistrates committed him for trial at the Assizes.

The trial at Stafford Assizes took place on Monday the 20th of July, 1857, before Judge Baron Bramwell. Reynolds was facing three charges as he had also been linked to the Birmingham offence. Mr. Whateley QC prosecuted and Reynolds was undefended.

Mr. Whateley explained to the jury that Reynolds used the same identical and distinctive modus operandi at the scene of all his crimes. He targeted licensed premises, purchasing ale for supposed local workmen and then paid by exchanging a forged note. Mr. Whateley said he could also prove that the notes used at every crime were printed from the same forgers plate, which he described as not 'first class.'

Several witnesses from all the offence locations identified Reynolds as the offender.

Reynolds claimed "he was as innocent as a child," as the identification procedure was flawed, because at Easter he had been in the Alma Tavern, when neither of the two women seemed to recognise him.

The Judge in summing up told the jury, that if they were happy with the identification they could find him guilty of uttering the forged notes, because guilty knowledge was perfectly clear. The jury took no time to find Reynolds guilty. Judge Baron Bramwell called him a 'trader in forged notes' and sentenced him to ten years imprisonment.

Mr. Whateley commented that Reynolds was the fifth member of a Birmingham gang who had recently been convicted for these offences and his Lordship said he was very glad to hear it.

Reynolds served his prison sentence at Millbank, Lewes, Chatham and Woking prisons.

Daniel Keyte continued to be an undesirable character, who was consistently on the police watchlist. He was convicted on the 8th of October, 1857 and then again on the 19th of January, 1858 for keeping a common bawdy house (a brothel). The first time his sentence was deferred, but the second time he had to secure a surety.

In 1858, Keyte tried his hand at Prize Fighting, with a contest against Henry 'Dragon' Baylis in London for £25. Keyte looked the odds on favourite during the early rounds, against an opponent ten years his senior. The experience of Baylis slowly began to tell as he ground Keyte down, knocking him out after one hour and fifty minutes of combat in the 64th round.

When Keyte was found guilty of forging a bank note in 1861, his luck finally ran out, he was transported to Western Australia for ten years. He sailed on the 'Clyde' on the 11th of March, 1863 and arrived in Western Australia on the 29th of May, 1863. Keyte became eligible for a 'Ticket of Leave' on the 21st of March, 1865, but nothing further is known about him, although a man by that name did die in Western Australia on the 20th of November, 1897. Maybe this time the pigeon never came home. [293] [294] [295] [296] [297] [298] [299] [300] [301] [302] [303] [304] [305] [306] [307] [308] [309] [310]

68. The Notorious 'Tom Duck' of Bloxwich Road - April 1857

On the night of Saturday 25th of April, 1857, Ralph Siddle and his master Thomas Goodall were socialising in Walsall. At about eleven o'clock they started to make their way home, walking along the main road towards Bloxwich. This area had a reputation for being rough at the best of times and they encountered a group of drunken Irishmen, one of whom was Michael Conroy. He walked over to Siddle and without any provocation whatsoever punched him, knocking him to the ground. Goodall asked what was going on, but he was threatened with worse if he didn't stay out of it.

A short time later, a boy named Thomas Plant walked along the same road. Conroy beat him savagely, smashing his stone bottle of beer in the road and stealing the cap off his head.

From the descriptions given to the police, they had a good idea that Conroy, nicknamed locally as "Tom Duck" was the offender. He was a notorious villain who the police considered dangerous, especially in drink. Conroy was fairly quickly located drinking in the Sportsman in Stafford Street, where he was arrested.

At court, Conroy claimed that on the night in question he was so drunk that he just couldn't remember anything.

Police Sergeant Wood was on the desk when Conroy was brought into the police station. He stated that although Conroy had been drinking, he was far from being so drunk he couldn't remember.

Superintendent Cater informed the Bench that Conroy was the notorious "Tom Duck," a well known character responsible for terrorising the neighbourhood of Bloxwich Road at night. People were in fear to go home that way from market, just in case they encountered him.

Conroy had two convictions from the previous year, so the Bench fined him one pound for each assault, or in default one month's imprisonment in each case. Needless to say "Tom Duck" waddled off to prison for two months. [311]

69. Two 'Brummie' Smashers - April 1857

Superintendent Cater and Sergeant Dackus were on duty on Tuesday the 30th of April, 1857, when Eliza Evans reported having received a fake half crown at her shop in St. Paul's Row. The two characters involved in uttering the counterfeit currency were still around town, so the officers went out on a detective mission to find the culprits before they struck again.

Sergeant Dackus spotted John Roberts and John Dolphin from Birmingham, two suspicious characters acting furtively. Sergeant Dackus and Superintendent Cater followed the men as they walked along Bridgman Street and into Wolverhampton Road. The policemen took a local short cut to get in front of them, near to the Cottage Inn public house on Wolverhampton Road. They waited for the unsuspecting crooks to arrive, then Dackus grabbed hold of Roberts, who instantly threw a package over a hedge and Superintendent Cater seized Dolphin. The package Roberts threw was retrieved and found to contain two counterfeit sovereigns and twelve counterfeit half crowns.

Roberts and Dolphin were remanded by the magistrates to appear before the Borough Quarter Sessions. When they appeared on Monday the 6th of July, 1857, they entered guilty pleas, Roberts was given twelve months and Dolphin six months, both with hard labour. [312] [313]

70. 'Irish Hotheads' and the 'Disfigured Man' - June 1857

Lower Rushall Street was a neighbourhood full of families with Irish descent and a well known place for trouble (see stories 53 & 55).

From mid-afternoon on Sunday the 31st of May, 1857, the White Rose beer house at 81, Lower Rushall Street was full of drunken Irishmen and women. By seven o'clock the drink fuelled belligerent Celts decided to settle some old scores and the place became a battle ground for a free for all fight, where the police had to be called.

The first officer on the scene was Police Constable Rabone who witnessed an all out riot taking place. Constable Rabone grabbed hold of James Friery to break up a fight, but was immediately attacked by William Conroy, who attempted to get his friend free. Badly outnumbered Constable Rabone determinedly managed to arrest both men, although he was nastily assaulted in the process.

Friery and Conroy were charged with assaulting a police officer and they appeared at Walsall Magistrates on Monday the 1st of June. Superintendent Cater said that some witnesses were afraid to give evidence against the two men for fear of reprisals, so asked the court to remand them in custody until Wednesday. He hoped to be able to convince the witnesses to give evidence, by assuring them positive action was being taken.

On Wednesday, three witnesses attended to corroborate that Constable Rabone was assaulted by Friery and Conroy. They were found guilty by the magistrates who fined them both two pounds each. They could not pay, so elected to walk the treadmill at Stafford Gaol for twenty-one days instead.

On Tuesday 26th of May, 1857, Superintendent Cater received numerous complains of a weird drunken man exposing his deformed and objectionable arm in public. The hideous John Smith was located in the market place, performing some kind of bizarre drunken show whilst begging for money. His public exhibition was put to an end when the strange man was taken into custody for the sake of public decency.

Smith an out of town stranger, pleaded with the magistrates to set him free. He promised to leave Walsall straight away and not to ever come back if they gave him their mercy. The Bench decided it was the best course of action, so they discharged him to perform his weirdness elsewhere. His harmless yet unpleasant problem was kicked down the road for another town to deal with. [314]

71. No Mercy for the Post Office Thief - June 1857

The Post Office was a British institution in 1857 and theft by an employee was not only a terrible breach of trust, it carried a considerable sentence. On first conviction an employee could expect to be transported for up to seven years, or be imprisoned for not less than three years.

When things started going missing at the main Walsall Post Office in 1857, it didn't take long for the pilfering news to filter down to the powers that be in London.

Henry Daly was sent to investigate the matter from the General Post Office in London on Friday the 7th of August, 1857 and his first port of call was to the office of Superintendent Cater. It was agreed that Superintendent Cater would personally post a controlled letter containing a marked florin that evening at the main Post Office in town. After the letter was dispatched, Mr. Daly travelled to Birmingham, to await the arrival of the relevant bag from Walsall. When it came the letter and the florin were missing.

The next morning, Mr. Daly and Superintendent Cater went to the Post Office as it opened. They suspected that thirty-three year old auxiliary carrier Samuel Smart was responsible, as he was on duty when the letter was posted. They asked him to turn out his pockets and one of the coins produced was the marked florin from the missing letter. Smart claimed he received the coin as part of his nine shillings and six pence wages.

On Monday the 10th of August, Samuel Smart appeared before the Mayor at the Magistrates Court.

Mr. Daly gave evidence that the marked florin was placed in a letter posted by Superintendent Cater to a bogus address in Cheltenham. Daly confirmed the letter never left Walsall and the marked coin was found the following day in the possession of Smart.

Superintendent Cater corroborated his evidence, stating that Smart alleged that he received the coin as part of his wages.

The Walsall Postmaster William Wainwright, confirmed that Smart would have handled the missing letter as he was the stamper, but he definitely didn't have the florin as part of his wages.

The magistrates committed him for trial at Stafford Assizes and bail was refused. A legal challenge was raised on the grounds that the letter was sent to a fictitious address, but this objection was overruled before the trial.

On Friday the 11th of December, 1857, Samuel Smart appeared at Stafford Assizes before Judge Baron Martin. Mr. Scotland prosecuted for the Crown and Smart defended himself. The prosecution witnesses gave their evidence and then Smart elected to address the Jury for his own defence. He denied any theft and maintained that the florin was paid to him in his wages.

After the Judge's summing up the Jury returned a "guilty" verdict. As was customary, the Judge asked Smart if he wanted to say anything. Smart begged the Judge for mercy, because since he had been in custody at prison, his wife had died leaving their two young children all alone.

The Judge told Smart that he wasn't entitled to any mercy, as he had neither shown any remorse nor admitted his wrongdoing by pleading not guilty. On the contrary, he had tried to implicate others for putting the stolen money into his pay packet. The Judge also pointed out that Mr. Daly only became involved, because other small amounts had gone missing previously. The Judge told Smart that he had been found guilty of a serious offence, where notwithstanding his personal circumstances and his previous good character, he must receive the same sentence as that given to others and that was a punishment of six years imprisonment.

In 1858, Smart was moved from Leicester to Portland Prison, before his final release on the 17th of June, 1862. Stealing two shillings was not a smart move in 1857. [315] [316] [317] [318] [319] [320]

72. Despicable Treatment of a Child - October 1857

Parts of the old town of Walsall hid the shameful secret of extreme poverty, where poor paupers lived in the most horrendous living conditions. Although some considered them the lowest of the low, they had standards and lived to a common code of decency. They may have become desensitised to their own situation, but unnecessary cruelty was sinful, especially if it involved the neglect and basic care of children. In the hardest of deprivation, child abuse was despicable, something even the most blighted people couldn't ignore. Ordinarily people often saw the authorities as the enemy, but blatant inhuman atrocities still got reported.

On Friday the 30th of October, 1857, Superintendent Cater was informed about the situation of a child, supposedly left alone in terrible conditions at a house in New Street. The Superintendent called in Mr. Purnell to assist him, he was a Borough Union relieving officer who had responsibility for child welfare. Together they went to the so called home of the child, where they were confronted with the most horrendous human spectacle of poverty and neglect they had ever seen. They found a young boy of about ten years of age, lying almost lifeless on an old filthy rug on the floor. The skin of his naked skeletal body was obviously riddled with some kind of untreated medical disease. Next to the emaciated silent child on the dirty floor boards was a small uneaten stale crust of bread. When asked, the whimpering child said, his mother had threatened to kill him if he ate it.

So completely shocked by what they had seen, the child was instantly removed to the Union workhouse for care and safety. Superintendent Cater ensured that the father, John Martin was arrested forthwith and brought into custody.

Martin, who the press described as a most repulsive looking man was put before the Walsall Magistrates. Having listened to the circumstances from Superintendent Cater, the justices were so sickened by what they heard, they refused to give Martin the opportunity to utter a single word in his own defence. He was sent straight to gaol for a month with hard labour. [321]

73. *The Ex-Cop & His Minder's Manslaughter - August 1858*

Tucked away up grimy and narrow back alleyways were Walsall's courtyard dwellings, some of the roughest and hardest places to live. Irrespective of the police, these dingy haunts had an extra layer of justice, the law of the jungle that reigned supreme. Local hard men called the shots in these little neighbourhoods, ruling with their reputations of fear and violence. People who stepped out of line or crossed the wrong person could expect some old fashioned summary justice, it was just the way of the world. The secret was knowing who and who not to cross, because these hot headed intemperate people had violent reputations and instant justice was dished out with a physical scrap to restore their own kind of status quo. The police were rarely involved, because their victims were scared to complain for fear of reprisals, so almost accepted it as a way of life. Shitting on your own doorstep had inevitable consequences in this toxic kind of society. It was only when fights occasionally went wrong or had unexpected results that the police got involved to pick up the pieces and punish the perpetrators.

Charles Welch the landlord of the Old Church and Bell public house in Church Street had a chequered past. Previously Welch had been a policeman who joined Walsall Borough Police in about 1847 and served under Superintendent John Rofe. Welch's ability was recognised by Superintendent Rofe and he was fairly quickly promoted to sergeant. It all went wrong in 1850 when the Watch Committee fell out with Superintendent Rofe. They forced Sergeant Welch to resign from the force and soon after Rofe went as well. Welch plays a part in the previous stories (19, 43, 44, 45, and 48), although the first one relates to an incident where he was acquitted at court before he joined the police.

When Welch left the force, he went into the licensing trade, which was not uncommon for ex-policemen. Unfortunately, Welch let his standards slip and started getting into things he once clamped down on, he was a gamekeeper turned poacher for sure. Welch already had the reputation of being a hard man when he left the police, so quickly adapted his skills to dispense the laws of the backstreet jungle instead.

In 1858, Welch then fifty-one years of age, still maintained his tough guy reputation, but now he had twenty-nine year old Richard Garbett as his minder to do the fighting and dirty work. Garbett was the front man for Welch's nefarious business enterprises, which included an unsavoury brothel at the rear of the Old Church and Bell pub.

Samuel Patten a local man, visited Garbett's brothel on the night of Saturday the 21st of August, 1858, but after leaving there at about three o'clock on Sunday morning, he realised his valuable watch was missing. He asked a fellow miner, forty-seven year old John Springthorpe for advice as he lived a few doors away from Welch in Church Street. Springthorpe had known Welch for years, so together they returned to the brothel to see if they could retrieve the watch, but without success. Patten offered a ten shillings reward, so Springthorpe sent his common-law wife of sixteen years Caroline Murray, to ask Welch if he could get the watch back for him. Welch agreed to do what he could and on Monday the 23rd of August, 1858, the watch was returned.

What happened next is uncertain, but it is fair to say that Springthorpe had infuriated Welch. Maybe Welch did not get his share of the reward, but whatever happened Springthorpe was in for it, the jungle police were looking for him.

At midnight on Monday, Welch and Garbett went round to Springthorpe's house banging on the door and threatening to teach him a lesson for not minding his own business. Garbett called Springthorpe out to fight, but the door was kept tightly shut and eventually they went away before they attracted the local bobby.

A nights sleep didn't calm Welch down and at about eight o'clock the next morning he went to Springthorpe's house again, shouting and threatening to kill him. John Springthorpe was out at the time, but returned to see Welch outside his house waiting for him. Welch made a run for him, but this time Springthorpe who was a big miner squared up.

Welch shouted to Richard Garbett who soon crawled out of the woodwork like his puppet. Springthorpe knew Garbett was a little rogue and bully and although he was far bigger in size, he didn't want to fight the thug. Garbett was Welch's hired fighter so when he screamed at him, " Now Dick, go into him, kill him," he immediately unleashed a savage blow, which knocked Springthorpe to the ground. Springthorpe got back to his feet, but the aggressive smaller man was like a wild animal. The level of violence took Springthorpe completely by surprise, Garbett grabbed him by the collar and aimed a powerful right fist at his face. Springthorpe's height difference meant the punch fell low of its target and sank savagely into his throat, knocking him backwards to the ground. Springthorpe staggered to his feet like a zombie, with his face going black and his neck swelling up. Welch continued shouting encouragement for Garbett to finish him off, but the damage was done, Springthorpe was totally unable to fight. Somehow he staggered back to his house, as Welch patted Garbett on the back and took him into the pub.

Springthorpe was fast approaching deaths door, he struggled to breathe as his constricting throat slowly began to strangle him. Sergeant George Wood and surgeon Mr. E. J. Marshall quickly arrived at the house, but the injury to his throat was so severe, they could not save him and within three-quarters of an hour Springthorpe died with his eyes bulging from asphyxia. Springthorpe was totally unable to speak a word before his death.

Sergeant Wood went looking for the suspects and found them together in Welch's pub where they were arrested. Garbett said to Sergeant Wood in the cells, "The superintendent would have done no more than I have done, which was in self defence."

They appeared together at Walsall Magistrates on Wednesday the 25th of August, 1858, Garbett charged with murder and Welch with aiding and abetting him. Some evidence was heard, but the case was adjourned pending a Coroners inquest.

The inquest was opened that afternoon at the Queen's Head, Church Street, before the Coroner, Mr. A. Fletcher.

Interestingly the previous inquest held at the Queen's Head in August 1854, involved seventeen year old James Barber, accused of killing John Nicholls, who had his head smashed open on a kerbstone after they had both frequented Welch's brothel. At the Assizes on the 12th of March, 1855, Barber was found guilty, but the Judge decided that he had served enough time on remand for him to be discharged without further penalty. James Barber's own father John, previously faced a murder charge after killing a man named Thomas Startin in a prize fight on the 19th of February, 1833 at Delves Green. Startin died in the forty-third round after an hour of scrapping in the fight arranged at the Blue Pig in Walsall. Barber was found not guilty at the Stafford Assizes in March, 1833.

At this inquest, several local people gave evidence about the fight taking place including, Maria Scully, Hannah Cooper, William Thomson, William Bird, Joseph Bartholomew and Isaac Whitlick. The surgeon Mr. Marshall conducted the post mortem examination and concluded that Springthorpe's death was caused by a considerable violent blow that threw the head backwards breaking the pyloric bone and smashing his thyroid cartilage. The inquest continued into Thursday, when the Coroner summed up and the jury retired to consider their verdict. It wasn't until half past eleven at night, after five hours deliberation that the jury returned a verdict of wilful murder against

Garbett and aiding and abetting against Welch. The Coroner issued his warrant for their committal to Stafford Assizes.

At the Magistrates Court on Friday the 27th of August, 1858, both men were sent to Stafford Gaol to await trial.

Welch's loss of control came at a catastrophic cost, less than ten years before he was the man taking the prisoners in irons to Stafford gaol by cart. How the mighty fall when a street fight goes wrong!

The murder trial before Judge Baron Bramwell was at Stafford Winter Assizes on the 29th of November, 1858. Mr. Scotland prosecuted, Mr. Motteram defended Welch and Mr. Hill appeared for Garbett.

Mr. Scotland started by informing the jury that they must decide on the evidence, whether the men were guilty of murder or the lesser offence of manslaughter with the assistance of the learned Judge.

At the conclusion of the prosecution case the Judge instructed the jury that the prisoners could not properly be convicted of murder, as there was no evidence to show any intent and no deadly weapon had been used to kill Springthorpe. The Judge however, directed that Garbett's actions were instigated by Welch and if they thought he had caused Springthorpe's death, then Welch was equally as guilty.

The jury returned a guilty verdict against both men and the Judge condemned Welch for hiring a bully to fight the battles he was too cowardly to fight himself.

In his own defence, Welch claimed to have been a man of excellent character and called Police Inspector Price from the County Police at Rushall as a character reference.

Inspector Price told the court, that Welch had been a sergeant in the police at Walsall and had received a reward of £20 for apprehending burglars, as well as several smaller gratuities for meritorious services. Price said that Welch had generally borne a good character and this sentiment was corroborated by Mr. Duignan, the Walsall attorney.

The Judge sentenced both prisoners to serve three months imprisonment with hard labour at Stafford gaol.

The license of the Old Church and Bell was removed while Welch was on remand, the magistrates describing the venue as, 'a disgrace to the town.' At some point the licence of the Old Church and Bell was renewed by Welch, but the place remained a problem and it was finally closed down in 1869. [322] [323] [324] [325] [326]

It's hard to believe that thuggish ruffians could get three months for killing a man in the street, while a Post Office worker got six years for stealing a florin that was recovered. Perhaps trust was valued more highly at the time!

74. Confounding the Cock Fighters - May 1859

In May 1859, Superintendent Cater received some information about an impending cock fight to be staged at John Flemming's, Ring of Bells in Hill Street. Superintendent Cater visited the premises and ordered one of his constables to remain behind to prevent anything from happening. John Flemming was furious about the constable being left at his premises, so marched around to the police station to have it out with the superintendent. He demanded that Superintendent Cater explain why a constable was at his premises, but he simply replied, he was there to prevent him holding a cock fight.

Flemming started gobbing off using abusive language, until eventually the superintendent had enough. He told Flemming that if he didn't desist, he would be arrested under the bye laws for disorderly conduct in the police station. Superintendent Cater then left the office for a while, to allow him some time to calm down, but Flemming continued his abuse and eventually he was taken to the cells. Flemming threatened to report Superintendent Cater's attitude to the magistrates.

When Flemming came up before the Bench, he was defended by Mr. Ebsworth, a man who held an obvious dislike for Superintendent Cater. Ebsworth contested that the power of arrest used by the superintendent did not exist. Ebsworth and Cater's personalities clashed and there was a collision of professional ego's. Ebsworth accused Superintendent Cater of arresting his client only after he threatened to expose him to the magistrates. Not only that he said, his client was deliberately subjected to false imprisonment and humiliation, after he was detained for several hours in a gaol with common criminals.

The Mayor Mr. Eyland, was unimpressed by Ebsworth's rant and fined Flemming twenty shillings or in default to seven days in gaol. The Mayor also told Ebsworth that he believed Superintendent Cater acted quite correctly and for his future reference, the Bench intended to punish all cock-fighting cases most severely. [327]

75. A Superintendents Good Thrashing - February 1860

On the afternoon of Wednesday the 22nd of February, 1860, John Kelly was drinking in the Dog and Partridge public house in Sandwell Street, run by Mrs. Emma Osbourne. Kelly was the worse for drink and at one point during his visit, he alleged that someone stole some sheet music from him. When he couldn't get it returned, he wandered off outside and began to stagger along the street.

By pure chance he bumped into Superintendent Cater and Sergeant Martin doing their rounds. Kelly excitedly requested them to accompany him back into the Dog and Partridge to help him recover his property. They went with him, but none of the music sheets were found and some of the customers stated that Kelly had exchanged them for drink. Superintendent Cater informed Kelly that under the circumstances there was nothing more they could do for him. Kelly followed Superintendent Cater outside the premises in a fit of temper and threatened to throw a stone he picked up. The superintendent told him firmly to put the stone down, but Kelly disobeyed him and smashed the pub window, while hurling abuse at the people inside. The superintendent was infuriated by Kelly's actions and lost his temper, so gave him a good thrashing with his walking stick, until it was reduced to splinters.

When Kelly appeared at court, Superintendent Cater was compelled to apologise to the Bench for losing his composure and acting under impulse. After a short consultation the lad was sentenced to pay a fine of one pound and costs or be imprisoned for twenty-one days. The Mayor said the Bench considered a sentence of six weeks, but reduced it to take account of the summary punishment already inflicted by Superintendent Cater. [328] [329]

76. The Lewd Snappers Ultimatum - March 1860

In March 1860, Superintendent Cater received some sordid information about a thirty-two year old photographer named Alfred Jones, the owner of a photographic studio in Bradford Street. He was supposedly involved in taking obscene nude images for customers as part of his business.

Superintendent Cater obtained a search warrant for the premises and duly raided his studio. Twenty-seven images, described as being of a 'disgusting nature' were found, some in a box and others in his laboratory with the chemicals.

When Jones appeared at the court he was defended by none other than Mr. Ebsworth, the superintendents nemesis. Ebsworth informed the magistrates that Jones only took the nude pictures at the special request of his customers and would be losing good trade if he refused. He contested that the Obscene Publications Act of 1857, initiated by Lord Campbell, was designed to stop such pictures being exposed for general sale or gain after the Holywell Street case in London. As these images were not sold to anyone but private clients it didn't apply and in any case the magistrates had no power to destroy the images found.

The Magistrates considered it for a short while but disagreed with him and ordered the pictures to be destroyed. The Mayor severely reprimanded Jones, saying he wished there were greater powers to punish him more severely. The Mayor suggested that it would be in Jones best interests to leave Walsall as soon as possible, if he had any plans to continue, because if he persisted in such a lewd trade and ever came before him again, he would be facing the full force of the law. It would appear that Jones did stay in Walsall after the case, so he either never got caught again or he modified his ways after his lewd ultimatum. [330]

77. Mr. Ebsworth's 'Prize Fight' Revenge - May 1860

Sporting men of all classes viewed the brutal art of prize fighting as a great source of entertainment and a chance to place some bets. Although impromptu fights were illegal, it didn't stop huge crowds descending on rural locations in secret to see the bouts take place.

The precise location of such contests was normally only disclosed at the last minute to prevent the police from stopping people attending the gatherings. Even if the police did turn up to interfere the contest would be postponed for another day and location as the cash prize funds were usually staked before the fight. Once a handshake had been made, there was no going back and the show must go on. Details of forthcoming events were announced in the publication, 'Bell's Life in London and Sporting Chronicle,' but not necessarily the exact locations.

In the edition for Sunday the 29th of April, 1860, an article appeared, "Joseph Amos of Bloxwich and David Welch of Walsall. These midland district men make their final deposit good to Mr. Hawkins, of Wednesbury, this (Saturday) evening for their fight, at catchweight, for £10 a side, which comes off tomorrow (Monday) within 12 miles of Walsall. Both men have actively trained for the event, and report speaks both men in excellent condition." David was incidentally the son of ex-sergeant Charles Welch (see story 73).

Colonel Hogg the Chief Constable of Staffordshire received information about the fight and Inspector Price from Rushall was asked to deal with the matter. Inspector Price, obviously knew Charles Welch very well as he gave a character reference for him in court. As the Welch's were a Walsall family, Inspector Price travelled to liaise with Superintendent Cater about the fight. Knowing where to look, it wasn't very long before the police observed known associates making their way towards the fight location at Barr Beacon.

At just before six o'clock on the morning of Monday the 30th of April, 1860, the police started making their way towards the Three Crowns on the Sutton Road, where a large crowd had already assembled. Fight day spotters saw the police coming and the crowd began to instantly disperse, with Welch running through the yard to hide beneath his cart. As he was the target of the operation, he was caught and arrested.

Welch appeared at Walsall court that morning, defended by Mr. Ebsworth. He instantly accused Superintendent Cater of bringing the lamest of cases and exceeded his authority in doing so. The professional animosity between the two men was clear to see, with Mr. Ebsworth saying he was determined to bring Superintendent Cater to account. Ebsworth said so long as Superintendent Cater was around, no one was safe to leave their own cart next to a crowd without being arrested and he accused him of bringing this case to court without the slightest shred of evidence to show that a prize fight was even about to take place.

This time after a short consultation, the Bench conceded that Ebsworth was right, so on the grounds of deficient evidence the case was dismissed.

David Welch walked away from court, but not from the fight. The two pugilists met at five o'clock at Kingswood Common in Staffordshire on another morning in early May. This time there were no police about and the two men got off to a timely start. Amos looked the favourite from as early as the fourth round, but despite showing early promise, he had to battle for another hour and twenty minutes as it wasn't until the 67th round that he finally knocked Welch out. [331] [332] [333]

78. Another Post Office Thief - October 1860

As we saw from our previous incident (story 71), theft in the Post Office was considered a serious breach of trust. The general public expected and believed that every man employed by the organisation was of the highest honesty and integrity. This belief was the bedrock of the organisation and why the public had confidence in the Post Office to safeguard the property placed in their hands.

On the morning of Saturday the 20th October, 1860, the General Post Office in London sent Mr. Thomas Jefferys to Walsall, to investigate complaints that letters had gone missing. Jefferys liaised with Superintendent Cater about the problem and gave him a test letter to post on his behalf containing a marked sovereign and a shilling.

Superintendent Cater duly posted the letter at Walsall and at half past five that day, he and Mr. Jefferys returned to the post office. The test letter and the shilling was gone, but the marked sovereign was found in the office cash box. The clear suspect was Nicholas O'Farrell, one of the clerks, so they went to his home address to see him. He denied knowing anything about the missing letter, but the marked shilling was found in his pocket. Just as in our previous case, O'Farrell claimed the coin was given to him as part of his wages paid on Saturday, but he was arrested and taken to the police station.

O'Farrell made an initial appearance before Walsall Magistrates on Monday the 22nd October, 1860, represented by Mr. Ebsworth.

Mr. Jeffreys was cross examined about the possibility of the coins just falling out of the envelope, but he said he had never known it happen before. Ebsworth picked up on the fact that O'Farrell was never cautioned properly before his replies were recorded and made a big issue out of it. Bail was refused and the case was adjourned until Thursday.

At court on Thursday, Mr. Wainwright the Walsall Post Master, said he saw O'Farrell leave the office at five o'clock on Saturday. He pointed out that O'Farrell's wages were paid on Friday night not Saturday and his pay packet did not include any shilling coins. Mr. Ebsworth complained that on a salary of just twenty-two shillings a week, O'Farrell was unable to afford a lawyer to defend him at the Assizes. True to form Ebsworth accused Superintendent Cater and Mr. Jeffreys of entrapping his client by resorting to diabolical methods and then not having the common decency to caution him properly before asking him questions. Ebsworth suggested the prosecution had conveniently overlooked the possibility that O'Farrell got the shilling coin by changing some of his own money. He made a final plea for the case to be dismissed due to a lack of evidence claiming there was reasonable doubt, especially with the methods used by the prosecution. Ebsworth did not convince the Bench, who committed O'Farrell for trial.

O'Farrell was found guilty at Stafford Winter Assizes in December, 1860 and was sentenced to four years imprisonment. It proved very costly for him as his reputation was torn to shreds and he lost his liberty for a significant time, but benefitted nothing as all the money was recovered. [334] [335] [336]

79. The Wilful Murder of James Flynn - December 1860

On the morning of Sunday the 23rd of December, 1860, a large contingent of the Irish community attended a Christening service and afterwards convened to an address in Green Lane. As was customary, especially amongst the Irish, the 'wet the baby's head' celebrations went on throughout the whole day and into the next.

At about quarter past two in the early hours of Monday morning, the party was still in full flow, but things were turning nasty. Tanked up men decided they were going to settle some old differences and about fifteen or so spilt out into the street to argue it out.

Police Constable 13 Beebee was walking his beat when he came across the large rowdy crowd gathered. One of the men, Richard Power was shouting about someone stealing his cap and threatening to make them pay. Constable Beebee's presence calmed the drunken group down and he continued on his beat, but he kept a watchful eye on things. After only going a short distance up the street a fight broke out, between two rival factions. Richard Power was the ringleader of one group, but several men were now fighting each other. Constable Beebee tried to break up one of the fights, but then heard James Flynn, cry out that he had been stabbed. All the fighting suddenly stopped and the constable saw that Flynn had a nasty open wound to his abdomen.

Flynn was asked to point out the offender, but said he could not see them. He denied it was Power and they actually shook hands on the fact. Flynn was taken home and a doctor was summoned to look at his injury.

One of the revellers named Bridget Keogh told the police that she was present when James Flynn received the cowardly stab to his lower belly. She heard Flynn cry out in pain and was convinced it was Richard Power who did it, as he immediately ran away.

Based on her account, Acting Sergeant Hudson, together with Constables Beebee and Hughes went looking for Power at his lodgings. Bridget Keogh pointed Power out as the person responsible and he was taken into custody and conveyed to the police station.

Flynn's condition began to drastically deteriorate and at about half past five that day, Superintendent Cater went to his home to record a dying declaration. Flynn was in total agony, wincing in pain with his intestines awkwardly protruding from an open wound in his stomach.

The statement started, "I believe I am in a dying state, without any hope of recovery." In his statement, Flynn did not point the finger of suspicion at any particular person. The doctor arrived to administer chloroform, in an attempt to give some relief, but the man was gravely weakened by the severe loss of blood. Flynn miraculously flickered in a dying state until Friday the 28th of December, but then his injuries forced him to succumb to death.

An inquest opened at the Bull's Head in Green Lane on Saturday the 29th of December, 1860. The only job for the jury on that day was the daunting task of viewing Flynn's dead body lying on a bench.

The inquest proceedings recommenced on Monday after a proper post mortem examination had been completed by Mr. Marshall a surgeon from Bridge Street. He examined the body of James Flynn and concluded that he died from inflammation from a one inch stab wound to the lower left side of the belly caused by a bladed instrument. He said that even if the bowels had been put back in immediately, there would have been little chance to save his life.

Superintendent Cater produced Flynn's heavily blood stained trousers and shirt and indicated to a one inch long cut through the shirt lining.

Mr. Ebsworth who attended the inquest to represent Power called Timothy Kyne as an alibi. Kyne said he saw the stabbing happen and Power was definitely not responsible. During cross examination, it became apparent that Kyne was lying and couldn't have possibly seen the stabbing from where he was standing.

The Coroner asked the jury to consider first of all, whether Power was the man who used the knife. If they thought he was the man responsible, then did he act in self defence, as a result of provocation, or did he intend to kill Flynn. In the first case it would be justifiable homicide, in the second manslaughter and in the third wilful murder. After a lapse of almost three hours they returned a verdict of "Wilful Murder."

Richard Power appeared before the Magistrates Court on Thursday the 3rd of January, 1861. Superintendent Cater explained that he was only seeking a formal committal to the Assizes, as the Coroner had already issued his warrant for wilful murder. The Bench agreed, but Mr. Ebsworth wanted it noting down that the Coroners verdict was given without him or his client being present.

Richard Power's trial commenced at Stafford Assizes on the 11th of March, 1861. Superintendent Cater started by telling the jury that some fresh evidence had come to light, since Power had been on remand at Stafford. On the night in question Power's landlady was handed a knife by a man named Michael Waney and it was dropped down a drain. The ignorant woman claimed that it never occurred to her that the knife might be the one the police were looking for! Superintendent Cater said all attempts to trace this Michael Waney had failed. After the stabbing he disappeared and his whereabouts are unknown, but enquiries suggest he absconded to the United States.

The trial continued, but at the end of the evidence the Judge summed up favourably in the interests of fairness to Power. After only a few minutes of deliberation, the jury returned a verdict of "Not guilty" and Power was discharged at once. [337] [338] [339]

80. St. Peter's Macabre Baby Bodies - March 1862

In March 1862 parishioners attending the service at St. Peter's church in Stafford Street got more than just the usual word of God. As they sat on the pews, the sermon was distracted by a strange poo of sickening effluvia wafting around the building. The rancid smell bore a likeness to death itself and complaints were made to Mr. J. Busst one of the churchwardens. After the service he set out following his nose to discover the source of the foul stink. To his absolute horror, he found the rotting bodies of several newborn babies in various stages of putrefaction, some of them he thought had been there for at least twelve months.

Mr. Busst summoned John Bentley, the thirty-two year old sexton who had been employed at the church for the last two years for an explanation. It was an accepted practice for still born baby bodies to be placed into the coffins of the recently departed before burial in the graveyard and this was one of the duties of the sexton. Bentley claimed that all the babies were still born, brought to him by various midwives for burial and he was just waiting for a convenient time to do it. John Bentley's explanation was unacceptable, as it was clear some of the bodies had been there for a long time. His answers were very vague and incomplete, so Mr. Busst immediately alerted the incumbent Reverend Charles Dunn of the grim finds, who in turn notified Superintendent Cater.

The suspicious circumstances warranted a thorough search of St. Peter's by the police, during which the horrific true extent of the matter came to light. The police search revealed, no less than thirteen tiny bodies, some in the tool shed, some in the meter cupboard and others below the staircase to the choir.

The disturbing finds started all kinds of bizarre and grotesque rumours to circulate around the town, including that Bentley was a grave robber collecting bodies. The story captured the minds of the locals who were eager to find out the truth about the morbid tales.

Mr. A. Fletcher, the Borough Coroner, had the prospect of conducting thirteen inquests on each of the bodies found. He opened the proceedings at the Sportsman public house in Stafford Street on the morning of Monday the 24th March, 1862. A large 'witch hunt' crowd formed outside in anticipation, such was the interest in the case. The first job of the Jury after being sworn, was to visit the porch of St. Peter's church where the tiny bodies in various states of decomposition, were all laid out in a row for inspection. After the ghoulish task was done they returned to the Sportsman.

Mr. Busst informed the Coroner that Bentley's explanations were very vague and didn't make complete sense. Bentley told him that one of the bodies came from Mr. Day at Bentley, one was from the midwife Mrs. Broadhurst, one was from Mrs. Stubbs another midwife, one was from Mrs. Jones and another from Mrs. Broadhurst's husband. Mr. Busst said that Bentley couldn't provide him with the proper certificates for most of them and it was very peculiar he did not know the names of the parents.

A surgeon David Smith Moore, said he conducted the post mortem on the body of a baby girl found in the tool shed. He considered the child was fully formed, but he believed it had been a still birth.

When the inquest ended that day, outside the Sportsman was like a scene from the middle ages. Numerous women had formed what can only be described as a 'lynch mob' and they were baying for his blood. Bentley had to be escorted back home under police protection for his own safety.

The inquest continued at the Sportsman on Thursday afternoon and started with John Bentley being called to explain the situation. Bentley gave an unsettling account of things, saying he usually kept the bodies of still born babies at the church, until he had the opportunity to bury them. Sometimes they were left at his house with his wife, but he could not remember how many. Bentley said that he received at least thirty or so still born babies that year and most of them were buried within two or three days, although he did have one at his house for a couple of months. When asked to explain the delay in burying the bodies found by the police, he simply said he just forgot. Bentley admitted taking one shilling and sixpence for each body to make all the arrangements.

David Smith Moore, was recalled and said that at least five of the babies must have been dead for over twelve months, because there was little more than a few bones to look at. He said the body of a fully developed girl suggested she was born alive, but died shortly after from hydrothorax or water on the lungs.

John Bentley appeared at the Guildhall on Friday the 4th of July, 1862, charged with refusing and neglecting to bury thirteen baby bodies. After all the facts were heard, the jury needed no time to deliberate and returned an instant "guilty" verdict. Bentley was sentenced to five months imprisonment with hard labour. [340] [341] [342]

81. The Wilfully Woeful Child Murder Case - 1866

This is another of those very sad and unfortunate cases where young women became the victims of the age. Unmarried women with children were frowned upon by society and very often abandoned not only by the father's, but also by their own families. Sometimes with no support, they were cast into a world of poverty, where they became the victims of unscrupulous people, who cashed in on their deprivation.

Elizabeth Burford was one of these women, thrust into motherhood as a teenager. By 1865, she was a twenty-two year old single mother with a four year old child and a six months old baby girl. As one of life's true unfortunates, Elizabeth Burford drifted into Walsall on the 31st of October, 1865, without a penny to her name and totally destitute. She was forced to seek refuge at Walsall Workhouse, but ashamed of being a fallen woman with two children in tow, she used the alias surname Dando. Single women with children were frequently forced into the workhouse, as they were unable to work and look after children at the same time. Workhouses were deliberately inhospitable and uninviting for a reason, it was a 'get on with it,' world, where people believed, 'you've made your bed now lie on it.' You have to remember, that this was a time when you were expected to pay for your own mistakes.

Elizabeth Burford stayed at the workhouse all winter until the 28th of February, 1866, when it appears she 'jumped out of the frying pan into the fire.' She took lodgings with Abraham and Maria Price at Bull's Head Yard in Upper Rushall Street, a notoriously rough area, full of Irish immigrants and other dubious characters. How she intended to pay for her stay is unknown, but soon after arriving Elizabeth Burford was seen associating with a very shady man, whose intentions were more than likely dishonourable.

Elizabeth Burford left Walsall with the man and her two children and went to stay at Mary Bagnall's lodging house in Wednesbury. The Saturday after arriving, the shady man vanished. Mary Bagnall instinctively knew the man had taken advantage of Elizabeth Burford's situation and sympathised with her desperate predicament. She was struggling and poverty stricken, so out of kindness Mary Bagnall wanted to help and tried to befriend her.

On Thursday the 5th of April, 1866, Elizabeth Burford's mood changed for the worse, she was extremely agitated and low spirited. Mary Bagnall sensed she was contemplating doing a flit and was so concerned for her welfare that she kept a watch. Sure enough at around seven o'clock her suspicions proved right, when she heard Elizabeth Burford at the door. She had the baby strapped to her breast and the four year old clinging on as she opened the door. The weather was horrendous outside, absolutely pouring down with rain. Mary Bagnall begged her not to go out into the cold wet night with the children, asking her to stay rent free if she had no money. Despite her very best efforts, Elizabeth Burford walked away into the night time storm, with the poor children hanging onto their troubled mother.

At eleven o'clock that night, Burford returned soaking wet at the lodging house of Maria Price in Bull's Head Yard and oddly she only had the four year old child with her. Maria Price was suspicious because the child was crying franticly, so Elizabeth Burford explained it away by saying "She is fretting about the baby" as it was dead and had been buried.

On Friday morning at five o'clock the picture became clearer, Thomas Rowson a furnace man was on his way to work when he saw a suspicious looking object in the Town Brook. When he took a closer look, he discovered an old black skirt wrapped around the body of a six months old baby wearing white socks and a brown bonnet. The child was very cold and dead, so he summoned the police and soon afterwards Constable Joseph Elkin arrived at the brook. The child was lying on its back, with its hands at the sides, without any obvious signs of injury. Constable Elkin noted that there was a trickle of milk coming from the child's mouth. He carried the little body back to the police station where enquiries began.

The word that a child's body had been found drowned soon travelled around the town and by nine clock that morning, Police Constable Dobbins was on his way to Maria Price's lodging house in Bull's Head Yard. When he arrived, Elizabeth Burford was upstairs in one of the bedrooms, dressing the four year old. The officer told her he had come about a very serious matter, because a baby girl's body had been found drowned in the Town Brook.

He formally cautioned her and asked if the dead child was hers, to which she replied, "It is not mine, I had a child, but it is dead and buried." She refused to tell Constable Dobbins where her child was buried, or where she lodged at Wednesbury, so he placed her under arrest and took her to the police station.

Later that afternoon, Elizabeth Burford was charged by Superintendent Cater with the wilful murder of her child, but she appeared strangely apathetic and made no reply. She was taken before John Shannon, a magistrate, who remanded her in custody until the following Thursday morning.

An inquest was opened at about half past six that evening at the Nags Head in Upper Rushall Street. A large group of people gathered outside the police station, hoping to catch a glimpse of the mother, but they were sadly disappointed. Only the evidence of Thomas Rowson who found the body was taken, before the inquest was adjourned to facilitate a formal post mortem examination.

The inquest resumed on Wednesday the 11th of April, 1866, when the surgeon Mr. F. P. Palmer, who completed the examination on the child's body was called to give evidence. He said that the child appeared to have been well nurtured, with mother's milk in its stomach, but said the child did not die from suffocation due to overlying. He concluded that the posterior part of the lungs were gorged with dark blood and the pulmonary vein was congested, suggesting that death resulted from drowning with violence.

In his summing up, the Coroner told the jury that Elizabeth Burford had tried to conceal the truth about the child's death to the police. If they were satisfied the death had been caused by violence, then they must return a verdict of wilful murder, but if they had any doubt, they must give her the benefit of it. The jury, only needed about a quarter of an hour to return a verdict of wilful murder and she was committed to take her trial at the next Stafford Assizes. Elizabeth Burford appeared very melancholy, but never raised her eyes throughout the whole of the inquest.

The following day on Thursday, Elizabeth Burford appeared in a crowded courtroom before the Walsall Magistrates, charged with the wilful murder of her child. She was allowed to sit while listening to the proceedings.

Overnight the surgeon Mr. Palmer seemed to have mellowed in his conclusions about the death. Palmer said that he could scarcely account for the fact that he did not find water in the child's stomach, which he would have expected in a drowning.

Mr. Matthews who was prosecuting, said that Mr. Palmer's evidence now suggested that the child's death looked less atrocious than it originally appeared to be.

Superintendent Cater produced a letter from the vicar of Frampton, which said that Elizabeth Burford and her mother were considered "half-witted," when they lived in his parish. This was a contemporary way of saying she had some learning difficulties.

At the close of the case, Elizabeth Burford was asked to stand for the Mayor, who had to inform her that she was being committed for murdering her own child. She fainted and was attended by Mr. Palmer the surgeon, until she recovered enough for the Mayor to finish his task. The woefulness of the proceedings seemed to move her and she cried out, "Oh, my poor child is dead, Oh, my dear child" then fell on the floor of the dock. The following day she was taken to Stafford gaol in a cab to await trial. [343] [344]

Elizabeth Burford's murder trial began at Stafford Assizes on the 20th of July, 1866, before the Judge Mr. Justice Shee. Mr. Motteram prosecuted and the Judge requested Mr. Brown act as defence counsel in the interests of fairness. The case continued for over three hours, but ultimately hinged on the evidence of the surgeon Mr. Palmer. When pushed, Palmer admitted it was impossible for him to say with any certainty, that the child had not suffocated accidentally prior to being placed in water.

Mr. Brown said it was perfectly probable for the child to have been accidentally smothered, whilst close to the breast on the walk from Wednesbury to Walsall. Furthermore, it was conceivable that realising the child was dead, Burford got herself into a terrible state of complete despair and placed the body in the brook without really knowing what she was doing.

The jury viewed Elizabeth Burford's case compassionately, believing her general lack of intelligence and understanding contributed to the terrible situation she found herself in. As Mr. Palmer's evidence left a reasonable doubt the jury returned a verdict of 'not guilty,' acquitting her of the terrible crime.

Superintendent Cater was obviously moved by the unfortunate woman's case and personally took charge of returning her back to Walsall. In the railway carriage on the way back to town, several gentlemen felt compelled to offer their charity. Mr. Matthews, the prosecutor and Mr. Palmer the surgeon both handed Superintendent Cater half a crown and he received three shillings and sixpence from two other travellers. When Superintendent Cater returned to Walsall he started a relief fund for her assistance, where contributions went towards helping the woman to rebuild her life. [345] [346] [347]

82. A Plague of Street Arabs - February 1867

At the presentation of the Chief Constable's report in February, 1867, Councillor John Wilkinson complained about an increase in 'Street Arabs.' This was a term used during Victorian times to describe a homeless vagabond or urchin, usually a child, who begged or stole from the street. Councillor Wilkinson said the prowling thieves plagued the town especially on market days, pilfering from stall holders and shopkeepers. He asked Chief Constable Cater to deploy a larger police presence to counter the nuisance during the day.

The Mayor said it was impossible for the Chief Constable to deploy extra resources, as policemen were also needed to keep the streets safe at night. The matter dropped when the Mayor said that stall holders created the problem themselves by leaving unprotected goods outside their shops. [348]

83. The Remarkable Thompson and Simpson - October 1869

Duignan, Lewis and Lewis, were a well established and trusted Walsall partnership of solicitors, practicing law in the town. On the afternoon of Friday the 15th of October, 1869, their good standing was rocked, when a package was stolen from a desk drawer during office hours. Shockingly it contained the whopping sum of £940 in various cash and money orders. (This would be worth about £125,000 in 2023)

The police immediately began to investigate, commencing with officers speaking to every member of staff on duty that day. One of them was sixteen year old junior clerk, Samuel Thompson, who lived at 7, Oxford Street. When Thompson was interviewed, he confidently in a 'butter wouldn't melt' manner, shifted the suspicion onto a client who visited the firm that day

Thompson wasn't a prime suspect, but he was a deceitful, cunning and convincing liar, who pulled the wool over everyone's eyes with a smoke screen of lies. Unknown to the police, Thompson had both the opportunity and a preconceived motive, he planned to steal the money to flee the country with a friend. The theft baffled everyone and with no real suspects, the desperate firm offered a reward of £50, for information leading to an arrest.

On Saturday the 13th of November, Thompson moved to the next step in his plan. He told his family that he had to travel on company business for a few days and although this was unusual the family thought nothing of it. However when he failed to return as planned on the Monday, his parents checked his room and found all his belongings were gone. Duignan, Lewis and Lewis told them that the whole story was false and he was now a suspect for the theft.

In what seemed like an unrelated matter another youth, Thomas Simpson went missing from his home in Walsall and unknown to everyone he was Thompson's partner in crime. Simpson's father made his own enquiries, hoping to shed some light on his son's mysterious disappearance. He found out that when he unexpectedly absconded from home, he caught a train to London. Determined to get to the bottom of his son's disappearance, he went in hot pursuit to London. It was there that he discovered the disturbing news, that his son had booked a passage to Australia with the missing solicitors clerk Samuel Thompson. The shipping company gave him an address of a coffee house, where the two youths were supposedly lodging, which he visited but neither of the boys were present. He did however uncover evidence of the boys deceit, they had planned everything very carefully, travelling to London on different trains by different routes, so as not to draw any suspicion. He waited for them to return to their lodgings, but they never came and eventually he left without seeing them. Thompson and Simpson soon realised they had been rumbled so hastily left London to avoid being arrested.

Back in Walsall the police were told that shortly before Thompson and Simpson left town, they had been seen digging something up in the grounds of Caldmore school.

Superintendent Cater travelled to London on Tuesday the 16th of November to make further enquiries to find the boys. It was revealed that the crooked duo fled via the underground to Fenchurch, where they got a cab to Euston Station and then a train to Birkenhead via Worcester. Superintendent Cater also found out that one of the £20 notes stolen from the solicitors office, was used at the shipping agents to book the passage to Australia. This confirmed beyond much doubt, that Thompson was a very devious young thief, who was responsible for stealing Duignan's money.

At about ten o'clock at night on Friday the 19th of November, the two suspects arrived at Woodside Vaults in Birkenhead. Mr. Simms was the landlord of these licensed premises on the opposite side of the River Mersey to Liverpool. In a most peculiar and bombastic display of theatre, the two suspects casually drank sherry, while smoking cigars in the bar. A man by the name of Parr, produced a newspaper with the story of the Walsall theft. Thompson, seized the moment by cooly taking the broadsheet from him and reading the article out loud in a theatrical presentation. After finishing the show to the mesmerised customers, he denounced the crime as heinous.

Mr. Simms, the landlord instinctively sensed there was something very odd about his visitors, so waited for them to leave and then followed them as they went to catch the ferry across the Mersey.

At the Ferry port, Simms pointed them out to Police Inspector Davenport, who stopped them to ask some questions. Confidently Thompson bamboozled him, managing to fool the inspector into letting them go on their way. Unfortunately for them, Constable Thomas Whereat overheard part of the conversation and wasn't so taken in by Thompson's spiel. Constable Whereat wasn't happy with their story or demeanour so went after them along the pier and spotted them at the landing stage. As Constable Whereat approached, Simpson realised the game was up, so discarded his share of the money by throwing it into the water. The constable grabbed hold of Thompson, who was also about to throw something into the water. His package turned out to contain fifty-one pounds and twelve shillings in cash and a book recording all the serial numbers of the stolen bank notes. Both youths were taken into the port office, where it was found that Simpson had a pistol and a police whistle in his pocket. Both were charged with committing the offence at the solicitors office in Walsall.

On the way to Bridewell police station, Constable Whereat took charge of Simpson and Inspector Davenport held Thompson. Thompson must have sensed that Davenport's grip was weak, so when the opportunity presented itself, he gave him the slip and legged it. The inspector's incompetence was compounded when he threw down his uniform coat to run faster. In the calamitous foot chase that followed an opportunist thief seized his chance to get a new coat and picked up the inspector's cast off. Luckily Constable Whereat realised the mistake as all the stolen money was in the pocket and retrieved it from the thief before he could make off. Thompson however was gone, easily outpacing the inspector.

Simpson appeared alone, before the Birkenhead stipendiary magistrate who ordered Constable Whereat to personally escort him to Walsall on the next available train.

Superintendent Cater was initially informed that both boys had been arrested at the ferry port and were expected to arrive in Walsall by train. In anticipation of getting a good look at the sensational thieves, a large crowd congregated at midnight outside Walsall train station to await their arrival. When they didn't arrive as expected, there was a rumour circulating that Thompson had committed suicide after escaping.

On Sunday afternoon, Simpson was expected to arrive from Merseyside by train again. A large and excited crowd assembled to witness the spectacle on the platform at the railway station. Amongst the reception party was the Mayor and the injured party Mr. Duignan, but Simpson did not arrive and eventually the disappointed crowd dispersed. The truth was Constable Whereat, had no idea which was the best route to take and he caught the Great Western train that arrived at

Wednesbury later in the day. From there Whereat took his prisoner in a cab to Walsall police station.

That Sunday night, Detective Sergeant Robert Drury from Walsall Borough Police, was dispatched to Birkenhead with a view to tracking Thompson down.

In the meantime, Thompson had made his own way to Chester, where with total bravado, he calmly walked into the local police station to enquire about good lodgings. He even managed to get one of the sergeants to show him where to go.

On Monday morning a massive crowd gathered outside Walsall Guildhall, hoping to hear about the details of the sensational case. Mr. Duignan could not sit on the bench as usual, due to his own personal interest in the case.

Constable Whereat informed the Bench that Simpson had made a confession. He was also keen for the court to understand that the escape of Thompson was nothing to do with him, because he personally warned Inspector Davenport beforehand, that he suspected Thompson might try to escape.

At the end of the court proceedings Simpson was remanded in custody.

While Sergeant Drury was doing enquiries in Liverpool, his wife received information that Thompson was going to collect a letter addressed to a George Wilkinson at Chester Post Office. Consequently, Detective Sergeant Drury made his way from Liverpool to Chester to follow up the lead and Detective Sergeant Wood was dispatched from Walsall to assist him. These two officers were perhaps the most experienced and capable officers in Walsall Police and they met and took lodgings at Nixon's Hotel, near the Chester post office. Together with local officers and post office staff they formulated a plan.

At seven o'clock on Tuesday morning, both officers went to the post office to wait. Sergeant Wood stayed inside where he could overhear anyone who came in asking for the letter and Sergeant Drury remained outside in readiness to prevent an escape. Sure enough at ten o'clock someone fitting Thompson's description approached and entered the post office. It was Thompson and he cooly asked the office clerk for George Wilkinson's letter. The game was up, seconds later Sergeant Wood's strong grip was firmly on his collar and there would be no escaping again. Thompson was taken to be charged at Chester Police Station, then conveyed back to Walsall by the borough officers.

As they drove up Freer Street to the police station, a huge crowd had assembled outside. Superintendent Cater was waiting to greet his men, no doubt pleased to see them return with the fugitive youth. When Thompson was escorted to the cells, he smugly smiled at everyone present, very happy with his self acquired notoriety.

On Thursday the 25th of November, Thompson and Simpson appeared together at Walsall Magistrates Court, where they were both remanded in custody until the following Monday.

At the Monday court, Mr. Dale the prosecutor produced a letter from Thompson to his father. It described how he escaped from the older policeman at the ferry port and running until half past four in the morning, before walking the remaining twenty-six miles to Chester. Mr. George Bytheway, from Duignan, Lewis and Lewis confirmed that the handwriting in the letter was definitely Thompson's.

Sergeant Drury produced a letter found in Thompson's possession, where his father asked him to come home and face the law. Mr. Dale confirmed that both sets of parents had done their utmost to get the boys to come home.

The prosecution wanted the trial to take place at the next Stafford Assizes, but Mr. Saunders defending asked for it at the Borough Quarter Sessions. He appealed due to the boys age, knowing there was a prospect for a more lenient sentence. After a lot of deliberation the magistrates decided to side with Mr. Saunders suggestion, but they refused Simpson's bail, mainly because he threw the money in the river.

At the Borough Sessions before Recorder Neale, on the 12th of January, 1870, Mr. Motteram prosecuted the case, Mr. Young appeared for Thompson and Mr. Warren for Simpson. Both defendants entered a guilty plea and threw themselves on the mercy of the court.

Mr. Motteram painted a very dark picture of their criminal exploits and their plan to flee the country with the money.

Mr. Young pleaded that the boys heads had been turned by reading trashy sensational novels exciting them into committing the crime. Mr. Young read out Thompson's confession statement. He claimed he had already agreed with Simpson to go to Australia, when he was tempted by the money in Mr. Bytheway's open drawer. He admitted burying the money in the school grounds for safe keeping and later purchasing the passage to Australia from Houlders of London. The rest of the statement describes his movements until his time of arrest.

Mr. Warren said a few words on behalf of Simpson, informing the court that he was of previous good character. The Reverend Motteram of Kidderminster and Mr. Irvine, headmaster of Walsall Grammar School both gave evidence of Simpson's previous good character.

The Recorder in his summing up, said he was unable to accept the submission that any novels had influenced their behaviour. He sentenced them both to nine months imprisonment at the Stafford House of Correction. [349] [350] [351] [352] [353] [354] [355]

84. Old Man Miller the Long Acre Killer - January 1870

This story is about a married couple Joseph and Elizabeth Miller, who in January 1870 resided in a small house in Long Acre. Joseph was a fifty-five year old unemployed coffee mill maker and Elizabeth was his second wife. Miller was a Coventry man who from the age of six worked as a brass founder. He married his first wife in 1840 at Handsworth Old Church and they had several children. Only three of them were still alive, a son and daughter in America and another son who lived in the potteries. Another son died in 1869 at West Bromwich Workhouse, having served most of his life in the army. In 1856, Miller was left a widower and he stayed on his own until he married Elizabeth on the 28th of June, 1869, at Whittington in Staffordshire. Elizabeth had two adult children from her previous marriage, a son, George Rogers who lived in Ryecroft Street and a daughter, whose little boy lived with them at Long Acre.

On the evening of Tuesday the 11th of January, 1870, George Rogers visited his mother and had supper with them. The next door neighbour, Mrs. Lucy Leeson saw them at eight o'clock that evening and all seemed "pretty comfortable."

At one o'clock in the morning, Mrs. Leeson was startled and woken by the sound of a loud thump, like a big sack of potatoes falling on the floor which shook the house. This was instantly followed by the bone chilling cry of a child calling, "grandmother murder!" The next thing she heard was a muffling sound followed by complete silence. She didn't know quite what to make of it and probably half thought she may have been dreaming.

On Wednesday morning the Miller house remained closed up and quiet, although the glimmer of a candle partly illuminated the upstairs bedroom in the evening. Lucy Leeson was suspicious and anxiously fretted that something might be dreadfully wrong. Eventually she summoned the courage to knock the door with a mop stick, but there was no reply, even after calling through the keyhole, "are you all dead." At about seven o'clock that night the sense of panic and worry overcome Lucy Leeson, when she heard the sound of footsteps in Miller's bedroom. She told her husband everything and he contacted the police. At nine o'clock, she told Police Constable Lakin about her suspicions and at ten o'clock, he went in company with Constable Willetts and they knocked Miller's door. Miller called out "who's there," but without waiting for a reply he rushed out into the street. He immediately declared, "I am your prisoner, I am your prisoner, I am your prisoner."

When they asked him what he meant, he confessed, "She cut my throat and struck me with the hammer as I lay in bed, and I killed her." Miller's chilling words sent a sudden rush of blood to Lucy Leeson's head as she realised her worst fears were true. In total shock she fainted and fell to the ground in horror. Constable Willetts seized hold of Miller, while Constable Lakin went into the house and climbed the creaking stairs. He found an appalling scene of carnage more hideous than he could have ever imagined. Elizabeth Miller's dead body was lying face up on the bed at the end of the room, her face was battered and bruised and covered with clotted clumps of blood. Next to her body was a macabre imprint in blood, where someone had been lying next to her corpse on the bed. At the side of the bed there was a bucket of crimson water and a mop, that had obviously been used to make the smeared wet bloodstains on the floorboards. At the other end of the room, Constable Lakin observed a heap of old clothes and a bag, on top of which sat the little traumatised and speechless figure of the five year old grandson. The poor child witnessed the entire violent and gruesome show and was now frozen with fear with his grandmother's corpse still in plain view.

While Lakin took in the reality of the situation inside the house, Miller said to Constable Willetts outside, "The way she has been on with me, I could not be doing with her, and you will find her dead enough." Miller pointed to some wounds on his throat and another on his forehead, which he said his wife did with a hammer. What precisely happened, nobody knows except for the occupants of that darkened room, one was dead, one was locked up and the other little soul scarred for life.

Constable Lakin took the prisoner into custody, while Willetts was left to guard the scene. On the way to the police station, Miller said, "If you had not come for me, I intended going tonight and throwing myself down a pit." Constable Lakin later returned to the crime scene and near the fireplace recovered a hammer and a knife, believed to be the murder weapons.

That same night, the surgeon Mr. F. P. Palmer attended the scene at the request of the police. He examined Elizabeth Miller's dead body, noting that her jaw was shattered and there were two serious wounds on her head caused with a blunt instrument. He concluded that she died at least six hours before he attended from the two head wounds, one on the rear upper part and the other over the ear.

At the police station, Mr. Palmer also examined the prisoner and found a 1¾ inch wound to his throat, requiring two stitches, but none of the principal blood vessels were injured. He also saw a wound to the forehead caused by a blunt instrument. Miller was later charged with murdering his wife, but he made no reply.

Miller appeared before the magistrates on Thursday the 13th of January, 1870, with a patch on his forehead and his throat bandaged up.

Only Constable Lakin and the Police Surgeon were called to give evidence, then Miller was remanded in custody until Monday, in order for the Coroner's inquest to take place the following day.

The inquest at the Chain Makers Arms in Green Lane, was opened on Friday by the Coroner, Mr. Fletcher. Joseph Miller was present in police custody.

The first witness called was Police Constable Lakin and after finishing his evidence, Miller said, "I have got to die. I don't want anything more. I have got to die that is all I can say, I don't want to live. I have nothing more to say."

Next up was, Mr. Palmer, who having completed the post mortem examination of Elizabeth Miller's body, described the severe head wounds to the victim and also some defensive bruises to her right arm. He believed that the hammer found in the room, was the weapon used to cause the head injuries. He concluded that Elizabeth Miller died from apoplexy, caused by a violent blow on the right side of the head. He said Joseph Miller's wound to his throat was self inflicted and possibly the injury to his head was the same. Miller called out, "Don't tell lies. I know I have to suffer for it. I have as good a soul as any one. Don't tell lies."

George Rogers confirmed that when he visited his mother's house on that night, everyone was sober. He heard them argue on the Monday before the incident, they often quarrelled, but he never heard Miller threaten his mother at all.

Lucy Leeson said the Miller's were arguing on the Tuesday evening in question, but it was before George Rogers arrived. She also detailed what she heard including the haunting cry of the child.

Lucy Carson another neighbour from Long Acre, saw Miller returning home at eight o'clock on Tuesday morning. His wife opened the door and said, "Where have you been all night with your bloody whores, you can go again."

Constable Willetts gave his evidence and then the coroner said he would adjourn until three o'clock on Monday afternoon. Miller said, "Well, I hope they will have the scaffold up on Tuesday morning, as I want to have it over soon."

Joseph Miller appeared before the adjourned magistrates court on the morning of Monday the 17th of January, 1870. The rest of the evidence was given and then Miller was committed to be tried at the next Stafford Assizes.

At three o'clock that afternoon the adjourned inquest resumed at the Chain Makers Arms. A large crowd assembled at the front of the premises and in the yard, where many were partaking of liquid refreshments.

Constable Willetts and Constable Lakin were first to give evidence. Superintendent Cater then introduced Ann Miller to the Coroner, who was the prisoners sister-in-law. She claimed that Joseph Miller had a stroke ten years ago, causing him to be of unsound mind. She said that Mr. Bullows and Mr. Shaw, two surgeons from Handsworth were prepared to testify to that on Miller's behalf at Stafford. She also believed that Mr. Withers, the relieving officer at West Bromwich, tried his best to get Miller into the 'Bastille' (Lunatic Asylum). A man with a van was actually sent to fetch him, but they couldn't get him to go.

The Coroner in summing up instructed the jury to dismiss from their minds, all idle gossip or exaggerated statements they might have heard. He told them it was their duty, if they believed Miller wilfully and maliciously inflicted the injuries causing the death, to return a verdict of wilful murder. After only a few minutes of discussion the jury returned a unanimous verdict of wilful murder. The Coroner also committed Miller for trial at the next Stafford Assizes, to which he said, "Thank you, thank you! When is it in March?" The Coroner issued the certificate authorising the interment of the deceased body.

Elizabeth Miller's funeral took place that day, with a long procession of spectators following the hearse from Long Acre, along the route to the cemetery. Bizarrely Miller passed the funeral cortege in the back of a cab, while being returned to the gaol from the Chain Makers Arms. The mourners spotted him and began to hoot and yell, creating an awkward last meeting between Miller and the coffin of his murdered wife going to its final resting place. The funeral procession terminated at the cemetery where the Reverend Thomas, curate of St. Peter's Church in Stafford Street performed a service.

The murder trial took place at Stafford Assizes on Monday the 7th of March, 1870, before the Judge Mr. Justice Lush. Miller entered a not guilty plea and was undefended. Mr. Neale and Mr. Forester prosecuted and out of fairness the Judge instructed Mr. Sawyer to watch the case on Miller's behalf.

After all the evidence was heard, the prosecutor Mr. Neale informed the jury, that it was within their power to reduce the crime to that of manslaughter if their conscience permitted.

Mr. Sawyer made a compassionate plea to the jury not to consign Miller to the scaffold, asking for a verdict to be reached in a merciful spirit.

His Lordship pointed out the distinction between the crime of manslaughter and that of murder, the first being an act committed in a fit of excitement and the other done in cold blood. If they thought Miller was attacked in his sleep and then he inflicted the injuries causing his wife's death, then they could be justified in finding him guilty of manslaughter, but if not, they could find him guilty of murder.

After only a brief period of consultation, Miller was found guilty of manslaughter. His Lordship, said he believed the jury had come to the right decision in exonerating him of murder, however in his opinion it was a case of gross manslaughter, where morally he was guilty of murder due to the degree of violence inflicted upon her. He sentenced Miller to twenty years penal servitude. Miller served his sentence at Chatham Prison in Kent. [356] [357] [358] [359] [360] [361]

85. The Dead Prisoner Who Failed To Appear - July 1871

On the night of Tuesday the 4th of July, 1871, forty year old George Jeffries, a groom originally from Stamford went to the lodging house of Mrs. Clarke in Walsall. Jeffries had no police record and was of previous good character, but he was totally destitute and had no money. Mrs. Clarke allowed him to stay the night only after pledging some of his clothing in payment. The true reality was that Jeffries was an alcoholic who was more than just down on his luck, his addiction had made him seriously ill. Medically, withdrawal from booze is more dangerous than most people could possibly know. Throughout the night Jeffries was delirious, constantly rambling in his sleep like an insane mad man and greatly annoying the other lodgers.

At six o'clock on the Wednesday morning, Jeffries got up and left Mrs. Clarke's house, wandering off down the Birmingham Road. Later that morning Jeffries was seen clinging for grim death to a telegraph pole outside the Lion's Den Cottage, near to the junction with Jesson Road. He was trembling almost to the point of fitting and looked terribly unwell. At about ten o'clock that morning, two policemen arrived and found Jeffries in a terrible state, so took him to the police station for his own safety.

Superintendent Cater was so concerned when he arrived that he immediately sent for Dr. Maclachlan to take a look at him. He diagnosed that Jeffries was suffering from delirium tremens (a disorder produced by alcohol withdrawal). The doctor continued to visit him hourly, the last time being at twenty to nine. At nine thirty a police officer checked Jeffries in his cell and found him dead. Dr. Maclachlan returned and was of the opinion that Jeffries died of apoplexy.

On the morning of Thursday the 6th of July, 1871, Superintendent Cater appeared at court to inform the magistrates, that George Jeffries who was on the list to appear, could not be present on account of him being dead. He explained that he had died in the police cell overnight, having been found wandering about in a state of supposed lunacy.

The Coroner Mr. Fletcher opened the inquest at the Dragon Hotel that afternoon. The jury returned a verdict that Jeffries died from natural causes, accelerated by excessive drinking. [362]

86. Attempted Sweetheart Murder - February 1872

This is the sensational story of Samuel Henry Cotterell, a twenty-three year old brush maker from Birmingham and his twenty-two year old sweetheart Sarah Ann Perrins. They had known each other for several years in 1872, but for the previous twelve months the prospect of marriage had been on the horizon.

At about four o'clock on Saturday afternoon the 10th of February, 1872, Cotterell visited Sarah Ann at 11, Mountrath Street her parent's house. They went into the kitchen together for tea and later retired to the parlour to relax. For several hours they sat talking, until shortly before ten o'clock, Sarah Ann said, "Come Samuel it is nearly ten o'clock, it is time you were going."

Cotterell replied, "If you will come and sit here till the clock strikes ten, I will go." They sat together in front of the fire and he gently rested his head on her shoulder. All seemed well, the cosy fire was making her tired and Sarah Ann closed her eyes for a moment, waiting for the clock to strike.

Suddenly without any warning, Cotterell forcibly wrapped his arm around her neck, while pressing a sharpened knife blade against her throat. The terrifying nightmare had begun, petrified she raised her right hand up to push the knife away, but lost her balance and fell onto her back on the floor. Cotterell was deranged, he jumped up to kneel astride her with the knife in his hand. Sarah Ann screamed in terror and began to struggle in a fight for her life. Endeavouring to save herself, she grabbed the blade of the weapon, just as he pulled it away slicing through all four fingers of her right hand. Mrs. Martha Perrins, Sarah Ann's mother heard the frightful cries for help and rushed into the room. Her motherly instincts prevented her from holding back as she pushed Cotterell off her daughter, enough for her to break free.

Shouting "Run," both women took their opportunity of escaping the madman by running out into the street. Mrs. Perrins saw spots of blood all over her daughter's forehead and looked back to see Cotterell coming out of the front door after them. He was staggering and groaning about twenty yards behind them, with blood streaming from a wound to his own throat. The traumatic and ghastly sight terrified the two women who watched as Cotterell slipped away and disappeared from view. After a short while they thought it was safe to return, so went back home and locked the door. There was a noticeable pool of blood and a stained knife on the parlour floor.

Police Constable Davies arrived at the crime scene and recovered the knife.

The surgeon Mr. Pharez Shore from 35, Bradford Street was summoned to examine Miss Perrins. He found her totally exhausted and pale from the loss of blood. He considered that Sarah Ann had been extremely lucky, as she had a four inch long incised wound across the front of her throat, right down to the thyroid cartilage. One of the throat veins was severed through, causing severe bleeding, but the artery was miraculously intact. Four fingers on her right hand were badly cut, with the index finger being very deep.

Cotterell was later taken to the Cottage Hospital by the police, after being found slumped in the street, having cut his own throat. The following morning the Reverend W. Allen, vicar of St. Matthew's church visited him and he asked him to tell Sarah Ann he was sorry and begged for her forgiveness.

On Wednesday night Samuel Cotterell was arrested and formally charged with attempting to murder Sarah Ann Perrins, but he had nothing to say.

On Thursday morning, Cotterell was escorted from the Cottage Hospital under police guard to the Guildhall. He appeared at court before the Mayor E. Holden, with Mr. Gillespie prosecuting, who described the attempted murder as most atrocious in character.

Miss Perrins said she believed the prisoner was very fond of her and she was very fond of him, right up until the day of the attack. On that terrible day she confessed to being rather cool with him and believed he may have been hurt as a consequence.

George Jefferies said he travelled on the Birmingham to Walsall train with Cotterell on the morning of the attack and recalled seeing him sharpening the blade of a pocket knife on a kerbstone at New Street Station.

Mr. Shore the surgeon said there was no permanent injury to Miss Perrins throat, but he could not be so sure about the wound on the right index finger.

No mitigation was offered by Mr. Dale defending Cotterell and he was committed to Stafford Assizes for trial.

The tragic attempted 'Sweetheart Murder' story was sensationalised by the press in newspapers all around the country, creating a lot of interest in the Walsall case.

Cotterell appeared before Judge Baron Cleasby at Stafford Assizes on the 11th of March, 1872. He pleaded guilty and was sentenced to five years penal servitude.

Sarah Ann Perrins, never married and died at Walsall on the 2nd of April, 1908, aged 58 years. Samuel Cotterell married twice after his release from prison and lived in Birmingham. He died in Handsworth on the 9th of October, 1934, aged 85 years, never having had any children. 363 364 365 366 367

87. Tipsy Prisoner Drops Down Dead - October 1874

At seven o'clock on the evening of Tuesday the 6th of October, 1874, Police Constable James Blewer found a sixty-eight year old woman named Elizabeth Whittaker lying drunk and legless in Park Street. She refused to see Dr. Maclachlan, despite the officers concerns and encouragement. Eventually, Constable Blewer obtained a stretcher and the assistance of Constable Arthur Thorpe to get the totally helpless woman to the police station. Elizabeth Whittaker was in a shocking state, her clothes were so filthy it looked like she had been wallowing around in a mud pit.

Police Sergeant John Childs was on the desk when she was taken in for being drunk and incapable. Elizabeth Whittaker told the police she was a dressmaker from Nottingham, but currently lived in Navigation Street. She had been in the cells the previous Friday, when Sergeant Childs allowed her to stay at the station overnight, before kicking her out on Saturday morning.

At nine o'clock that night, Sergeant Mason took charge of the cell block from Sergeant Childs, at which time Whittaker appeared alright. Harriet Preece, one of the female police searchers visited Whittaker in her cell at quarter past nine, when she was still drunk and unable to stand, but appeared otherwise well. Police Sergeant Mason visited her every hour during the night and at about ten minutes past six in the morning, he sent Police Constable James Chandler downstairs to let the prisoners out to wash. Whittaker asked him if she could, "Stay a minute," so he left her for a while longer. He returned at half past six, this time she walked towards the wash area, but looked very frail and almost fell down, so he helped her back to the bench in the cell and gave her some water. She started looking very unwell, so he left her and went back upstairs to inform Sergeant Mason of her condition. By the time they returned Elizabeth Whittaker was quite dead and there was nothing they could do. The police surgeon James Maclachlan arrived about twenty minutes later to pronounce life extinct and he was of the opinion that she died from syncope caused by drunkenness and privation.

An inquest was held at the Dragon Hotel by the Coroner Mr. Fletcher that Wednesday afternoon. Dr. Maclachlan said that drunkenness often obscured more serious disease, making it very difficult to determine between drunkenness and apoplexy. He concluded that once alcohol had entered her system, no medical aid could have helped after several hours had passed by. The jury, returned a verdict based on the testimony of Dr. Maclachlan and exonerated the police of all blame. The Coroner said the police had only done their duty. [368] [369]

88. The Slaying of 'Hampton Jack' - February 1875

John Corbett, alias 'Hampton Jack' was a forty-six year old miner from Tipton, who lodged in Victoria Terrace, North Walsall (now called St. Peter's Terrace).

On the evening of Saturday the 20th of February, 1875, Corbett went out drinking at the Horse and Jockey in Bloxwich Road, leaving just before eleven o'clock. He returned to Victoria Terrace, where Mrs. Elizabeth Davis his landlady gave him his supper. After finishing his food, Hampton Jack decided that his night was not over and he went out again to meet up with three other drunken men not far from the Horse and Jockey.

You might recall what happened in the story of 'Tom Duck' (story 68) on the road between Walsall and Bloxwich in 1857. The area hadn't improved crime wise since then and it was still notorious for drunken gangs harassing anyone who dared to travel that way at night. What Hampton Jack's intentions were are uncertain, but he probably had nothing good in mind.

Sometime between eleven and twelve o'clock that night, John Stokes was on his way home from Walsall to Goscote. Stokes was a thirty-six year old married man of good character, who worked as a boiler maker. As he approached the Horse and Jockey public house, four drunken men tried to rough him up, one of them being 'Hampton Jack.' Stokes broke free and ran, but he heard them chasing behind and one of them shouted, "Stop the bastard, we'll give him something." After a hundred yards, three of them caught up and there was a scuffle where Stokes billycock was knocked off his head. Stokes took out a knife fearing for his life and attempting to scare them off shouted "I will give you this." His attackers relentlessly went at him oblivious to his threat, until he jabbed out sticking the blade in Hampton Jack's face. At that point Stokes was able to get free and made his escape.

Hampton Jack staggered drunk and injured back to his lodgings in Victoria Terrace, just off Proffitt Street. He frantically banged on the front door and Mrs. Davis looked down from an upstairs window and saw him bleeding profusely. He shouted up, "Landlady, do come down for I am stabbed with a knife." In the dead of night, she ran down the stairs to see the blood soaked Hampton Jack on her front step. It was a scary sight, he just about managed to say he was stabbed near to the Horse and Jockey, then dropped down dead on the doorstep.

The stabbing took place on the main road between Walsall and Bloxwich, which was inside the borough of Walsall, but Victoria Terrace where the death occurred was in Ryecroft, at that time covered by Staffordshire County Police from Rushall. Sergeant Arnold and Constable Williams from the County Force arrived, closely followed by Superintendent Cater, Detective Sergeant Drury and Acting Sergeant Salt from Walsall Borough Police. A murder investigation commenced, but at that point the police had no suspects.

Throughout Sunday the murder was the talk of the town and the events of the previous night, no doubt played heavily on John Stokes mind.

On Monday morning Stokes spoke to his brother-in-law John Benton about what happened and confessed to being in a fight somewhere between the Horse and Jockey and North Walsall railway station. He said the unknown men roughed him up and stole his hat, so to get away he was forced to stab one of them, before making his way back to Goscote over the Forest. Stokes was terrified at the prospect of facing the hangman's noose, but they thought the best course of action was to go to the police and tell them the truth

At around quarter to nine that morning, John Stokes went with his brother-in-law to hand himself in at Bloxwich police station. On arrival he gave Constable Thomas Mayo his knife and asked to speak with Sergeant Martin, who everyone knew was the Sheriff of Bloxwich. Sergeant Martin took down Stokes written statement under caution, he couldn't name the man he stabbed, but explained what happened. Sergeant Martin took Stokes to Walsall cells and liaised with Superintendent Cater about the confession. Of course Superintendent Cater knew all about the death, so it was easy to put, two and two together to make Stokes the prime suspect. Stokes was charged with wounding an unknown man near to the Horse and Jockey Inn, on the evidence of his own admission.

When Stokes appeared before Walsall Magistrates, Superintendent Cater informed the court that a man was stabbed near to the location described by Stokes and had subsequently died. He requested a remand in custody until Friday, so that enquiries could be made to determine whether the two incidents were related.

On Monday afternoon an inquest was opened by Mr. E. Hooper, County Coroner at the Bird in Hand, James Street, Ryecroft. Ann Jones, identified her deceased's half-brother. She said Corbett's real name was Bridgewater, but he always went by that name as his mother remarried when he was very young.

Samuel Emery of Harden Lane, said he had known Stokes for twenty years. On the night in question they had been drinking together until about ten o'clock at Mr. Holder's, Odd fellows Arms in Town End Bank. He left the pub after Stokes, but he did see four men knock down a man named Gee in Stafford Street at about eleven o'clock. They approached him, but must have decided to leave him alone. Shortly after he bumped into Stokes, who told him four men attacked him and gave him a right good hiding, blacking his eye and stealing his hat.

The inquest was adjourned until Monday to enable a post mortem examination to take place.

Stokes appeared back before the Magistrates Court on Friday, where Mr. Gillespie appeared for the prosecution and Mr. Rhodes for the defendant.

Dr. Maclachlan who conducted the post mortem, said 'Hampton Jack' died from a one inch deep wound on the left side of his neck, which severed the carotid artery and damaged the jugular vein. He concluded that it would have been impossible for him to survive that injury with the loss of blood.

Mr. Rhodes contested that there was no evidence for a charge of murder and a strong case for self defence against one of manslaughter. The case was adjourned until Monday with £50 bail and two £25 sureties.

On Monday the case continued, but there was an uncomfortable atmosphere in court. The Mayor and other magistrates were obviously sympathetic towards Stokes, knowing only too well what types of ruffians and vagabonds hung around in Bloxwich Road at night.

Mr. Rhodes asked to call a single woman named Mary Slaney, who lived at Harden. Mr. Gillespie the prosecutor successfully argued the evidence was hearsay and irrelevant and it was deemed so by the Magistrates Clerk. Despite this the Mayor and other magistrates overruled them and insisted on hearing what she had to say.

Slaney said that she was walking past the Horse and Jockey on the night in question, when she saw four or five men hiding under a hedge. Two of them came out with their caps covering their eyes, she knew the one to be Daniel McQue. He said, "Oh, is that you Mary. Make the best of your road up the Forest, for we don't wish you to be hurt, and they mean stopping everyone because one of our gang has been stabbed."

The Mayor felt very uneasy about the case and openly admitted he personally wouldn't commit Stokes to the Assizes, as he believed he was harmless and acted in self defence. He thought the magistrates were being compelled to send Stokes to the Assizes on the evidence of his own confession and that was wrong before the Coroners inquest had concluded. All the other magistrates sympathised with Stokes predicament, but that was the law and they had no choice but to send him to the Assizes. Stokes was granted on the same terms as previously.

That afternoon, the County Coroner resumed the inquest at the Mission Room, in James street, Ryecroft. Superintendent Cater attended on behalf of Walsall Police. The Coroner read through the depositions taken at the magistrates court. He then told the jury that the object of the inquest was to determine when, where, and by what means the deceased came to his death. Stokes confession suggested that he had inflicted the wound causing the death, but they had to consider the circumstances at the time it was done. If he acted in self defence, it would amount to simple homicide. If he inflicted the stab wound during an argument, it would be the more serious charge of manslaughter. It could only amount to murder, if the jury thought the attack was premeditated. It did not take the jury very long to deliver a verdict of 'Homicide by misadventure,' a decision that confirmed they believed John Stokes, acted in self defence.

This case attracted widespread sympathy around Walsall and further afield. The Coroners Court had determined that no murder took place, yet Stokes was awaiting trial for murder. Some of his friends raised a subscription to help with his defence and Mr. Rhodes his solicitor of 66 Park Street, agreed to receive contributions from people who wanted to assist him.

On the 8th of March, 1875, John Stokes appeared before the Stafford Assizes charged with the manslaughter of John Corbett. Mr. Justice Archibald was the judge, Mr. Motteram prosecuted and Mr. Young defended. Mr. Motteram said Stokes had voluntarily made a statement at the police station, where he admitted to stabbing an unknown man. The only question for the jury to consider, was whether he was justified in using the knife or not.

Several witnesses came to give evidence and all of them spoke highly of Stokes good character.

Mr. Young, described Stokes as a sober man with a quiet and harmless disposition. Bloxwich Road, he said was a very lonely and dark place at night, where ruffians assembled to abuse anyone that passed by. He suggested that the people who attacked Stokes were undoubtedly such a class of characters.

In summing up, the Judge said that Stokes would have been perfectly justified in using the knife, if he could not have reasonably escaped from serious injury, without using it. If the jury believed this was the case then he was entitled to be acquitted. The Jury returned a not guilty verdict and John Stokes was discharged from the court a free man. He went back to his wife and family at Smith's Cottages, Goscote. [370] [371] [372] [373] [374]

89. Doveridge Scrap Ends in Disaster - August 1876

The baking hot sunny weather of Wednesday the 16th of August, 1876, attracted lots of men to Charles Poppleton's, Crown and Anchor pub on the old West Bromwich Road at Doveridge. At the rear of his premises there was a popular skittle alley, lined each side by thick hedges offering welcome shade from the red hot sun.

About twelve o'clock that afternoon, John Giles a twenty-two year old bit maker from Little London, went into the tap room with a number of other men. At first everything seemed good with everyone drinking and singing, but after an hour and a half, Giles began swearing and Mr. Poppleton told him to leave, if he couldn't behave himself.

James Cardwell, a bit filer from 17, Spout Lane left the tap room and went into the bar, where thirty-three year old William Bond, a bit maker from Spout Lane and James Elkin, a shoemaker from Vicarage Place, were singing songs and enjoying themselves without any trouble. At about three o'clock, Bond and his group moved out to the bowling alley to take in the sun. Cardwell then went into the kitchen, where he overheard Giles talking about a fight for money and running Bond down, over some old grievance.

At half past four, Giles went outside into the bowling alley looking for Bond, revved up and ready for trouble. He found Bond lying on the grass bank and accused him of saying something that might have got him six months in gaol. Giles picked up a bowling ball, threatening to break Bond's legs and challenged him to a fight by producing some stake money from his pocket. Bond was not interested, he had a wife and family to keep so stayed on the bank taking no notice. Giles relentlessly goaded Bond, calling him a coward and using bad language because he wouldn't fight even for money. Giles public provocation caused others to sneer at Bond and eventually it became too much for him to bear, his resolve gave way and he stood up to fight. Eager to get stuck in, Giles threw down his hat and coat tying a white handkerchief round his waist. Adjacent to the skittle alley was a small piece of ground covered in weeds, where they moved over to fight. Giles father was egging him on, but there were no regular seconds present.

The men locked together falling on the bank, but they got back up to fight three or four rounds. About six minutes into the scrap, Bond cracked Giles with a tremendous right hand, dropping him towards the ground. On his way down, Bond followed up with a big left connecting just below the right ear, knocking Giles out cold. He fell like a sack of spuds and stayed down completely motionless.

Henry Butler, a collar maker from Spout Lane ran to get some brandy and to tell Mr. Poppleton about the fight. By the time they arrived back with the brandy, it was too late, Giles was dead.

Mr. Poppleton sent out for a surgeon and the police, telling everyone to remain at his premises until they had arrived. Bond very calmly took a seat and made no attempt to leave. Patrol Sergeant Thomas Bailey, Detective Sergeant Robert Drury and Detective Thomas Salt arrived at the scene to start the investigation and found the deceased still lying on the bowling green where he fell. Patrol Sergeant Bailey went into the kitchen, where Bond said, "I am here," and surrendered himself. The corpse was brought into the public house and Bond was taken into custody.

On Friday morning the magistrates remanded Bond in custody until Monday. At five o'clock that Friday afternoon, the surgeon James Maclachlan completed a post mortem examination, some forty-eight hours after the death. He noted bruises around Giles face, body and both hands consistent with being in a fight. He concluded that Giles died from a violent blow under the right ear, causing the rear part of his brain and the veins around it to fill with blood. He said that heavy drinking contributed to the blood vessels being unhealthy and rupturing more easily.

John Giles inquest was opened on Saturday afternoon at the White Hart Inn in Caldmore by Mr. Fletcher, the Borough Coroner. After all the evidence had been given, the Coroner said there was little doubt about who, when, or how, John Giles met his death, but he believed Bond had no intention to kill him and could not have anticipated the result of the fight. The Coroner judged there was no evidence to justify a verdict of wilful murder, but said there was no escaping one of manslaughter. The jury retired at half past six and ten minutes later returned a verdict of 'Manslaughter,' but commented on the level of provocation involved. Bond was committed for trial at the next Stafford Assizes, with the Coroner saying he would bail him for £100, with two £50 sureties after his appearance at the magistrates court. The proceedings were then adjourned until four o'clock Monday.

A large number of orderly people turned out for John Giles funeral on Sunday the 20th of August, 1876, along the route and at the cemetery.

On Monday, William Bond was back in court at the Guildhall charged with manslaughter. The evidence given at the Coroner's inquiry was read out and Mr. Checkley, the Mayor said he would be prepared to grant bail on the same terms as the Coroner. At four o'clock that afternoon the adjourned inquest at the White Hart reopened, with Bond appearing in the custody of Detective Sergeant Drury. Numerous people helped raise the bail money and Bond's father and Levi Evans provided the two sureties of £50's each. Bond was released from custody to attend the Assizes.

The trial was at Stafford Assizes was on the 2nd of March, 1877, before Mr. Justice Lindley. Mr. Rose prosecuted and Mr. Underhill defended. The jury decided that Giles was the author of his own misfortune and found Bond 'Not Guilty.' [375] [376] [377] [378] [379]

90. The Sadistic Pleck Baby Slayer - May 1879

Twenty-three year old, Robert Fosbury Lines was a young looking coach smith, born and raised in Wednesbury. Appearance wise, he was a thin man, five feet six inches tall, with a sallow face, slight moustache and an habitual anxious expression. On the 7th of October, 1878, he married a Walsall girl named Emma Russell at Rushall and shortly afterwards they both moved to Albert Street, Wednesbury, near to where he worked. [380]

On Boxing Day 1878, the couple moved in with Emma's parents, Mr. and Mrs. Russell, who had a small cottage on the Wednesbury Road, nearly opposite the junction with Oxford Street. Money was tight and Emma was pregnant and expecting their first child. [381]

A full term baby boy, John Thomas Lines was born at half past five on the morning of Friday the 25th of April, 1879. That morning Robert Lines went to work at Wednesbury after the birth as usual, but he had convinced himself the baby wasn't his, because they only married in October. He returned to Walsall at around five that evening, but before going home he went to the Rose and Thistle on the Wednesbury Road, Pleck, run by Samuel Middlebrook. Lines told Middlebrook that the child wasn't his and he had a good mind to throw it and his wife through the window.

Lines returned home in a temper and repeatedly threatened to split Emma's face open if she refused to give him the baby. He threatened violence, saying he would "finish" the baby, by smashing its brains out, but despite his threats she wouldn't let him near the child and he didn't assault her at that time.

On Saturday Lines left the house at half past seven in the morning and stayed out all day. Mr. and Mrs. Russell were going to the market on the evening and were concerned about leaving their daughter and the child alone in the house. They asked a local woman named Phoebe Burns from Oxford Street to come around to look after them. Mrs. Burns arrived just before seven o'clock, with three young children that she was looking after for another family.

When Robert Lines returned home at about ten o'clock that night, he appeared to be quite sober and in a calm mood. But this was the calm before the mother of all storms, he had other evil plans in mind for that night. He confirmed with Mrs. Burns that his mother-in-law was out before asking her to fetch him a quart of ale. From upstairs in bed, Emma Lines heard him come into the house, but was surprised when she heard the door close again. Now Mrs. Burns was out of the way, the coast was clear for him to complete the real intention of his awful plot. Virtually as soon as Mrs. Burns went out, Emma Lines heard him creeping slowly up the stairs. She could see very little as she lay awake in bed as the bedroom was almost in pitch darkness. She asked Lines to fetch her a lamp when he walked in and he momentarily disappeared back down the stairs. Moments later the shadowy figure of Robert Lines returned to the doorway of the room and he began walking towards the bed. She glimpsed the horrifying silhouette of a wood chopping axe being raised above his head as he stepped towards her and he menacingly said, "This is the lamp glass you've got to have, I must be hung for you." Lines launched a furious attack on the defenceless woman, violently slamming the killing tool down towards her. Trying desperately to defend herself, the first strike crashed against her arm breaking through the skin. The second shot was intended to smash her brains out, but luckily she managed to grab hold of the handle of the weapon. The petrified woman wrestled with him for her life, begging him to stop before he killed the baby who was on the bed. Maliciously and spitefully Lines told her that he was going to kill the baby, but first he wanted to see her die. In the frenzied tug of war, he wrenched the chopper out of her grip and she fell awkwardly down the side of the bed, almost fainting with exhaustion. Now defenceless and semi-conscious, she heard an indiscriminate thudding sound as Lines hacked away aimlessly at the bed in the darkness where the baby was lying. With only the darkness for protection, she heard him say, "Prepare for it, for now you've got to have it." The realisation of impending death, chilled her senses into fight or flight mode. Unable to battle any more, she made a last second desperate dash for the top of the stairs. Half way down the stairs she stumbled, tumbling the rest of the way and falling flat on the hard kitchen floor. Almost frozen with fear, she heard his footsteps closing in from behind her. Scrambling to her feet, she ran as fast as she could go, out of the back door and into the garden, wearing nothing but her night dress. The three small children, Mrs. Burns brought with her were traumatised by a screaming woman and a chasing mad axeman, the oldest was only seven. Emma Lines screamed as she ran towards the back gate, it was locked so she frantically began banging on it to get out. Luckily, Matthew Walters from Pleck Road was walking by at the time and heard her haunting cry, "Oh, he has killed my child." Walters ran over and quickly kicked the gate open, freeing her to flee to the safety of a neighbours house. Robert Lines headed towards him, with a chopper in one hand and a poker in the other, threatening to "cut her head off." Walters blocked Lines path and firmly told him that he would have to come through him to hurt the woman. Lines chose not to take Walters on in a fight and remained in the back garden.

Very soon afterwards, Patrol Sergeant James Alden arrived to find Lines at the garden gate. He said, "What's the matter here?" Lines replied, "I've killed the child." Together they went back into the house, now in complete darkness apart from a few flickering embers in the fire grate. Alden turned on his police lamp and they went up the stairs, but nothing could have prepared him for the horrifying scene of carnage that he was about to witness. There had been a desperate fight, but he was sickened by the sight of a blood soaked bed, with a twitching baby in a state somewhere between life and death. The tiny thing had two tremendous wounds on its head, which had clearly smashed out some of the poor souls brains, which were now sticking out precariously. The little baby boy's life blood was draining away with every second that passed and there was nothing anyone could do for the mite, his death would certainly come soon. Switching into work mode, the shocked Sergeant Alden took Lines back down the stairs and told him he was under arrest. The murderous chopper still dripping with blood was on the kitchen floor, sending a chilling reminder to Sergeant Alden of what had just taken place.

Lines was taken to the police station and when he was charged with killing his child, he replied, "It is not my child, it's my wife's."

Patrol Sergeant Alden and Dr. James Maclachlan returned to the murder scene at about half past twelve that night. Matthew Walter's informed Sergeant Alden that he saw Lines with a poker, so the officer seized the one from the fire.

The doctor examined the dead child, but it was obvious what caused the death. He found two three inch cuts, one on the forehead and one on the face, both penetrated through the baby's skull. The doctor also examined the grieving mother, who had a cut on her left arm and a severe bruise on her right arm. He noted that she was pale and suffering from the exhaustion of postnatal haemorrhage.

On Monday the 28th of April, 1879, Lines appeared before Walsall Magistrates court, charged with murdering his two day old child and attempting to murder his wife. Crowds formed both inside and outside the Guildhall, but the only witnesses called were Patrol Sergeant Alden and Dr. Maclachlan. Lines didn't ask either of the witnesses any questions and was remanded in custody for a week. Superintendent Cater made the arrangements for the prisoner to be taken before the Coroner's inquest that afternoon.

The inquest was held at the Hope and Anchor Inn on the Wednesbury Road, Pleck by the Coroner Mr. Fletcher. Again large crowds assembled to see Lines attend in the custody of Detective Sergeant Drury and Superintendent Cater. Just before the inquest opened, the members of the jury were ushered to Russell's cottage almost opposite the pub. There they witnessed for themselves the lifeless little corpse lying in a pool of its own blood on the bed. Superintendent Cater made a special plea for the Coroner to spare Emma Lines giving evidence on the first day.

After hearing the evidence of Phoebe Burns the Coroner adjourned until Thursday afternoon, for a proper post mortem to be done.

Dr. Maclachlan conducted the procedure on the baby's body which was only five pounds in weight, that very night. The infants death was obviously caused by the two serious wounds on the child's head made with a chopper. The first was across the forehead, running from an inch above the right ear down to the nose, splitting the skull and entering the brain. The second started over the right eyelid and terminated on the left cheek. The right arm was also broken and Dr. Maclachlan concluded that the child had no chance of survival with the severity of the injuries.

On Thursday the 1st of May, 1879, the inquest resumed with even more people gathered than previously. Detective Sergeant Drury had charge of Lines custody and Mr. Ebsworth from Wednesbury came to defend the prisoner.

The first witness was Emma Lines, who was in the bedroom of an adjacent house, still unable to get up. Mr. Ebsworth protested at her speaking from the sickbed, but the Coroner insisted and overruled him. The Jury shuffled into the bedroom to hear her evidence in the strangest of circumstances, then afterwards returned to the Hope and Anchor Inn. Mr. Ebsworth insisted on being given an opportunity to cross examine Emma Lines before the jury reached a verdict, claiming that it would be, "a day after the fair," otherwise. Meaning it would be too late to act.

Dr. Maclachlan gave his finding from the post mortem, which was followed by a big debate between the Coroner and Mr. Ebsworth over a form of words that the doctor could use in evidence. Eventually they agreed upon the following words, "I am asked to suppose that the man and woman were wrestling with the chopper and in the course of the wrestle, came in contact with the child's head. I am of opinion that the wounds might have been produced in that way, that it is possible they might. The wounds on the woman were very superficial. The one on the arm was compatible with her having been struck with the chopper. It must have been produced by a sharp edged instrument. The wound on her arm might have been produced with the chopper, or it might have been done by a knife or a razor, but it could not have been done with a blunt instrument. The wound on the woman's other arm was a contusion. It might have been produced by a fall downstairs."

It was agreed to adjourn the inquest until four o'clock on Monday, to give Emma Lines sufficient time to recover.

After the proceedings concluded that day people continued to hang around outside out of morbid curiosity, because they wanted to witness the departure of the little one's funeral cortege.

On Monday the 5th May, Robert Fosbury Lines reappeared before Walsall Magistrates defended by Mr. Ebsworth. More of the witnesses were heard and Lines was remanded in custody for a further week to conclude the coroners inquest.

One week later on Monday the 12th of May, Robert Lines appeared back before the magistrates, with Mr. Gillespie prosecuting. Mr. Ebsworth mistakenly understood the case would be adjourned until after the inquest on Wednesday so was absent. The Bench refused to postpone the case just to accommodate Mr. Ebsworth, deciding that if he wanted to cross examine Emma Lines, he would have to do it at the coroners inquest.

Emma Lines was the first witness, who appeared in a plain black dress to give her evidence and the press described her as being very attractive?

At conclusion of the proceedings, the chairman of the bench Captain Newman committed Lines to Stafford Gaol. There were two distinct charges, one for murdering his child and the other for attempting to murder his wife. Lines said, "I am innocent of a good deal of what she swears to be true. A good deal of what she says is false." Superintendent Cater was then tasked to take Lines to the inquest, which was about to continue.

Detective Sergeant Drury took Lines to the inquest in his custody that afternoon and Mr. Ebsworth turned up to defend him. One juryman wanted to know why they were bothering, when the magistrates had already committed Lines for murder. Mr. Ebsworth heavily criticised the magistrates for the discourteous way they decided the matter in his absence. He blamed it on the jealousy and competition between the magistrates and the coroner courts.

Emma Lines told the coroner that she had courted Lines for about four years on and off, mainly due to him working out of town. In fact, they had a still born child together three years previously. She said that intimacy took place between them on the 9th of September, last year at the Wednesbury Wakes and there was no doubt in her mind whatsoever, that Lines was the father of the dead child.

The Coroner in summing up said there could be no doubt as to who caused the child's death and by what means it was clear and decisive. The Coroner told the jury they only had to decide whether the act was wilful or not, because if Lines intended to kill his wife, but actually killed the child it was still murder.

The jury retired to deliberate, but after about three quarters of an hour the foreman returned to say they could not all agree on the verdict. The foreman, Mr. Edwards said seven were for wilful murder and six for acquittal. The Coroner expressed his complete surprise, that with all the evidence anyone could even contemplate acquittal, as in his opinion there was no doubt the child had been murdered. He told Mr. Edwards that they would be locked in their room until they did agree a verdict. One of the jurymen asked what would happen if they still could not agree after another three or four hours? The Coroner said if they could not decide after forty hours they would be kept locked in without food, light, or fire until they did arrive at a verdict. Amazingly after only fifteen minutes the foreman said they were unanimously agreed on a verdict of wilful murder. A Coroner's warrant for committal was then handed to the Chief Constable.

The murder trial was at Stafford Assizes on Saturday the 19th of July, 1879, before Mr. Justice Hawkins. The indictment was one of murdering a male child born of Emma, his wife on the 26th of April, 1879. In a clear and distinct voice Lines pleaded "not guilty" and the Judge allowed him to sit throughout the trial proceedings. Mr. J. W. Nelsen Neale conducted the prosecution and Mr. Darling appeared for the defence. Mr. Neale started by praising the police for not interrogating Lines, saying it altogether reflected the highest credit upon the authorities in Walsall.

All the witnesses gave their evidence, followed by speeches from the prosecution and defence counsel's. Finally, the Judge summed up the case, clearly stating what constituted murder in regard to the law. He informed them that if Lines intended to kill the baby it was murder. If he wanted to kill his wife or do her bodily harm, but killed the baby by mistake, that would still be murder in the eyes of the law.

It only took the jury fifteen minutes to return a guilty verdict of murder, but with a strong recommendation for mercy. When asked, if he had anything to say as to why the sentence of death should not be passed upon him, Lines made no reply. His Lordship placed on the black cap and pronounced, "Robert Fosborough Lines you have been found guilty by a very humane and favourable jury of the wilful murder of this poor little infant. I say a very humane and favourable jury, because they were a long time in deliberating on the facts which, to my mind, could leave no doubt. I know they were struggling within themselves to see whether there was any ground by which they could reduce the crime and they have coupled with their verdict that recommendation, which I will take care to forward to those who alone have power to attend to it. For myself, I can say nothing as to whether those to whom I forward it will think that the circumstances are such as to justify a remission of any portion of the sentence. Let me appeal to you, therefore, to prepare to meet your God. You have been found guilty of a fearful crime under any circumstances, even supposing the woman had been unfaithful to you, as to which it is not right that anyone should express an opinion. As for the poor little child it had never done you any harm, and one can but wonder how any man could raise so murderous a weapon as this for the purpose of destroying the life of the poor little thing. I do not desire to harrow up your feelings and I have but one terrible and imperative duty imposed on me by the law, and that is to sentence you to die. The sentence of the court is that you be taken to the place from whence you came, and thence to the place of lawful execution, there to be hung by neck until you are dead, when you are to be buried within the precincts of the gaol, and may the Lord have mercy on your soul, Amen."

The words seemed to slightly daze Lines, who stood up to leave the dock with an almost unmoved demeanour.

That week a petition was raised in Wednesbury on behalf of the condemned prisoner. One of the supporters was W. J. Nelson Neale, the Recorder of Walsall and the man who prosecuted the case at Stafford. On the first day of the petition one thousand signatures were given and soon after it exceeded five thousand. The petition was personally presented to Mr. Cross, the Home Secretary by Mr. Brogden MP, who explained the circumstances directly.

The sentence of death was scheduled to be carried out on Tuesday the 5th of August, 1879 and Lines had to wait until the Sunday before for the communication regarding the appeal arrived from the Home Secretary. The instruction sent to the county prison said, "the execution of the sentence in this case has been respited with a view to its commutation to one of penal servitude for life."

Whether Robert Fosbury Lines ever thought a life in gaol was preferable to death at the time is uncertain, but in reality he only served twenty years behind bars and was released from Pankhurst prison on the 14th of July, 1899. In 1901 Lines was forty-five years old and living back in Wednesbury. What happened to Lines after that, is as yet unknown, he may have emigrated or changed his name only time will tell. As for Emma Lines, we will catch up with her later (see story number 93). 382 383 384 385 386 387 388 389

91. A Serial Gaol Breaker - April 1884

Frederick Wallis, Samuel Shaw, Samuel Jackson, Andrew Kenyon, Charles Marshall, Charles Davis and Joseph King are just some of the names used by the same notorious criminal. Who knows what his real name was or the exact number of convictions he accumulated, but it's certain he appeared at many courts in many counties before he passed through the gaol at Walsall in 1884.

This story starts on the 25th of July, 1882, when using the name Andrew Kenyon our artful pickpocket, dressed as a 'swell mobs man,' with a smart walking cane and prowled the Birmingham markets. He was seen practicing his trade on several victims and was taken into custody. At Birmingham Court he was given three months imprisonment and sent to Winson Green Prison.

Kenyon hatched a secret plan to escape and he confidently persuaded the warders into thinking he was a trustworthy and skilled painter. His trick worked and he was given work painting the outside of the governors house, which was on the inside of the prison walls. On the 2nd of August, 1882, his opportunity came when he was left unsupervised for a few minutes. Kenyon slipped inside the governors house, where he quickly changed into one of his suits and put a dark overcoat on. There were dark clouds outside and it had just begun to rain, so he put up an umbrella and walked across the yard to the prison gates. Kenyon completely fooled the warders when he said "Good day," they thought he was the Governor and opened the gates for him to walk out unchallenged. His gaol break was quickly discovered and the facts were telegraphed to Detective Inspector Black and Detective Sergeant Bennett at Moor Street. A short time later Kenyon was spotted in Wrentham Street and apprehended, when they asked him why he absconded he said, "the food was not good enough." After a short stop off at Moor Street Lock-Up, he was returned to Winson Green after an absence of only two and a half hours. [390]

On Tuesday the 22nd of April, 1884, almost two years later, police at Walsall spotted an artful dodger pickpocketing in the town. They moved into arrest him, but unknown to the officers, this was our prison breaker previously known as Andrew Kenyon. This time he gave the name of Charles Davis and after appearing at Walsall Magistrates Court he was confined to the cells. Prison life was obviously not to his liking and on Wednesday morning, Davis spotted a weakness in the security. Builders had been working in the exercise yard to measure for a new staircase and had loosened one of the iron bars. Our prisoner casually asked the gaoler if he could have some fresh air, so was let out to sweep the exercise yard. When the gaoler was preoccupied getting the other prisoners breakfasts, Davis got a trestle being used by the builders and reached up to the iron frame covering the exercise yard. He clambered up to the loose bar where he managed to squeeze himself through. He spotted the servant girls at the Dragon Hotel watching him, so cockily and cooly smiled at them and kissed his hand. He then dropped twelve feet down from the top of the wall into the Dragon's yard, from where he calmly stepped out into Goodall Street and walked away.

At the next meeting of the Watch Committee, the matter was brought up, but it was decided that under the circumstances no blame could be proportioned to the gaoler. Our prison breaker remained at large from the authorities for several years. [391] [392]

Our mans next incarnation was as Captain Joseph King of the Royal Horse Artillery. On the 10th of July, 1889, he deceived Fanny Farmer the landlady of the Farmers Arms in Hay into giving him food and lodgings. His scam was discovered, he was arrested and remanded in custody to await trial at the next Quarter Sessions.

King was detained at Brecon Gaol, but again he planned to escape. At lunchtime on Thursday 29th of August, 1889, he rang the cell bell to alert the gaoler and Thomas Griffith the fifty-seven year old warder, went to see what he wanted. King asked Griffith to help him write a letter to his wife, but as the cell door opened he brutally battered him over the head with a stool, knocking him to the ground. Griffith put up a gallant struggle, but King took the large metal keys and repeatedly beat him about the head until the older man lost consciousness. Griffiths lay incapacitated in a pool of his own blood and King used the keys to make his way to freedom. Another prisoner smashed a window to alert Governor Mynard and he came to find Griffiths lying on the cell floor. Chief Constable Gwynne attended with the police surgeon and enquiries revealed that King had made off towards Hereford. [393] [394]

Deputy Chief Constable Chip at Gloucester received information that King was in his area and he briefed his men to watch for him. On Saturday the 31st of August, Joseph King was recaptured in Barton Street, Gloucester by Police Sergeant Williams and one of his constables who placed him in handcuffs. At Gloucester Magistrates on Monday the 2nd of September, King was remanded to await his transfer back to Brecon. Superintendent Thomas Flye and Warder Jonathan Peacock collected him and he was returned to Brecon at twenty-five past five that evening. A large crowd assembled outside the gaol hoping to see the notorious criminal. [395]

His case was heard at the Brecon and Radnor winter Assizes on Friday the 13th of December, 1889, before the Judge Sir. Henry Hawkins. Mr. W. Benson prosecuted an undefended King who pleaded not guilty. After hearing all the evidence, King was found guilty and sentenced to five years imprisonment. On the other charge of obtaining lodgings by deception he was sentenced to one days imprisonment, the Judge taking into consideration the four months served on remand. [396] [397] [398] [399]

92. Brutal Attack on a Walsall Detective - April 1885

At five o'clock on the evening of Friday the 24th of April, 1885, Joseph Henry Mellor, locked up Henry Lavender's architect offices in St. Paul's Chambers, where he worked as a clerk.

Joshua Hopkins, a wine merchants clerk at Smith and Company also at St. Paul's Buildings, heard a noise in Mr. Lavender's office at about half past eleven that night. Concerned something was wrong he went and found Detective Officer John Smith who was in Park Street. Hopkins had the keys to the offices and opened the door to let them in. They went up the stairs towards Mr. Lavender's room, where Mr. Hopkins lit the gas light. Detective Smith immediately saw two men hiding under the table and a third in the corner of the room. Before he had the chance to react, the man in the corner rushed at him and belted him two or three times over the head with a life preserver. Detective Smith fought bravely back with his thin walking stick, but an accomplice from under the table struck him a violent blow with a heavy object, rendering the him unconscious.

Joshua Hopkins screamed "murder" and "police" attracting the attention of Police Constable Ingram who was on duty nearby. He dashed to the premises, just in time to see Henry Fenton run out of the office door and another man drop from the window above. Fenton threw a tripod at Constable Ingram and the two burglars ran off into St. Paul's Terrace. The officer shouted them to "stop" and gave chase knocking Fenton down with his staff. As Fenton tried to get up, he struck him again this time on the arm. Fenton grabbed his police staff with both hands and shouted to his accomplice, "Come back, he's got me." In the struggle Constable Ingram grabbed Fenton around the throat and pinned him up against the wall. Fenton surrendered saying,

"Don't hit me, I'll go with you." The other man got away, as did the third man who was chased up Bridge Street by Joshua Hopkins. Police Constable Willetts joined them and while the handcuffs were being put on, Fenton dropped a burglars wedge down on the floor.

At twenty past twelve Acting Sergeant Cliffe went to the offices and found ten skeleton keys, a pick lock, a wedge and a bull's eye lantern, all left by the offenders. He saw blood spots sprinkled on the floor and the office had been ransacked. The safe had been dragged out to the middle of the floor where they had attempted to open it and there was a small bottle of some sort of acid next to it. All the office drawers had been forced open and the petty cash was gone. Several architects instruments had been taken out of their cases and put near to the fireplace and a tripod was missing.

Detective Smith was seriously hurt with a severe down to the bone two inch wound above the left temple and a smaller wound at the back of the head. He was treated by Dr. John Wood, the acting police surgeon to the force.

On Monday the 27th of April, 1885, Henry Fenton, a thirty-four year old labourer from Fenton was charged with feloniously entering the offices of Henry Lavender and violently assaulting Detective Officer Smith.

Fenton accused Police Constable Ingram of being, "A very good liar," claiming that he was in pursuit of the real offender when Ingram caught him and hit him over the head, allowing the real burglar to get away. He accused the officer of planting the burglars wedge on him, after it was found by an unknown member of the public. Police Constable Ingram said he never lost sight of Fenton and that he dropped the wedge when handcuffed.

Superintendent Cater said that Detective Smith's injuries were so severe they prevented him from attending court. He requested that Fenton be remanded in custody for a few days for the officer to recover.

Fenton was formally committed for trial at the next Borough Quarter Sessions when the case was heard on Friday. One of the magistrates Dr. Day, wanted to know why Detective Smith only had a small stick to defend himself. Detective Sergeant Drury said that every detective did have a truncheon, but Smith's was cracked so he left it in the office.

Superintendent Cater promised to ensure that all his detectives were better prepared in the future.

In the hunt for the outstanding two offenders, they concentrated on the good description given by Detective Smith of the second attacker, who had a peculiar and distinctive squint. Photographs of possible suspects were obtained from other forces and a thirty-four year old Bristol man named William Maurice Phillips, alias Hughes was identified.

Sergeant Smith from Bristol Police arrested Phillips at his lodgings, where he found two skeleton keys and a locked box. This contained a copy of the Walsall Observer from the 2nd of May, with an account of Fenton's appearance at the magistrates.

Sergeant Drury travelled down to Bristol on Wednesday the 13th of May, 1885 and saw that Phillips had a fresh wound on his head, which he claimed was an old injury caused by a block of wood some years ago. Phillips was taken back to Walsall police station, where Detective Smith identified him as the other man who attacked him.

Dr. Wood was of the opinion that the two inch wound on Phillips head, bore a remarkable resemblance to the one on Detective Smith's head and was almost certainly inflicted at the same time.

On Friday the 15th of May, 1885, Phillips appeared before Walsall magistrates charged with burglary at Mr. Lavender's premises and assaulting Detective Smith in the execution of his duty. It was alleged that a tripod valued at twenty five shillings was stolen.

Detective Smith said he was certain that Phillips was the other man who assaulted him, because of his distinctive squint in one eye.

A witness named James Russon, a cart gear maker from St. Paul's Street, said he saw Phillips and Fenton with another unknown man on the Wednesday before the robbery. They were standing in Park Street outside the Three Cups, not far from the Bridge, sometime between eleven and twelve o'clock. Then on the day of the robbery itself, he saw the same three men again between the Swan with Two Necks and

Mr. Paine's pork shop in Park Street wearing brown raincoats. He said he positively identified Phillips as one of them at Walsall police station on Thursday night.

Fenton and Phillips were tried at the Borough Quarter Sessions sitting at the Guildhall on Friday the 17th of July, 1885. The first charge was for feloniously breaking and entering into the office and counting house of Henry Edward Lavender on the 24th of April, 1885 and stealing a tripod valued at twenty five shillings and other chattels. The second charge was for assaulting Detective John Smith, a police officer, acting in the lawful execution of his duty. Mr. Kettle prosecuted and Mr. Herbert defended Phillips.

The first witness, Joshua Hopkins identified Phillips as the man he saw on the night of the burglary attacking Detective Smith.

Detective Officer Smith confirmed that Phillips was the man who rushed from the corner of the room and struck him on the head with a life preserver. He said Fenton came from under the table and hit him on the side of the head rendering him unconscious.

In cross examination, Detective Smith said he had no recollection from the time he was struck until about three hours afterwards and could not remember getting home that night. He distinctly remembered everything however, up until the assault happened.

Dr. John Wood, said that Detective Smith was compelled to stay for several days at his own surgery in order to recover.

Joseph Mellor identified the tripod thrown at Constable Ingram as the one stolen from the office, but said the skeleton keys and bull's eye lantern found by Acting Sergeant Cliffe did not belong to Mr. Lavender.

Police Sergeant Childs said that on the night when Fenton was charged, he gave his name as "Bill Phillips."

Fenton accused Detective Smith of lying and denied being at the offices at all. Mr Herbert defending, contended that the identification evidence against Phillips was insufficient for a jury to convict him.

After the Recorder's summing up the jury returned a guilty verdict. Fenton had a previous conviction under the alias of James Barker, for a similar offence at Manchester and another conviction for felony. Fenton denied the convictions were his, but they were proved when a warder from Manchester gaol identified him. Phillips had some less serious previous convictions recorded against him. Fenton was sent to gaol for seven years and Phillips for eighteen months with hard labour. [400] [401] [402] [403] [404]

Phillips didn't learn his lesson, he got ten years for breaking into a warehouse in Birmingham in 1889. [405]

93. A Murderer's Wife, a Constable and a VC Winner - 1887

This tale demonstrates just how extraordinary things can happen as the everyday web of Walsall life is woven.

We return to Emma, the wife of murderer Robert Lines who was sentenced to death for murdering his baby and attempting to murder her in 1879 ('The Sadistic Pleck Baby Slayer' story 90). Robert Lines was an evil and cowardly man, who endeavoured to taint Emma's reputation by cruelly portraying her as a loose woman. To cover for his horrendous crime, he tried to make himself look like the victim of her alleged infidelity. Robert Lines sentence was subsequently reduced to one of life imprisonment, leaving poor Emma in eternal limbo, unable to legally remarry for as long as he remained alive in prison. Robert Lines was the guilty one, but she would always be remembered as the 'Murderers Wife' and his soiled goods. As divorce was beyond the realms of the working classes, Emma Lines was seemingly stuck in the shadow of the dreadful man.

The next party in this story is Benjamin Arthur Thorp, who was born in Tipton in 1845. He had a challenging life too, his first wife, Sarah who he married in 1868, died in the workhouse at the age of twenty-two. He married his second wife, Harriet in 1872, but sadly she also died a few months later at Alvechurch on the 16th of May, 1872 aged twenty-nine. [406] [407] [408] [409]

In 1873, Thorp decided to make a fresh start and joined Walsall Borough Police as a constable. He married his third wife Hannah Delagrade Long at St. Michael's church in Rushall on the 2nd of March,

1874. She was twenty years old and originally from Guernsey, but the marriage was not made in heaven and not long after she left him. At the time of the 1881 census, Benjamin Thorp was lodging with a police colleague in Regent Street and although he was listed as a married man, there is no sign of Hannah being with him. [410]

So Emma Lines and Benjamin Thorp were technically married when they got into a relationship, which must have started sometime after the sensational Robert Lines case of 1879. It may well have been through his police connections to her as a victim, we just don't know. Either way, Thorp would have known that Robert Lines was still alive in prison and his own wife may have been alive, even if he didn't know for sure.

At the beginning of 1882, Thorp must have decided it was time to move on, as he married Emma Lines at West Bromwich on the 31st of January. Thorp stated he was a bachelor and she used her maiden name of Russell, suggesting they were less than truthful, but it's fair to say that bigamous marriages were quite common in Walsall, because many believed it was better to take the risk of getting caught than have illegitimate children in the eyes of god. [411]

To be fair, Emma Lines probably considered Robert Lines was dead to her anyway and there was a rule of not prosecuting for bigamy if you had been estranged for over seven years and you believed your spouse was dead.

The couple started living a fairly normal 'married life' and over the next four years they had three children together. However, life was going to drastically change for them both, someone had snitched about the bigamy to the Walsall Watch Committee and they instructed Chief Constable George Tewsley to investigate the matter and suspend Constable Thorp from duty.

On Wednesday the 16th of February, 1887, Benjamin Thorp (known as Arthur), of 7, Bescot Street and Emma Lines of the same address appeared before the Mayor W. Kirkpatrick, B. Beebee and Captain Brookes at the Guildhall. Thorp was charged with marrying Emma Lines, while his wife, Hannah Thorp, was still alive and Emma Lines for marrying while her husband was still alive in prison. Mr. H. Jackson from West Bromwich appeared to defend both defendants.

Mr. Loxton, the Magistrates Clerk, said the police wanted a week's adjournment for other evidence to be brought, but Mr. Jackson complained that would put his clients to much more expense and he suggested the case be withdrawn and started again when the police were ready.

Mr. Loxton explained that charges against a serving officer could only be initiated by the Watch Committee and once brought could not be withdrawn.

Mr. Jackson expressed his surprise to find the police taking the matter up in the first place, but Mr. Loxton's explanation certainly made things clearer as he was unaware the Watch Committee had turned themselves into public prosecutors.

Mr. Jackson complained that Thorp had not received his police wages to which the Chief Constable said he could collect his pay up to the time of his suspension from the office.

Mr. Loxton said that several of the magistrates were also members of the Watch Committee and could not get involved in the case. The matter was then adjourned until the following Wednesday. [412] [413]

On Wednesday the 23rd of February, Benjamin Thorp and Emma Lines appeared again for feloniously marrying on the 31st of January, 1882. The magistrates were Dr. Day and Captain Brookes. Mr. R. W. Gillespie prosecuted and Mr. Jackson defended the couple once again.

Mr. Gillespie announced that the prosecution intended to offer no evidence against Emma Lines and withdraw the charge against her. He said that under the circumstances that her husband was sentenced to life imprisonment for murdering their child and three parts murdering her it was not appropriate to continue.

Mr. Gillespie said that Thorp married Hannah Long at Rushall Church in 1874 and the witnesses were John Garbett, the parish clerk and Emma Bills, Thorp's sister. Thorp then married Emma Russell on the 31st of January, 1882, while Hannah Long was still alive.

Police Sergeant Collins produced the two marriage certificates to Hannah Long and Emma Lines.

John Garbett the Rushall parish clerk from Westbourne Road, produced the register of marriages for 1874 with an entry of a marriage between Arthur Benjamin Thorp and Hannah Long. He said he witnessed the marriage, solemnised by the Reverend Littlecot and identified Thorp as the man involved.

Emma Bills Thorp's sister from Ocker Hill, stated that she was present at the marriage to Hannah Long, but that shortly after the wedding they separated and had remained apart ever since.

John Keyte of Queen Street, said he was Thorp's friend and attended his wedding with Emma Russell on the 31st of January, 1882. He was one of the witnesses and was aware Arthur Thorp described himself as a bachelor. He said Thorp and Emma had lived together amicably as a couple for several years without any problems.

Thomas Plant, the West Bromwich parish clerk produced the register of marriages for 1882, between the Thorp and Emma Russell.

Mr. Jackson, addressed the Bench for the defence and pointed out that the Watch Committee had initiated a vindictive prosecution, as nobody denied the second marriage took place. He said that if they knew the whole facts and circumstances they would only commiserate with his client. Jackson mentioned a similar trial at Liverpool, tried by Judge Hawkins, where he blamed the magistrates for sending a case that should never have been brought and refused to sentence the prisoner to even an hour's imprisonment. He appealed to the Clerk to advise the Bench that no prosecution could proceed if the offender had not seen his wife for seven years and did not know if she was alive. Mr. Jackson said as far as he was concerned, the prosecution had failed to give a scintilla of evidence that his Hannah Thorp was still alive or even if she was that he knew about it. On those grounds he thought that the case must be dismissed.

After a short consultation in private the Bench decided that a prima facia case had been made out and committed Thorp to the Assizes for trial. Mr. Jackson reserved his defence and bail was allowed for £30 and one surety the same amount. [414]

At Stafford Assizes on the 6th of May, 1887, the Grand Jury threw the bill of indictment against ex-Police Constable Thorp and he was acquitted of bigamy before any trial. [415 416 417]

Benjamin Thorp and Emma continued with their lives after this, but not surprisingly he never went back to policing. In 1891 they lived at Sedgley where he laboured at the ironworks and then in 1901 he was working as a drayman at a brewery and living in Wolverhampton. He was still a drayman living in Wolverhampton in 1911, but had retired by 1921. The couple had six children between 1882 and 1894, Benjamin Thorp died in 1922 aged seventy-five and Emma in 1926 aged sixty-nine. [418 419 420]

So you are probably left wondering what happened to the illusive Hannah Thorp, the wife who strangely never turned up to give evidence against him. The curious reality was that Hannah still lived in Walsall, and had been in an 'over the brush' relationship with a man named James Bullers since at least 1878. Bullers originally from Coton in the Elms, was twenty-three years Hannah's senior and a war veteran who had been invalided out of the 1st Battalion, of the 60th Rifles on the 28th of January, 1859. Bullers had been married twice, his first wife Maria died in 1870, aged thirty-one after having six children and his second wife, Mary, who he married at All Saints Church, Bloxwich on 24th November, 1874, died two years later in 1876 aged twenty-nine. As can be seen from our story, women did not have the greatest life expectancy.

In 1881 the couple lived at 2, Tantarra Street, with their two year old son Joe and Hannah's sixty-four year old widowed mother Elizabeth Long. Hannah and James Bullers eventually had at least four sons together between 1879 and 1885. [421 422 423]

The twist comes when our last character, William James Thompson from Yoxall enters the story. He was also a distinguished war veteran and army pensioner, who also served with the 1st Battalion of the 60th Rifles the same as Bullers. At the siege of Delhi on the 9th of July, 1857, Thompson saw the life of Captain Wilton was in grave danger, when he became surrounded by the enemy. He dashed out from the lines under severe fire and despite being severely injured himself, he managed to kill two enemy soldiers and bring his captain safely back to the lines. Thompson lost his right arm as a result of his injuries, but was awarded the Victoria Cross for gallantry on the 9th of December, 1860 by Queen Victoria at Windsor Castle, having been nominated by the privates of the regiment.

When Thompson left the army he moved to Walsall, where his first wife Dinah died in early 1890. Within a few months of Dinah's death, William Thompson married Hannah Thorp, who was twenty-two years his junior at Walsall. Although she was still technically married to Benjamin Thorp, she must have felt free to remarry after the case against him was thrown out of court.

In April 1891, Hannah and William lived at 51, Marlow Street, but the short marriage ended when Thompson died aged sixty-one on the 5th of December, 1891 at 57, Dudley Street. Thompson was buried in Queen Street cemetery, where a blue plaque celebrates the Victory Cross he was awarded. [424] [425] [426]

Why Hannah married Thompson is uncertain, but he must have known Bullers who also served with the 1st Battalion of the 60th Rifles.

The next peculiar fact is that on the 19th of March, 1892, three months after Thompson's death, Hannah married again at St. Michael's Church, Rushall, the same church she originally married Benjamin Thorp. This time it was to the father of her children and life long partner Joseph Bullers. Hannah Delegarde Bullers died age forty-six years at Walsall in 1898. [427] [428]

This was one of the hardest stories to unravel, but basically Police Constable Benjamin Thorp, married Hannah who later married a Victoria Cross hero and then married Emma who was the wife of a murderer. That's strange even for Walsall!

94. The Ablewell Street Hoard of Gold - January 1889

At about midday on Wednesday the 9th of January, 1889, labourers demolishing an old building in Ablewell Street, must have thought their 'ship had come in' when they uncovered a hoard of between £100 and £200 in gold coins (over £30K in 2023). The six men who found the money decided against reporting it to the authorities and divvied it up between themselves. The men immediately went on a spending spree and for the rest of the day and the following morning, the men 'made hay while the sun shined.' Their spendthrift behaviour soon attracted Chief Constable Christopher Taylor's attention. When he heard about the mens good fortune, he had them arrested to find out what was going on and recovered fifty-eight pounds cash in the process.

The building being demolished was occupied for a number of years by a well known and eccentric saddler named John Owen. After Owen passed away, his trustees sold the property to Walsall Council in November, 1886, who subsequently sold it to the current owner Mr. Joseph Dixon. The labourers all worked for Mr. Mallin, a West Bromwich contractor employed by Dixon to demolish the property to enable road widening. Of the three Owen sons who originally inherited the property, one was in the workhouse, one was dead and the remaining son, John Owen claimed the gold was hidden by his late father sometime towards the end of his life. [429]

On Friday the 11th of January, the six labourers appeared in court charged with stealing at least eighty pounds in gold. The Chief Constable said he had yet to establish the rightful owner of the gold, but he was currently making enquiries to ascertain if the money could be declared as 'treasure trove.'

Mr. Jackson who represented the interests of the contractor Mr. Mallin, claimed that the demolition materials were owned by him under the terms of the contract.

The Chief Constable said he expected an interpleader dispute at civil court over the ownership of the cash, between the owner of the property, the contractor and the Owen family. He asked for one of the men, John

Moran to be remanded in custody on the grounds that he had hidden about ninety pounds, which hadn't been recovered. Moran was remanded in custody and the others released with £5 bail.

When the six men appeared at the Guildhall on the 16th of March, 1889, the Chief Constable asked for a further remand as there had been no agreement over the ownership of the money. Mr. Newman, the presiding magistrate decided that it would be unfair on the men and the Bench agreed to discharge them all. [430]

The Chief Constable informed May's meeting of the Watch Committee that there were currently three claimants for the £58 in gold. The first was Joseph Dixon, the current owner of the property, the second was the contractor Mr. Mallin whose contract gave him all the building materials in part payment of his fees and finally John Owen, who contested that his father hid the money, so it rightfully belonged to the family. The Chief Constable said, all three claimants initially indicated they were going to sue the police if the money was not returned, but a resolution had now been agreed between them. The Owen family trustees would take half the money and the other half would go to Mr. Dixon, who would settle with the contractor directly.

Councillor Beddows suggested that the Watch Committee authorise the Chief Constable to return the money with an indemnity from the claimants about taking any legal action against the police. The suggestion was carried, although Councillor Roper refused to vote, saying no proper claim had been made out for the gold. [431]

95. Brutal Bridge Street Wife Stabbing - October 1891

John Johnson, was a forty-seven year old hawker who lived at the Cross Keys Inn, in Lombard Street, Lichfield. He had been married to his wife Elizabeth for twenty-one years and they had five children together. Towards the end of 1890, Elizabeth Johnson ran away to live with another man in Short Acre, Walsall, taking the young children with her. John Johnson had subjected his wife to terrible domestic violence over the years and had become progressively more dangerous due to his excessive drinking.

They had been estranged for twelve months in October, 1891 and had not seen each other since March that year. John Johnson was however a jealous and vindictive man, who harboured evil thoughts about his wife and was determined to drag her back one way or another. Johnson's pent up anger consumed him and eventually he lost all control when he decided he was going to make Elizabeth pay for his short comings.

On Tuesday the 20th of October, 1891, Johnson visited William Mills, a well sinker, of 3, Cottonshop Yard, Lombard Street. He asked him if he had an old knife to open mussel shells and Mills gave him one with a squared off broken blade. Johnson told him that he intended to find his wife in Walsall, but he strongly advised him against it as it would get him into trouble. Johnson took the broken knife to Sampson Holland a grinder in Green Hill, Lichfield, who sharpened and rounded off the square blade to make it suitable for opening mussels. That night, Mrs. Eliza Wright the landlady of the Cross Keys Inn, noticed Johnson seemed more excitable than usual. Johnson burst into tears and said, "She has been the ruin of me" and "I'm going to Walsall. I've got something in my bosoms and I'll put an end to her." In a disturbing way he told Eliza Wright, "You can look out, and you'll see it in the paper." She gave him his food, but instead of eating it, he put it in his pocket saying, "If I do eat it I think it will be the last I shall ever eat."

The next day, Elizabeth Johnson was walking down Park Street with her young son, when she saw her husband coming towards her. She attempted to avoid him by going into the Earl Grey public house, but he saw her and followed. He asked her if she wanted a drink, but she knew his turning up out of the blue only spelt trouble and refused. Johnson demanded that she go to Cannock with him and threatening to give her "one of the old ones," if she refused. Johnson was an intimidating bully who threatened to follow her about for ever, unless she did what he wanted. There was some angry words exchanged over the separation, where she sensed he was going to beat her, so holding the frightened child's hand tightly, she walked away down Park Street towards The Bridge. She knew that in the past when he didn't get his own way, he had become extremely violent and stabbed her.

Police Constable Curtis saw them having words near the coffee shop, where Elizabeth Johnson said, "I don't want this man to follow me, I don't want a knife into me." This was a time when the police avoided getting involved in domestic dispute's between husband and wife, so the officer suggested they should go outside the police station if they were planning a row. Elizabeth Johnson walked off with the child, but Constable Curtis stayed close and watched Johnson as he followed her into Bridge Street.

At about quarter past twelve, Johnson caught up with her again near the fruit shop in Bridge Street, opposite the chapel. Elizabeth was horrified to see the outline of a knife in his pocket and asked him, "You have a knife here," to which he replied, "I've got it for you."

Instinctively Elizabeth Johnson feared the worst and turned to escape him. As she moved, Johnson drew his knife and plunged the blade deep into her neck. Elizabeth fell to the ground, where Johnson held her down with his left hand and he repeatedly stabbed her dagger fashion in the head and face with his right. She let out a shrill and terrifying scream, which alerted Constable Curtis, who ran over as fast as he could. On the way he drew his staff and gave the insane man a vigorous blow on the side of his head. Johnson was momentarily dazed, but the crazed man recovered quickly and lifted the weapon towards the constable. Curtis was ready for him and before he could take a stab, he whacked him across the wrist forcing him to drop the knife. Alarmed passers by feared for Elizabeth Johnson's life and rushed over to assist Constable Curtis. With Johnson disarmed, the constable made the arrest and secured his man. Johnson had managed to inflict some terrible injuries in the space of a few seconds and blood streamed down from the open wounds on Elizabeth's head and face.

On the way to the police station Johnson said to Constable Curtis, "I wish you had let me kill her."

Mr. Jackson a solicitor followed them with the injured woman. At the police station, the police surgeon Dr. J. Scott Wilson, examined the large wound across her throat and immediately took her to the Cottage Hospital. He carefully examined her and found six distinct incised wounds, one in the front of the neck between the windpipe and the large veins was about two inches deep. Another in the left cheek, cut into the mouth and injured the bone of the upper jaw. There was a three inch long, quarter inch deep scalp wound above the right ear, that ran down the back of the neck. Both thumbs were cut with what appeared to be defence wounds. The doctor considered that Elizabeth Johnson was very faint from blood loss and needed to remain in hospital for rest and recuperation.

John Johnson appeared on Friday before Walsall magistrates, W. Bayliss, J. Newman, W. E. Blyth and Dr. Phillips at the Guildhall on the Friday morning charged with attempted murder.

The Chief Constable Christopher Taylor said that Elizabeth Johnson was still in hospital and unable to attend court, so he only intended to call enough evidence to justify a remand in custody.

Police Constable Curtis described how Johnson used an extreme level of violence to cut his wife's throat and stab her in the head using a knife. In a short time he created a scene of carnage before he could be arrested.

Dr. Wilson confirmed that Elizabeth Johnson was still under his personal care at the hospital and the wounds to her throat and head prevented her from attending court. He thought that she might be incapacitated for at least another week, but he no longer feared her life was in danger. No objections were made and John Johnson was remanded for a week. [432]

On the following Friday, Johnson appeared back before the magistrates, W. Bayliss and W. E. Blyth and Dr. Phillips. This time the Chief Constable asked for a further remand in order to trace potential important witnesses in Lichfield and Johnson was accordingly remanded until the following Wednesday. [433]

At that Wednesday court, John Johnson appeared before the Mayor Alderman Russell, B. Beebee, J. Thorpe and J. Lindop.

Elizabeth Johnson gave her evidence sporting some hideous injuries to her head and face. She told the court about her marital background and horrendous events of the ill fated day, where she nearly lost her life. Elizabeth said she couldn't risk Johnson finding out where she lived, when asked why she didn't just go home after seeing him in Park Street.

Police Constable Curtis outlined his involvement in the arrest and Dr. Scott Wilson, described the injuries and the care given.

Eliza Wright from the Cross Keys Inn, spoke about the conversation she had where John Johnson threatened to do something silly on the night before the attack.

William Mills and Sampson Holland both talked about the knife that Johnson supposedly wanted to open mussels and identified the one recovered by Constable Curtis as one and the same.

Ultimately when the magistrates committed Johnson for trial at the Assizes, he had nothing to say.

The Chief Constable warned that some newspapers reported that Johnson had some serious previous convictions, where he got long terms of imprisonment. He wanted to make it clear, their stories were untrue and very unfair as could possibly influence a jury. In this respect the Chief Constable was misinformed and the papers were right, Johnson had been convicted before and soon the truth would come out.

The Mayor and magistrates personally thanked Constable Curtis for the promptitude in acting to save the woman's life. [434]

At the next meeting of the Watch Committee, it was agreed to grant Constable Curtis a gratuity of £2 for his brave actions and they also sent their thanks to a member of the public named Mr. Walker, who assisted the officer in the arrest. [435]

Johnson appeared at Stafford Assizes on Tuesday the 15th of December, 1891 before Judge, Mr. Justice Day and Mr. Lewis prosecuted.

The jury found Johnson guilty, but before passing sentence the Judge enquired about his antecedents. Elizabeth Johnson insisted he had been convicted of stabbing her previously at Derby, but the police didn't seem to know anything about it. The prisoner admitted that he had lived in Derby for five years, but denied the offence. The Judge was very displeased by the lack of clarity and adjourned the case until Wednesday for enquiries to be made with Derby police. When Johnson faced the Judge the second time, his conviction for attacking his wife with a knife previously at Derby was confirmed. In consequence the Judge sentenced John Johnson to twelve years imprisonment.

Johnson was a serial drunk who was sent straight back to prison for theft after being released on licence. He amassed over a dozen convictions for drunkenness and even stole from the Workhouse in 1909. [436] [437]

96. The Walsall Anarchists - January 1892

The case of the Walsall Anarchists is arguably the most notorious crime in the towns criminal history. The facts show how a band of revolutionaries came together in Walsall with the intention of making bombs for the cause. Their plot was uncovered after a decorated Scotland Yard detective infiltrated the terrorist organisation with an informant. The full account of how these Victorian terrorists were finally brought to justice could fill a book itself, so luckily my 'Walsall Borough Police and the Hotbed of Anarchy' (2023) tells you all about the intriguing arrests and trial in full. The story also plots the rise of Socialism in Walsall starting with Haydn Sanders, the first ever Socialist Councillor in England. The Anarchists case is included here, as it would be a crime to miss it out.

97. Matrimonial Misery, Murder & Suicide - December 1892

This story highlights how a disastrously tragic and sad end can come from a miserable marriage, destroying not only the life of the murder victim, but the entire family left behind to grieve. Even more heart wrenching, is the fact that this hideous crime was committed on the

Sunday before Christmas, 1892, leaving two little children orphaned without a mother or father.

The couple involved are thirty-one year old William Joseph Bate and his twenty-eight year old wife Charlotte, who were married at St. Paul's church, Walsall on the 25th of November, 1883. Joseph worked as a slater for Mr. Lynex builders and Charlotte was a harness stitcher, in the employ of Mr. Roberts. [438] [439] [440]

The Bate's initially lived at 29, North Street, Ryecroft and had two children, a daughter Henrietta born in 1885 and a son William born in 1891. It was not a happy home, William Bate was a man of intemperate habits and had a violent temper that got increasingly worse with time. This was compounded by an unfounded streak of jealousy on his part, which mixed up a dangerous cocktail of emotions. On one occasion in a fit of rage at North Street, William threatened to kill Charlotte and planned to do it by hiding razors and a sharp knife under the bed. Luckily, that night she discovered them and risked his wrath and potential violence by refusing to give them back.

In 1892, the couple moved to West Bromwich Road, but things didn't get any better, with physical and emotional violence increasing with the drunkenness. At the end of November, 1892, Charlotte couldn't take any more, so she took the children and left him, determined to make it on her own. This was actually the fifth time in twelve months, but this time she meant it and she wasn't going back. On one previous occasion William Bate sold all the household furniture and spent the money going to America. Unfortunately for her, he came back, bringing his cold, cruel and controlling attitude with him.

Charlotte and the two children went to stay with her parents, Charles and Louisa Busst at 100, Hospital Row, Love Lane, Whitehall. At that time, William Bate was working on some improvements to the New Inn, in Horseley Fields, Wolverhampton and lodged at 26, Mary Ann Street, with a work mate named Ward.

On Tuesday the 13th of December, Bate told his workmate Ward, "I'm going to Walsall by the next train."

Ward asked "Oh whats the matter? What time shall you be back?" Bate replied "I shall be back tonight if I don't get locked up."

Bate went to Walsall where an altercation took place, Charlotte was assaulted and he snatched both children from her and took them both to his parents. Thomas and Eliza Bate's his parents lived at 79, Wolverhampton Road. At about nine o'clock that night Bate met Ward again at the New Inn and told him, "Well I've put it all right. I have put the youngsters away now, and I don't care."

Charlotte had threatened to summons Bate for assault and he told Ward, "She's going to summon me and if she does I shall do for her." Ward told him not to be silly, but Bate determinedly said, "I shall."

The next day, Charlotte went to Walsall court to obtain a summons for assault against him. She was determined to challenge his behaviour and get the children back. Police Constable James Pritchard served the summons on Saturday the 17th of December, 1892 at Bate's parent's address.

Charlotte's employer Mr. Roberts advised her to give her husband another chance, but she said he would surely murder her if she dared to. Unimpressed with his advice, she quit the job and moved to the establishment of Mr. Macfarlane.

At midday on Sunday, Bate visited a work mate named Bullock who lived at 10, Birchills Street and calmly told him that he would not be going back to work on Monday or ever again.

Bate's murderous plan commenced shortly before ten o'clock that night, when he turned up drunk at his father-in-laws house, looking for his wife, Charlotte, who was out with her married sister, Louisa Osbourne. Bate walked in through the back door and awkwardly took a seat and although he spoke on friendly terms with Mr. and Mrs. Busst, you could have cut the atmosphere with a knife. They could see he had been drinking, so when he asked for beer, Mrs. Busst would only give him some tea. It was an uneasy situation and due to his general attitude and disposition, the parents feared there would be violence if Charlotte returned. Mrs. Busst secretly sneaked out into the street, where she waited to warn Charlotte to stay away from the house. When she arrived Mrs. Busst implored her not to go in, but Charlotte would have none of it, telling her mother, "I may as well face him as not." Charlotte drank the ale she brought home with her for a bit of Dutch courage, before entering to face him.

She walked in, and said, "What brings you here?" She then looked at her father and said "Turn him out father."

Charles Busst, had been unwell for several weeks and was physically incapable even if he wanted to, so Bate laughed at her, treating her comments as a joke. She point blank refused to kiss him when he asked and said she would never return home to live with him again. It was awkward when Bates said, Charlotte was "a pretty girl" and other things in front of her parents. Mr. Busst sent his other daughter Louisa to fetch his medicine, but Bate seized the opportunity to occupy the empty seat next to Charlotte and he asked her for a kiss again. Charlotte stood up and defiantly refused, moving to stand in the corner. Bate stepped in front of her and put his arm around her neck, as if to kiss her, but he pulled a razor from his pocket and without any warning, sank the blade and swept it powerfully across her throat. Charlotte let out a blood curdling scream when she instantly realised what he had done. Warm blood spurted out in a great stream, running down and soaking the front of her dress. Mrs. Busst grabbed the poker to hit him, but Bate drew the blood stained razor across his own throat and slumped into the couch dropping the blade. Charlotte had an horrendous gash across her throat and her last gurgling words to her mother were, "Oh mother, I'm dying" and "God have mercy on me."

Neighbours who heard the screams ran in and hurriedly tried to get her to the Cottage Hospital, but their efforts were in vain, after only a few yards Charlotte was dead. They returned her corpse to the house where Bate was still alive.

Police Constables Albert Severn and John Brierley arrived a few minutes later, to see blood everywhere in the house, which looked like an abattoir. The policemen only had a few months police experience between them, but managed to get hold of a folding bedstead and began to carry Bate to the Cottage Hospital. Bate never made it and was dead long before they reached the institution.

Dr. Riordan was called to the crime scene, but there was nothing he could humanly do, Charlotte was quite dead.

An inquest was opened by the Borough Coroner, Mr. T. H. Stanley at the police court on Tuesday the 20th of December and started with the jury boarding vehicles to visit the bodies of the two deceased. William Bate lay at the mortuary of the Cottage Hospital and Charlotte was at her father's house at Whitehall. When the jury returned from their gruesome mission, the Coroner told James Frakes, the foreman, that he proposed to accept all the evidence for both deaths together as they were so entwined.

The first witness was Charles Busst who identified his daughter's body. He said she married Bate nine years ago, but they had lived apart for the last three weeks. On Sunday night, just before ten, Bate entered his house through the back door and came into the front room where he sat on the couch. He said "How do Bill? How are you getting on?" Bate said "Middling." Bate asked, if there was time for a quart of ale, but he said "no." Bate drank two cups of tea and then Mrs. Busst left the room, to prevent Charlotte walking in on them. Just when Bate decided to return to Wolverhampton, Charlotte came into the room with her sister Louisa. Bate asked her for a kiss a couple of times, but she refused and would have nothing further to do with him, so he lit his pipe. After a while, Bate approached her again, this time she got up to avoid him and the next thing was he heard a scream. When he turned around he saw blood gushing from his daughter's throat. Bate threw himself on the couch, where he saw another pool of blood. His daughter was taken out, but he remained with Bate until the policemen arrived. It was then he saw the razor on one of the chairs. Charles Busst had an injury to his forehead and said his wife accidentally hit him with a poker intended for Bate. He said Charlotte had a thorough dread of Bate, he was violent towards her and had beat her more than once without any reason. He knew that Bate had threatened Charlotte previously with razors and that she had taken out a summons for assault, which was due to be heard in court on Monday. Charles Busst conceded that his daughter could use bad language at times.

Charlotte's mother, Louisa Busst, greeted Bate on Sunday night with, "Why William what wind has blown you here?" He didn't answer the question but when he asked for some beer, he was given two cups of tea instead. Bate had been drinking, but she had seen him far worse in the past. About half an hour after arriving, Bate started to enquire about Charlotte's whereabouts and at that point she went to the end of the field to meet her two daughters, Charlotte Bate and Louisa Osbourne when they came back. When Charlotte returned she begged her not to go in, but she wouldn't listen. She heard Bate say, "Charlotte come and sit by the side of me." She answered "No." He enquired, "Why not?" And she replied "I have a reason, I shall not sit by the side of you anymore." Bate got up and lit his pipe and after throwing the empty box on the fire, said "If you won't come and sit by me, come and kiss me." Bate said to Mr. Busst, "Father, she's a pretty girl ain't she?" When Louisa got up to get her father's pills, Bate took Louisa's seat next to Charlotte. She got up and moved to the corner by the door and he said "Don't go from me, kiss me." She said, "No William never no more, never no more, I have done with you." He put one arm on her shoulder and the other round her neck, slitting her throat. Charlotte screamed out, "Oh, mother, mother I'm a murdered woman. God help me." Mrs. Busst remembered saying, "He has killed my daughter, and I will kill him," and picked up the poker to hit him. By mistake she hit her husband, who cried out "Don't, don't he's done himself, look at the blood." Bate fell on the couch with blood gushing out in a stream. She helped to take Charlotte outside, intending to get her to the Cottage Hospital, but she died in the arms of Mr. Clarson just in the field only a few yards from the door.

Police Constable Severn said at about twenty-five minutes past ten on Sunday night he heard screams of "Murder" and went to Mr. Busst's house. By the time he got there, three or four neighbours were bringing Charlotte Bate out into the yard, with blood all over the front of her dress and a deep cut to her throat. She was not dead, but was past speaking. He went inside the house and saw Bate lying on the couch with his throat cut and a blood stained razor wide open on the chair.

Police Constable Brierley went to fetch a doctor and then they put Bate on a folding bedstead to carry him to the Cottage Hospital. He was dead before they got there and they found the summons to appear at court on Monday for assaulting his wife in his jacket pocket.

Dr. Riordan said that when he arrived shortly before eleven o'clock at the house in Hospital Row, Charlotte's body was laid out on the couch. She had only been dead a few minutes, but died from the haemorrhage of blood from a deep throat wound caused by a very sharp instrument. The extensive grisly wound ran from below the left ear and all round the neck to the other side, terminating between the corner of the jaw and the right ear. The internal jugular artery and the deep veins on the left side were completely severed as was prominent cartilage at the front.

Dr. Riordan also viewed Bate's body in the hospital mortuary. He had a straight wound right across the throat a little higher up than in the other case, but also died due to haemorrhage from the large jugular vein on the left side.

Eliza Bate, William Bate's mother identified his body and said she was unaware they had separated, until Bate asked her if she had seen the children. Jokingly, she asked if he had lost them and then he told her they had split up. She wished they could live peacefully, but Bate said, "I cannot, mother, because she is so irritable." Bate accused Charlotte of being the worse for beer with a female relation when he got home.

The Coroner said there were other witnesses, but after the evidence already given he didn't think it would be necessary to call them. Summing up the evidence, he said the jury could really come to no other logical conclusion than they both died from the wounds inflicted by William Bate. In respect of Charlotte Bate, he expected them to deliver a verdict of wilful murder. In regard to Bate's death, it was necessary to consider his state of mind when he inflicted the terrible injury. The evidence shows he was separated from his wife and he had a summons to appear at court the following morning in his possession for assaulting her. The only unusual item in his possession when the act was committed was the razor. Mrs. Busst said he had been drinking, but at the same time it was safe to say he knew what he was doing. Remarkably no one either saw the razor in his hand or saw him use it. It was for the jury to determine whether Bate was of unsound mind or whether it was simply felo de se (suicide).

The jury unhesitatingly returned a verdict of "wilful murder" in respect of Charlotte Bate, but in the case of William Bate there was great difficulty in deciding. The difference between insanity or felo de se was discussed at great length, but eventually the they found that Bate committed suicide, as there was no evidence to show his state of mind at the time.

A joint funeral took place on the afternoon of Thursday the 22nd of December, with immense crowds lining the route at various points all the way along to the cemetery. When the two coffins were lowered down into one grave, the Bate's were joined eternally in death, something which proved impossible in life. There was no disturbance or excitement amongst the mourners, it was just a very sombre occasion. [441] [442] [443]

Their daughter Henrietta Bate was brought up by her paternal grandparents, Mr. and Mrs. Bate until she married. William Bate, their son, was brought up by his paternal aunt, Henrietta Cook his father's sister.

98. The Park Street Bomb - October 1894

After the dreadful excitement of the Walsall Anarchist Bomb Plot in 1892, suspicions ran high in town about potential terrorists. Few people foresaw the extreme event taking place and when Joseph Deakin from Walsall was convicted, it left a nasty taste in the mouth. Walsall was branded the 'Hotbed of Anarchy' in the newspapers, a slur most people just wanted to forget and move on.

That was until the night of Thursday the 11th of October, 1894, when twenty year old Clement Westbury, of 41, Upper Rushall Street, made his way down Park Street near the corner with The Bridge. His attention was suddenly drawn to a small scintillating light on the window sill of the Metropolitan Bank, behind the ornamental ironwork. The street was full of people passing by, but his curiosity drew him to take a look. On closer inspection he saw a burning fuse protruding from an eight inch long piece of iron piping, about an inch in diameter. Mr. Westbury, a brushmaker, immediately suspected that it was "an infernal machine." Without a seconds thought for his own safety, he selflessly snuffed out the fuse with his finger and thumb, causing some nasty burns to his hand. With the contraption extinguished, he placed the pipe into the horse road and summoned Police Constable Smith. The officer took charge of it, but the general consensus was that it was a prank, a stupid and harmless hoax.

In the morning Chief Constable Christopher Taylor examined the pipe and a very different picture emerged. He found the pipe was capped at each end with plaster of Paris, with a layer of wadding underneath, through which the fuse mixed with chlorate of potash passed. The pipe itself was charged with gunpowder, mixed with large shot, tacks and small bullets. Threaded through the pipe was a spiral twisted piece of copper wire. Far from being a harmless hoax or joke, the bomb could have potentially exploded causing serious or fatal injuries to many innocent people walking past the bank. Luckily the prompt and courageous actions of Mr. Westbury prevented a disaster.

Unfortunately the mysterious bomber left no clues whatsoever as to their identity or motivation for this diabolical act, which is impossible to conceive. [444]

In the aftermath of the story there were people in the town who wrongly accused Clement Westbury of being associated with the 'Walsall Anarchists.' This was mainly due to the similarity of his name to John Westley, a Walsall man charged and acquitted of anarchism in 1892, who was also a brushmaker.

Clement Westbury wrote to the local papers pointing out that his name was not Westley and that he had no association with any of the Anarchists whatsoever. He also claimed that the whole incident had traumatised him and ever since the experience he had suffered from what the Germans call 'vorstellung' vivid mental pictures of what could have happened if the bomb had gone off. 445

Westbury died on the 27th of April, 1939, at 49 Adams Street aged sixty-four.

99. *Murderess or Melancholy Mother? - May 1895*

Sarah Jane Bache married Walter Frank Kendrick at St. George's Church, Walsall on the 6th of February, 1893. Sarah Jane was heavily pregnant with their first child, Grace Janette who was born on the 16th of March, 1893, a month after the wedding. Immediately after the birth Sarah began to suffer from severe melancholia requiring her sister, Phoebe Bache to move into the marital home at 105, Whitehall Road to support her. In 1894, Sarah fell pregnant again and had a second daughter, Dorothy Mary at the end of that year. Unfortunately, Dorothy died only a few months afterwards in February, 1895. 446 447 448 449 450

Twenty-five year old Sarah Jane was traumatised by the child's death and suffered terribly from the enormous loss of her baby daughter. This impacted on her delicate mental state that chronically worsened. At the end of April, Sarah Jane began to act more strangely than usual, her condition was worsening, but the family tried to help her through it.

On the afternoon of Tuesday the 30th of April, 1895, a neighbour Matilda Jeffries was disturbed by the strange groaning noises emanating from 105, Whitehall Road. She had only known Sarah Jane for about six months, but knew she was prone to act in a strange manner. Apprehensive about the noises, she called another neighbour Ellen Compton, from 111, Whitehall Road for assistance, who had known Sarah Jane all of her life. Together they went to the front door, which was locked and bolted from inside, but they could hear the sickening groaning coming from an upstairs room and knew they had to get in to investigate. Ellen Compton managed to climb in through the kitchen window and she opened the door to let Matilda Jeffries in. Slowly and apprehensively, they scaled the stairs to find Sarah Jane sitting scarily at the top. The groaning stopped and Sarah Jane told them, "I have done it. I have killed the child." Sarah Jane, looked very wild and there was a red mark around her throat. As they entered the bedroom they saw the harrowing sight of her two year old daughter Grace lying dead on the bed. The whole scenario stunned the two women, who saw a carving knife in the bedroom with some traces of blood on it. Ellen Compton warily asked what she had done to the child? "Strangled her" she replied and then said, "I want to die now the child has gone."

A man named Clews came in and agreed to stay with Ellen Compton while Matilda Jeffries went to get Dr. Riordan. Sarah Jane began shouting deliriously at the top of her voice, she was out of her mind and totally deranged. When Dr. Riordan arrived at the address, he saw Sarah Jane lying on the bed upstairs with the dead child beside her. He found her crying and talking incoherently and answering his questions automatically and unconsciously. The dead child had strangulation marks around its throat and Police Inspector Gore escorted Sarah Jane to the police station.

On the following Wednesday morning, Sarah Jane Kendrick appeared at the Magistrates Court, before B. Beebee, J. Lindop, and H. D. Clark, charged with the wilful murder of Grace Kendrick, her two year old child. Sarah Jane sat in the corner of the dock, supported by the lady police searchers. She was constantly moaning and obviously unable to comprehend what was going on.

Chief Constable Taylor apologised to the Bench for having to bring her to court in such a condition and believed it would be preferable to take her to a place of safety. The chairman of the Bench, Mr. Beebee was very sympathetic.

Phoebe Bache her sister was the first witness, who said she lived with Sarah Jane as she suffered from melancholia and needed support. Over the last few days her sister had been in a very strange condition.

Ellen Compton said she had known Sarah Jane all her life and about eight or nine years ago a blood vessel burst during an illness, which made her very weak. After Sarah Jane lost a child in February, she was stricken with grief and her condition became considerably worse. Ellen

Compton described going into the house with Matilda Jeffries and finding Sarah Jane at the top of the stairs, where she said, "Oh, I have done it Ellen, I have done it." Sarah Jane told her she had strangled the child, but looked wild and had a mark on her throat. After Matilda Jeffries went for the doctor, Sarah started shouting and screaming and was out of her mind. Matilda Jeffries, corroborated her evidence.

Dr. Riordan said he found Sarah Kendrick on the bed totally unintelligible and incomprehensible, with the dead child lying next to her. It was clear that the child had been strangled from the marks around the throat. There was also a visible mark on the right lower lip, where it had been pressed against the teeth by force and some slight discolouration of the thighs, but the child was otherwise quite normal. Having conducted the post mortem examination, Dr. Riordan said he found the lungs were in a state consistent with strangulation or suffocation and the brain showed similar signs. He concluded that death was caused by strangulation. The doctor stated that the defendant had tried to cut her own throat, but the injuries were of a very superficial nature. He did ask Sarah Jane why she killed the child and she said, "Because I could not kill myself," which he thought accounted for the self inflicted injuries. When he asked her to explain she told him, "I have killed the child, won't they kill me now?" It appeared that she killed her child in the hope that she would be hanged for the crime. The doctor asked her why she wanted to kill herself, she said, "Because I cannot do my duties." Dr. Riordan believed Sarah Jane had no concept of what was going on around her and was in a dazed and incoherent state.

The magistrate Mr. Lindop asked, "Do you think strangulation was brought about by pressure on the windpipe?"

Dr. Riordan said there were pressure marks across both sides of the throat, so yes he believed that to be the case. He also thought that the mark on the lip, was caused by the mother's finger and thumb to stop the child screaming out. Dr. Riordan told the jury that Sarah Jane was not in a proper or normal state of mind and was completely upset.

Inspector Gore said that after arresting Sarah Jane he conveyed her to the police office. Throughout the whole time she was in his custody, she appeared very distant and unable to understand what was going on. As a consequence he didn't formally charge her.

Sarah Jane was committed to take her trial at the next Assizes and after the magistrates hearing concluded, an inquest was opened in the Sessions Court, by Mr. T. H. Stanley, the Borough Coroner. The evidence given was virtually the same as that heard at the magistrates court.

One jury member asked Phoebe Bache, if Sarah Jane and her husband lived unhappily together, as they had heard a rumour. Miss Bache firmly said there was not the slightest grounds, they never had a wrong word and if all men were like Mr. Kendrick, there would be many more happy homes.

The Coroner told the jury, that they did not have to consider her state of mind at that time and if they thought she caused the child's death by strangulation, then their verdict must be one of murder.

Cornelius Stanton the foreman of the jury held a consultation with the rest of the members and after a minute or two said they were all agreed, with the exception of one.

One member David Enos, said, "I object to that verdict."

The Coroner Mr. Stanley replied, "That does not matter, you are by yourself." The jury then returned a verdict of wilful murder against Sarah Kendrick, and she was committed with the coroner's warrant.

The Chief Constable said he thought it was inadvisable to take Sarah Jane to Stafford by train in the usual way, so it was agreed Inspector Gore and the female attendants would go with her in a closed carriage.
451

The case came up for trial at Stafford Assizes on Friday the 26th of July, 1895, before Judge, Mr, Justice Hawkins. Sarah Jane Kendrick was indicted for killing her two year old child, Grace Janette on the 30th of April, with malice aforethought. She appeared to be very faint and weak in the dock and was allowed to sit supported by a female attendant.

When the clerk asked, she pleaded guilty, but everyone could clearly see she was utterly confused and bewildered. She was asked if she knew what she was guilty of, but she had no idea. The stress of the question proved too much, she fell immediately into some kind of perfectly helpless stupor, without the slightest understanding of what was going on.

It was pitiful and the Judge indicated to the prosecutor, Mr. Lawrence that the defendant could not comprehend the proceedings. The Judge said that he thought it not only unseemly, but inhuman under the circumstances, to try her for a capital crime, which might end in a conviction.

Mr. Lawrence said two medical witnesses entirely supported his Lordship's view, attributing her condition to mental disorder.

The Judge said, "If her mind is so unhinged from disease or any other cause that she cannot comprehend what is going on, and cannot defend herself, that is an entirely good ground for postponing the trial, or taking the course of having the jury sworn to consider what her state of mind really is, in order that she may be removed to a place where she may, at all events, be taken care of for a time."

Dr. James Beveridge Spence, Medical Superintendent at Burntwood Asylum was called. He said that at the request of the prosecution, he visited Sarah Kendrick at Stafford gaol on the 23rd of May. He made a long and careful examination to ascertain her state of mind and determined that she was suffering from melancholia. He told the Judge her condition was likely to last for some considerable time, as it had improved very little since he saw her. He said Sarah Jane had no glimmering idea of why she was a prisoner and believed the child was quite well at home.

Dr. Spence was asked if she could appreciate the details of her trial, to which he replied, "I don't think she has mind enough to appreciate the enormity of the offence. She is quite unfit to follow the details of the trial." Turning to the Judge he said, the woman was in "a very bad way" and physically unfit to defend herself.

After hearing this evidence the jury came to the conclusion that Sarah Kendrick was insane and unfit to plead.

The Judge used his powers to detain her indefinitely at Her Majesty's pleasure. He said that if she ever recovered the Secretary of State would deal with her as he thought right, but he personally thought that if that happened, she should be released without ever being tried again. [452] [453]

Later in 1895, Phoebe Bache, married Albert Edward Kendrick, Sarah's husband's brother. [454]

100. Storm in a Teacup - Reddick v. Evans - December 1896

This is the curious tale of a clash between the founder of a well known dynasty of local solicitors and a Walsall Borough police officer. The two parties involved in this affair were Enoch Evans, aged thirty-seven a solicitor and John James Reddick, aged twenty-eight a police constable in Walsall Borough Police. Enoch Evans started the law firm in 1884 and by 1896 it was a successful practice. Police Constable 45 Reddick joined the force on the 10th of January, 1894, so had just short of two years police service when this happened. I don't think it would be unfair to say that there was a significant difference in the two mens social status, but who was to blame remains open for debate, the circumstances however suggest this really was a 'storm in a teacup.'

The circumstances for the epic saga were set in motion on the night of Monday the 16th of November, 1896, when Police Constable Reddick paraded for duty at ten o'clock. It just so happened to be his first shift on a new beat.

Just before five o'clock the following morning, he was working his way back to the police station, when he noticed a light at the rear of Dundrennan House on the Wednesbury Road. Apparently unknown to Constable Reddick, this was the home address of Enoch Evans and his family. He went to check everything was in order and found the back door was slightly ajar. As he got closer, he was greeted by two servant girls, twenty-one year old Eunice Brittain, the nurse from Westbourne

Street and twenty year old Alice Shingler, the cook from the Sandhills. The two girls had stayed up all night without going to bed and were lighting the fire, but everything was in order. At this point, it would have been prudent for him to have continued on his beat, but the servant girls offered him a cup of tea, so having broken the ice on that freezing cold morning, he accepted. The girls made some casual small talk about their crochet work and marriage to pass the time, but Reddick did not sit down and after five or six minutes, he finished his tea and went out the door to leave.

As he was walking away, Constable Reddick heard a woman call from an upstairs window, "Get back" and as he looked up, Enoch Evans ran out through the kitchen into the yard, striking him with a metal poker. That much is agreed by all parties, but did Enoch Evans strike the second blow before or after he asked the officer for his police number. Enoch Evans said that he struck Reddick twice at the same time, but Constable Reddick's account is that he supplied his number after the first blow and was then struck again. Who was right only they know, but Enoch Evans demanded his number and ordered him to report to his sergeant. Also undisputed is the fact that Reddick's shoulder was badly swollen and the poker used was bent to indicate the force.

The following day, Chief Constable Christopher Taylor wrote to Enoch Evans, asking for his account of things. He wrote back accusing the constable of misconduct for being in the company of his servants so early in the morning. Evans didn't deny striking Constable Reddick, but informed Chief Constable Taylor that he had already sacked both girls from his employment and implied that he might do the same with Reddick.

The Chief Constable having listened to the facts decided to side with his man Constable Reddick, but still discussed the matter with the Town Clerk, the town legal advisor, prior to any prosecution. The Town Clerk spoke to Enoch Evans suggesting an apology on his part would suffice, but he allegedly refused, so a summons was issued for him to attend court for assault.

Enoch Evans appeared before Walsall Magistrates Court at the Guildhall on Tuesday the 17th of November, 1896, charged with assaulting Constable Reddick with a poker. The Bench consisted of Alderman Newman, W. E. Blyth, G. A. Phillips and T. A. Hill. The Town Clerk, Mr. J. R. Cooper prosecuted and Mr. Plumptre appeared for the defence.

Police Constable Reddick said he walked to the side entrance quietly in case there were any burglars at work and saw the two girls who invited him in, but he wasn't aware the tea would be at Mr. Evans expense. He didn't personally know either of the two servant girls and hadn't seen them either before or since the incident. Reddick categorically denied any larking about with the girls, he said he was on his way back and was off duty at six when this incident happened. Reddick said that Mr. Evans hit him, then asked for his number, then struck him again. When Mr. Plumptre cross examined, he denied seeing any lights at the front of the house, but admitted with hindsight, that it was wrong for him to have taken the tea .

Sergeant Curtis and Inspector Gore both said they met with Constable Reddick during his tour of duty and he was working his beat responsibly.

Dr. Scott Wilson described the injury to Reddick's shoulder as a severe bruise, most probably caused by the poker.

Eunice Brittain and Alice Shingler, both said they didn't go to bed that night and at twenty past three they went into the kitchen to make up the fire. At ten to five they heard the police officer's footsteps outside, so they opened the door to offer him a cup of tea. Just as he was leaving, Enoch Evans ran out after him. The girls both denied knowing the officer or that any improprieties took place. Eunice Brittain said that when Mr. Evans returned he said, "I've bent this across his back" and showed her the poker.

Mr. Plumptre admitted that Enoch Evans hit the officer, but said the circumstances warranted the case to be dismissed. He said that Mr. Evans was awoken by his wife, who saw a man leaving the house, so he ran down stairs and armed himself with a poker. He saw the large man walking away and struck him, not realising he was a policeman. When he realised he was a constable he demanded his number and told him he would report the matter to the Chief Constable. He contested that Mr. Evans showed great courage and the officer only had himself to blame for his improper conduct. Mr. Plumptre said, Enoch Evans noticed that his servant girls hair was down when he saw the strapping man leaving his house and believed he had been acting inappropriately, so quite rightly gave the fellow a couple of stripes on the shoulder. Mr. Plumptre thought that the Watch Committee would have been a better way of dealing with this matter.

After ten minutes of private consultation, the Bench decided to fine Enoch Evans five shillings and costs, but that wasn't the end of it. [455] [456]

Enoch Evans was obviously aggrieved by the decision of the magistrates and wrote a letter to the editor of the Walsall Advertiser as follows: -

"Sir, Permit me to thank you for the very kind remarks you made concerning me in your last issue. The rest of your "leaderette" only aggravates the conduct of the Town Clerk and Chief Constable in the matter, as I think you will admit after reading my letters. It has been a great consolation to my family and myself to know that not only the Press, but the public generally, have so unmistakably shown their sympathy with us. I was placed in a situation, which I trust none of your readers will ever find themselves in, especially if they consider that I had a wife and several little children under my protection. From the numerous expressions of goodwill towards me, I am glad to know that there are today in Walsall many gentlemen who would adopt the course I did, if they should unfortunately be placed in the same position that I was.

I think I may reasonably complain that neither the Chief, nor our worthy Town Clerk adopted the course, which I pointed out to the latter, before the summons was issued, of bringing the matter before the Watch Committee, so that both my wife and myself could give evidence, and I believe the people of Walsall generally will consider their conduct 'un-English" in issuing a summons, which practically shut the mouths not only of myself, but also of my wife, the only person who could give evidence on my behalf. If the course suggested did not meet with their approval, a civil proceeding in the County Court would have fully elucidated all the facts of the case, and all the evidence could then have been heard upon oath.

Without in anywise reflecting on the magistrates, I may say I naturally regret, under all the circumstances, their decision. It is very repugnant of me to have to move further in the matter, but as the magistrates did not think fit either to "commend" or "reprimand" the officer, I consider it is a duty I owe not only to myself, but to my fellow townsmen, to formally call the attention of the Watch Committee to the facts so that they may judge for themselves what the conduct of the Police has been in the matter, and have accordingly addressed a letter to the chairman, of which I enclose a copy. Yours Truly, Enoch Evans, the 27th of November, 1886."

He was very upset that Chief Constable and Town Clerk decided to take action against him in the first place, but when the magistrates fined him he was even more aggrieved. He believed public opinion was on his side and he intended to take the matter further by reporting the circumstances to the Watch Committee.

This is a copy of the letter sent to the Chairman of the Watch Committee via the Town Clerk, J. R. Cooper.

"Sir, Before five o'clock on the morning of the 17th inst. P.C. Reddick (45), instead of being on his beat, was admittedly for some 10 minutes in my kitchen with my two maid servants, who had not been in bed through the previous night, drinking my tea, which my servants had no right to give him.

The discovery was made in consequence of my wife being awakened at half past three o'clock by hearing one of the children crying in the nursery. She went up to the second floor, and into the night nursery, where there are three beds, one of which should have been occupied by the nurse, but her bed had not been slept in that night.

My wife returned to our room, but could not sleep for thinking where the nurse should be, as both the servants always retired before I did. At that hour there is a full night light on in the night nursery fronting the street and a smaller light burning in the day nursery, which also fronts the street.

Sometime afterwards my wife again left her bed to ascertain if the nurse was sleeping with the cook, and as she was crossing the landing she heard, to her horror, a man's voice in the kitchen. Thoroughly alarmed now, she again came back to our room, but for some time was unable to speak in consequence of the fright. When she recovered herself somewhat she awoke me and told me the nurse was not in bed, and that she had heard a man's voice in the kitchen. I at once slipped on some portion of my dress, and, picking up the bedroom poker, which was the only defensive weapon at hand, I hurried downstairs. As I opened the door leading from the hall to the kitchen I saw the door on the other side of the kitchen on the swing and passing quickly through, I observed in the darkness of the morning a big man hurrying down the sidewalk. My wife, who had opened the bedroom window over the kitchen, screamed at the man, "I see you, you are seen" as I came through the door. He took no notice, his intention evidently being to get away without being identified, and hurried underneath the window out of my wife's sight.

I was after him as fast as I could go, shouting at him, "You infernal scoundrel" and almost in a moment overtook him halfway down the walk, not knowing but that he might possibly be armed and have a confederate, I struck him quickly twice. He then stopped, turned round, and I for the first time saw that he was a policeman.

Astounded at such conduct by a policeman, I seized him by the collar and demanded to see his number. He replied, "Here it is; take it then." I told him what a cur he was, and that he must report himself immediately to his Sergeant, as I should tell the Chief about him. He offered no explanation whatever of his conduct. At the Police court last Friday the officer stated I struck him again after I had taken his number. I hereby pledge myself, and am ready to state on oath, that this statement of his is not true. I did not strike him at all after taking his number.

The officer also swore that he was not in my house more than ten minutes, and that all he received was a "cup of tea." This will be for the committee to enquire into. He further admitted that he heard a "bustling" noise in the house, and I submit to the committee on hearing this, if he had been so innocent as he would have the public believe, he should have waited to see what it meant, and not tried to "sneak" away.

If he had waited but for a few seconds longer, he would still have been in my kitchen when I entered. I should have seen who it was, he could have given his explanation, and I could then have enquired into the truthfulness of his statement.

My wife, in consequence of the fright she received, was compelled to put herself under the care of her medical adviser, but if she is well enough, she will attend before the committee to give any information that may be required from her, and I shall only be too glad to have the opportunity of doing so.

In making this request for an enquiry by the Committee, I do so on public grounds, believing that such an enquiry will be the means of bringing about a better state of affairs in the good government of the town and in the police force in particular. Yours obediently, Enoch Evans. Dundrennan House. Walsall. 27th November, 1896." [457]

The letter accused the officer of theft of his tea and then making off when he called him. Mr. Evans said he thought the man might have an accomplice and they could have been armed and that is why he struck him. For whatever reason, the matter was becoming something of, 'a mountain out of a molehill' and now it was being escalated.

A special meeting of the Watch Committee was held on Tuesday the 1st of December, 1896. The Mayor Councillor Smith, ex-Mayor Councillor Noake, Alderman Roper, Councillors Brownhill, Dean, Hughes, Clare, Pearman-Smith and Cotterell were present. Enoch Evans and John Reddick were also present throughout the inquiry.

Enoch Evans said he had not been treated fairly by the officials, as Constable Reddick had been in his house without his permission, yet it was him who had been charged with assault. He alleged the Chief

Constable was set on convicting him to save his officer and the Town Clerk aided him with it.

The Town Clerk suggested they should look at the briefing notes made when he first spoke to Mr. Plumptre about the case, to see what he said then.

Mr. Evans said that idea was very unorthodox, it was legal privilege, but said he had no objection.

Everything really revolved around the question of whether he struck the officer after he gave his number. The legal brief was read out, but it only said that he hit him twice, with no other details.

The Town Clerk said he did suggest to Mr. Evans when he first spoke to him that an apology might end the matter, but he refused. He informed him then, that under the circumstances he had no alternative but to issue a summons, but he still had the opportunity of addressing the Bench.

Councillor Cotterell said that Mr. Evans had everyone's sympathy and Councillor Clare said he would have acted exactly the same.

Constable Reddick was asked if he knew who lived at the address, but he denied knowing that Mr. Evans lived there and apologised for being in the house. He said again that Mr. Evans did hit him after getting his number.

Mrs. Evans said she heard two strikes before the officer gave his number.

The Town Clerk conceded that the constable should have left after he realised there was no need for his services, but Councillor Hughes said he was wrong from beginning to end and Mr. Evans should have finished him.

The hearing went on for over three hours, until the committee went to consult in private for another half an hour. The decision was to severely reprimand Constable Reddick, by fining him a week's pay and reducing him a class in rank. The committee then apologised to Mr. and Mrs. Evans for their trouble.

Mr. Evans said he never wanted to see the officer dismissed and put down the fact that he stuck to his story, as a sign he was confused.

The Mayor finished by threatening Reddick that if ever came before the committee again, he would be discharged. [458] [459]

It looked to many that Reddick was made a scapegoat for the whole thing, where the middle class men stuck together and punished the working man for doing his job. That was certainly the opinion of Mr. Duignan the notorious solicitor and historian, who claimed in the local newspaper that Constable Reddick must have been born under a very unlucky star, to have received such a punishment. He urged the Watch Committee to urgently reconsider their unfair position. [460]

At the Watch Committee meeting on Monday the 14th of December, the Town Clerk presented a signed memorial received from forty-six members of the Police Force.

It read: - "To the Watch Committee of the Borough of Walsall. This petition of the Police Force humbly showeth that they have learned with regret the decision come to by you in the case of Police-constable Reddick, and most respectfully request you will kindly re-consider that decision, whereby three punishments have been inflicted for one offence namely, a reprimand, a fine of one week's pay and a reduction in grade, making together a sum of £14 to £15 and all that for the simple offence of accepting a cup of tea and being off his beat for a few minutes. Your petitioners would most respectfully point out that the offence charged was only supported by the evidence of a person who had been fined for assaulting the officer on the occasion when the offence was said to have been committed, and his wife, and that their statements were at variance with the evidence given on oath when the case was heard by the borough justices. Under all the circumstances your petitioners would most respectfully submit that the officer having been reprimanded by your honourable body and assaulted by his accuser, has been sufficiently punished, and that therefore, they sincerely hope you may see your way clear to temper justice with mercy by reinstating the officer and returning him the sum he was fined. And your petitioners in duty bound will ever pray. &c."

Councillor Hughes demanded to know who initiated it, but both the Town Clerk and the Chief Constable could not, or would not give an answer. Councillor Pearman Smith said, he hoped for the sake of the force, that the men who did sign it had not read it beforehand, or he would be very annoyed at the discourtesy to the committee.

Councillor Hughes said he wanted Reddick dismissed, but Councillor Cotterell said he regretted supporting the punishment as he thought it was too severe and a reprimand would have sufficed, like the Ex-Mayor proposed.

The Ex-Mayor said he thought that the officer had committed an offence, but to fine him twenty-seven shillings, reprimand him and lower his grade was too severe for what he had done.

Councillor Brownhill said the dignity of the committee could be upheld, if they couldn't stick to what had been decided.

The Mayor thought the committee would have dismissed Reddick had he not apologised, as there was no doubt he should not have gone into the house.

Alderman Baker thought that once the committee had reached a decision, it was the duty of the minority to abide by it.

Councillor Brownhill said he objected to the decision being a result of a compromise.

Councillor Clare thought Reddick would have been sacked for all the wrong some of them thought he had done.

It was unanimously agreed to ignore the testimonial and move on to the next business. [461]

There was obviously a lot of differing views on the rights and wrongs of the matter. The men of the police force was aggrieved at Reddick's treatment and the Chief Constable and Town Clerk supported him, but certain factions within the Watch Committee were determined to punish him, possibly through an allegiance to a legal man?

In February 1899, the Watch Committee formally reinstated Police Constable Reddick to the grade he was reduced from in December, 1896. Enoch Evans had already intimated that he had no objections providing the officer's subsequent conduct entitled him to it. [462]

Police Constable John James Reddick proved to be an outstanding officer, staying with Walsall Borough Police for the rest of his life. He died at the age of forty-seven from throat cancer on Saturday the 23rd of November, 1912, whilst still a serving officer. He served with the force for nineteen years and had been a prominent member of the police band playing clarinet.

Reddick's funeral was on Wednesday the 27th of November where the Reverend John Fenwick Laing, vicar of Rushall officiated. His father and son attended, together with about sixty police officers, including retired officers and senior officers, such as Chief Inspector Ballance, who later became the Chief Constable. [463] [464] [465]

101. The Mysterious Constable Conundrum - March 1898

This is the extraordinary case of Police Constable 34 Sidney John Charlesworth, who joined Walsall Borough Police early in 1898. Charlesworth was twenty-six years old, six foot one and a half inches tall, an ex-soldier and the son of a Shropshire Police Constable. On the face of it he had all the credentials of a good recruit.

In March, 1898, a story circulated around the town that a duo of dangerous masked burglars were operating in the area. Surprisingly when the press made enquiries with Walsall Borough Police, they said there was no truth in the rumours and denied the story.

Curious, local reporters made their own enquiries and a very different story emerged. They got their story from the occupants of an address in Mellish Road and one of the Walsall constables himself. Police Constable Charlesworth alleged that at four thirty on the morning of Wednesday the 16th of March, 1898, he saw a light in the breakfast room of Mr. Hurst's residence at 31, Mellish Road. Creeping up he saw two masked men, gathering up their valuable swag, including a handsome presentation clock. He waited until one of the burglars climbed out from a window, then grabbed him and got into a wrestle to get the handcuffs on. As he was struggling, the second masked villain came to his partners aid armed with a poker and struck Charlesworth over the head, knocking him unconscious. While on the ground, Charlesworth said he was kicked violently in the stomach and while incapacitated, the two men made their escape through the garden gate. During the commotion, Mrs. Sarah Hurst was woken and she sent her husband, Edwin to see what was amiss. He went downstairs and saw that things in the room had been disturbed during the night and the window was wide open. Police Constable Charlesworth was lying on the ground outside groaning in pain. Mr. Hurst's adult son, Charles ran out into the street and bumped into Sergeant Alfred Williams, who was only a short distance away. After the Sergeant arrived, Constable Charlesworth came to his senses and they later returned to Walsall Police Station to speak with Inspector George Ballance.

Having got their story, the reporters went back to Chief Constable Taylor who originally denied the incident. He then gave what he believed were the true facts. He said that Constable Charlesworth started working his beat at ten o'clock on Tuesday night. At about ten to four in the morning, Charles Hurst informed Sergeant Williams about the incident and together they went to the family home in Mellish Road. The sergeant arrived to find Charlesworth lying on his back on the lawn groaning. He found the constable's helmet with the top smashed in and his whistle and handcuffs on the ground. Nearby there was a poker and a couple of silver items from the house, but he could not find any signs of a forced entry to the premises, or any trace of the alleged offenders. When Charlesworth recovered he told the sergeant he had struggled with the offenders, but they had knocked him unconscious and escaped.

The Chief Constable said that when they returned to the station Inspector George Ballance requested that Charlesworth see the police surgeon, but refused. As a result, Chief Inspector Thomas Gore was called for and he ordered him to go. When the doctor examined him he found no injury on his head, but there was a small bruise above the right groin, but nothing to cause unconsciousness. The supervising officers examined his helmet and concluded that it was so badly damaged, it was impossible not to have sustained a head injury, if his account was true. They suspected that something was not right and when the Chief Constable was appraised of all the facts, he came to the same conclusion.

On Wednesday night, the Chief Constable accused Charlesworth of having committed the offence himself for the sake of gaining notoriety, which he denied. There had been two previous incidents that gave cause for concern, the first was the previous week when Charlesworth called at Mr. Greatrex's house and warned the servants that a suspicious character was loitering about, when no such report had been made at the police office. The other was an alleged burglary at the Green Man, in Dudley Street, where Charlesworth fell chasing a suspect who got away. As a result of all these concerns the Chief Constable informed Charlesworth to return his uniform on Thursday, as his services were no longer required.

After being dismissed Sidney Charlesworth, gave his own account to the press. He said the police surgeon ordered him to stay in bed, but the Chief Constable insisted he got up and appear at his office at six thirty on Wednesday evening. He was in no fit state, but the Chief Constable accused him of dishonesty and dismissed him at a moments notice, without allowing him to recover. Charlesworth claimed that Mr. Hurst and Sergeant Williams could clearly see there had been a desperate struggle and that his actions prevented the thieves from stealing the booty, but the Chief Constable rewarded him with instant dismissal. Charlesworth told reporters that the matter was in the hands of his solicitor. [466]

Sergeant 9 Alfred Williams also wrote to the editor on the 24th of March, pointing out that Charlesworth's account was incorrect. He could not confirm there had been a struggle, because he had been sixty yards away from Mr. Hurst's house in Mellish Road, when it happened. He said that if the two offenders had made off through the gate as Charlesworth alleged, he would have certainly seen them, but there was no sign of anyone. Sergeant Williams said that the first he knew of things, was when Charles Hurst ran up the street towards him. He did see Charlesworth lying on the ground apparently unconscious, but could not confirm that any struggle had taken place.

Sidney Charlesworth wrote a letter to the papers on the 26th of March. He said the Chief Constable accused him of breaking in, but

Sergeant Williams clearly stated he found no trace of a forced entry, so how was he supposed to have done it. He never refused to see the police surgeon, he just didn't want to trouble him, which is not the same as refusing. Charlesworth said, Chief Inspector Gore did not order him to see the doctor, as he was only too willing to go. The doctor found a small lump on his head, but he was saved from the worst by his helmet and he also had a nasty kick to the abdomen. He contended the shock of concussion could cause unconsciousness on its own, without any injury. Charlesworth concluded by saying the Chief Constable alleged he didn't deny the accusations, but that was wrong, he actually told him to his face it was a real burglary. [467]

At the monthly meeting of the Watch Committee on Monday the 11th of April 1898, the Town Clerk reported that he had received numerous letters in relation to the recent case of the alleged masked burglars and Constable Charlesworth. Some of them wrongly accused the Chief Constable of being unfair and acting in haste, but the Mayor had read the correspondence and did not consider the letters merited a special meeting to discuss them.

Councillor Noake implied that the Chief Constable had been uncivil to Mr. Hurst, accusing him of making up the masked burglars story. The Chief Constable said he always received information fairly if given in a proper spirit.

Interrupting, the Town Clerk informed the meeting that Mr. Hurst had since withdrawn most of his allegations about the matter, including the one where he accused the Chief Constable of being unjust. There was no grounds for any of the allegations of unfairness levelled at the Chief Constable and the Mayor had come to the same conclusion. The Town Clerk said he had discussed taking action against Charlesworth with the Chief Constable, but they had decided not to take any formal proceedings at that time. The Town Clerk revealed that it had come to light that Charlesworth was now wanted by Staffordshire County Constabulary in connection with some forged references to gain employment. When his application to join Walsall Borough Force was checked he had done the same and they could consider taking action against him for that.

Alderman Baker believed they should make an example of the man, especially as he had done the same thing elsewhere. He said they had a duty to protect the public from people becoming police constables using false representations.

The Town Clerk said they didn't want to make it look like they were just shutting Charlesworth up.

The Chief Constable confirmed Charlesworth had produced references from Wiltshire Police and a magistrate from that county, in relation to his appointment at Walsall, but he had no idea that he had been in the Staffordshire Police as well. Charlesworth's army discharge papers had been altered to appear his character was better than it was.

The Watch Committee agreed to defer any decision about taking proceedings out against Charlesworth until a later date. [468]

The truth was Charlesworth had a chequered military career. On 24th of October, 1892, at the age of eighteen, he joined the 3rd battalion of the King's Shropshire Light Infantry, but was discharged as medically unfit on the 4th of March, 1893. He re-enlisted with Shropshire Light Infantry on the 17th of February, 1894, then transferred to the Royal Artillery on the 14th of November, 1894. In 1895, a military court sentenced him to twenty-eight days imprisonment for an unspecified crime and on the 15th of September, 1896, he was discharged again for being medically unfit. [469]

In August, 1898 it became public knowledge that ex-police constable Charlesworth, was wanted by Staffordshire Police for making a false declaration to enter their force and by other police authorities for various crimes. Charlesworth went on the run to evade arrest, but astonishingly appeared in Oxford, where he joined the county constabulary. Not only that on the 15th of August, 1898, Charlesworth married Annie Maria Froggatt at St. Thomas's Church, Oxford. He gave his occupation as police constable in the county constabulary and she gave her address as H.M. Prison, Stafford, where she was a nurse. [470]

On the 27th of August, 1898, Sidney Charlesworth was arrested in Oxford for obtaining twenty pounds by false pretences from a Chester moneylender, named Wolfe Jackson. He pleaded guilty at Chester Court on the 20th of October, 1898, and sentenced to twelve months imprisonment with hard labour. It was then revealed he had a conviction for the theft of a rabbit in 1893, where he was fined. He served his time at Knutsford Prison and was released on the 6th of September, 1899. [471] [472]

This sequence of events exonerated the Chief Constable's decision to sack Charlesworth, his judgement of character had proved right. Charlesworth's deceit and dishonesty strongly supports the view that he staged the burglary at Mellish Road after all.

You might think that Charlesworth would have learnt his lesson, but some people never learn. On the 18th of July, 1900, he enlisted with the 2nd Life Guards at Regents Park Barracks, only to be discharged on the 16th of August the same year as not likely to be an efficient soldier.

The 1901 census shows him living with his sister at 259, London Road, Davenham and employed as a footman, then on the 28th of May, 1901, he and Annie had a son Frederick John Charlesworth.

He always appeared to be running from something and on the 7th of January, 1902, Charlesworth joined the Imperial Yeomanry at St. Albans. Whilst at Aldershot on stable guard, a horse supposedly kicked him in the stomach and he landed on his head. He said he woke up in hospital remembering nothing and stayed there for couple of days.

After leaving hospital he was posted to South Africa during the Boer War and in May he was promoted to Lance Corporal. Charlesworth's storytelling wasn't over yet, on the 9th May, 1902, whilst in Victoria, he claimed he fell whilst having a fit rendering himself unconscious.

At the Military Medical Board of enquiry, he blamed the incident where he was kicked by the horse at Aldershot. He told the board that soon after arriving in South Africa, he started sleep walking and on one occasion the sentry shot at him, waking him up in a fit. The army recommended that he was medically discharged, diagnosing that epilepsy was a permanent disability. He was returned to England and left the army on the 16th of September, 1902. [473]

He returned to live with his wife in Stafford, but things did not go well. On the 31st of December, 1906, Annie Marie Charlesworth filed for divorce, painting a very dark picture of him being a serial adulterer and a brutally cruel wife beater, with a catalogue of physical assault and mental cruelty. The marriage was finally dissolved on the 3rd of February, 1908. [474]

On the 2nd of May, 1907, Charlesworth broke into Lammascote House in Stafford belonging to George Earl, Superintendent of the Prudential Assurance Company and stole the safe.

He was arrested and appeared at court on the 3rd of May, where he pleaded guilty. It was revealed that at various times, he had managed to join no less than five police forces and several army regiments. This time the Judge gave him five years, to which Charlesworth said, "My Lord, you have pronounced my death sentence." [475]

He went to Parkhurst prison on the Isle of Wight and was released on the 19th of May, 1911 with the intention of travelling to London. His freedom was short lived, because on the 30th of June, 1911, he was arrested for a burglary in Ipswich and sentenced to a further five years, plus he had to serve the remainder of his previous sentence. At some point while serving this sentence at Parkhurst Prison, he convinced the doctors that he was insane, so they moved him to Melton Asylum, in Suffolk, although he may have spent a short stint at Broadmoor. When his sentence finally expired on the 11th of August, 1917, he was offered work as a clerk at Melton. [476] [477] [478] [479]

When Charlesworth was released, it was at the height of the Great War and he went on his travels again. On the 19th of September, 1917, at the age of forty-one he joined the Army Service Corp at Bath. Four months later on the 29th of January, 1918, he married a widow Mary Jane Holbrow at Bath. [480]

The army discharged him again on the 17th of July, 1918, as medically unfit due to 'moral deficiency.' This term was used to describe a person who lacked honesty, integrity, shame, guilt or lacked control. The medical officer suggested that enquiries be made at Broadmoor Lunatic Asylum, as to whether they knew anything about him, indicating things were not right with his head.

On the 12th of May, 1919 he was convicted at Bath Court for giving false information to gain employment at the Royal Mineral Water Hospital and sentenced to one month imprisonment. [481]

What happened to Charlesworth after this is uncertain, he was not with his wife in Bath at the time of the 1921 census, although she is listed as married and not widowed, suggesting that he was still alive. By 1939 she is recorded as a widow, but this may have been wishful thinking on her part!

Charlesworth simply vanished, he could have died unknown, changed his name, left the country under a pseudonym or ended his days in the darkened cell of a lunatic asylum, we just don't know.

We do know that he was a very troubled man with the inability to distinguish between fact and fiction, a man who acted out his fantasies in an unconvincing way and a very unsuccessful master of deceit and deception. Charlesworth lacked a sense of reality and I'm guessing his luck finally ran out!

The End

In the relay of life,
Learn from the past,
Live in the present,
Prepare for the future,
Pass a better baton on!
PR © 2023

About the Author

Paul Reeves was born in the early 1960's in Walsall Wood, Staffordshire and was educated at two local schools. For more than two hundred years, his ancestors forged strong affiliations with the town of Walsall and made it their home.

Paul worked at West Midlands Police for thirty years as a police officer until retirement in 2016, with his final day being at Green Lane, shortly before the stations demise. The vast majority of his service was as a detective and in that role he became a successful investigator, experienced in building up hundreds of criminal cases of evidence. Since retiring Paul has channelled his skills into a hobby as an investigative historian and genealogist. He searches for historical facts to recreate stories from the past, using years of genealogical experience and his case building expertise. He puts the flesh back on the bones of the people he writes about, to bring their stories back to life.

This is Paul's third book and follows, 'Remember Me - The Life of A Walsall Lad' (2021) and 'Walsall Borough Police and the Hotbed of Anarchy' (2023). All the books have been self written and edited, and independently published on Amazon Books. 'Walsall Borough Police - 101 Historical Cases from 1832 to 1898' continues in the theme of honouring the diverse social history of Walsall people. It chronologically runs through a selection of crimes and events from 1832 to 1898, to demonstrate how policing evolved and crime and punishment changed.

Dedication

This book is dedicated to the early pioneers of policing, the thin blue line, who made the system work in the face of adversity. Over many years those officers built up a bond with the public, who came to trust and believe they protected the virtues and values of society without fear or favour. They produced an organisation that became the envy of the world, based on the nine Peelian principles issued to every police officer in 1829, called the 'General Instructions.' These principles set out the ethos that only 'policing with the consent of the public' could succeed and confirmed the historic tradition, 'that the police are the public and the public are the police.'

There will always be those who mistrust or dislike the police, but so long as the majority support them, modern day freedoms will be maintained. Robert Peel said that maintaining law and order was incumbent on every citizen, the police were only citizens who gave it their full time attention! - Paul R.

In writing this book, I'm fully prepared to stand corrected if any of the sources used prove to be factually incorrect, or if additional material was inadvertently overlooked or undiscovered. By relying on historic sources, there is always the possibility it may be wrong, or in the case of newspapers articles, tainted or biased by the political or personal views of the authors. I always welcome being informed of any mistakes identified!

Acknowledgments

First of all I would like to acknowledge the hundreds of people who have either purchased, showed an interest, or offered valuable feedback and reviews for my first two books. It's great to know that there are so many people who enjoy your work, so a big thanks to everyone for the encouragement.

I would like to thank the many social media pages, that give their permission for authors to promote and advertise their books. In this respect the local Walsall pages have been especially supportive. This undoubtably demonstrates that the great and diverse Walsall community appreciate the rich history of the town and have a hunger to find out more about it.

I have to acknowledge a special thanks to Phil Buckley chronicler extraordinaire (Karma Times), for his continued assistance and help in promoting my work. Many may already know that Phil is an accomplished photographer and the front cover of this book is one of his great original snaps of the Guildhall entrance on High Street.

Finally no book is ever created without a group of supporters around the author and in this I have been lucky. My wife Paula and her wonderful sister Jenny have spent hours proofreading this book to iron out the many mistakes and there were quite a few. The title and versions changed weekly just to confuse them, but they kept at it and I hope it reads okay.

Further Reading

The research for this book has been completed using many internet based resources, too exhaustive to list, but include the following: -

The British Newspaper Archive
Ancestry
Find my past
Wikipedia
FreeBMD
The National Library of Scotland - Georeferenced Maps
Hitchmough's Black Country Pubs

I have referred to very few articles and books in the creation of this work, relying heavily on internet based resources, but have read: -

- A History of Walsall and Its Neighbourhood by Frederic William Willmore - 1887
- Enoch Evans 1884-2000 by John Evans - 2006

I would also recommend that people visit and support the local museums, libraries and archive services across the region. These places are under constant threat and face financial challenges, year in year out. This history is yours, if you lose it, it will be almost impossible to replace. Take your children, grandchildren or mothers and fathers and enjoy what the past has to offer.

Signposts to the Past - Source Records

[1] A History of Walsall and Its Neighbourhood by Frederic William Willmore - 1887
[2] Evening Mail - Monday 17 December 1832 - Page 2
[3] Staffordshire Advertiser - Saturday 15 December 1832 - Page 3
[4] The Examiner - Sunday 16 December 1832 - Page 9
[5] Staffordshire Advertiser - Saturday 15 December 1832 - Page 3
[6] England & Wales, Criminal Registers, 1791-1892 - Class: HO 27; Piece: 46; Page: 199
[7] Home Office: Convict Prison Hulks: Registers and Letter Books; Class: HO9; Piece: 3 & 4
[8] UK, Criminal Records, 1780-1871 - The National Archives; Kew, Surrey, England; HO 13 Home Office: Criminal Entry Books; Reference: HO 13/63
[9] Criminal Records, 1780-1871 - HO 13 Home Office: Criminal Entry Books; Reference: HO 13/63
[10] New South Wales, Australia, Convict Indents, 1788-1842 - State Archives NSW; Series: NRS 12189; Item: [X636]; Microfiche: 708
[11] Australian Convict Transportation Registers – Other Fleets & Ships, 1791-1868 - Class: HO 11; Piece: 9
[12] New South Wales, Australia, Convict Registers of Conditional and Absolute Pardons, 1788-1870 - State Records Authority of New South Wales; Kingswood, New South Wales, Australia; Card Index to Letters Received, Colonial Secretary; Reel Number: 783; Roll Number: 1250
[13] New South Wales, Australia Convict Ship Muster Rolls and Related Records, 1790-1849 - New South Wales Government. *Musters and other papers relating to convict ships.* Series CGS 1155, Reels 2417-2428. State Records Authority of New South Wales. Kingswood, New South Wales, Australia.
[14] New South Wales, Australia, Convict Indents, 1788-1842 - State Archives NSW; Series: NRS 12188; Item: [4/4018]; Microfiche: 689
[15] New South Wales and Tasmania, Australia, Convict Pardons and Tickets of Leave, 1834-1859 - Class: HO 10; Piece: 53 & 54
[16] The Sydney Mail Saturday 23 January 1875- Page 123
[17] New South Wales, Australia, Convict Registers of Conditional and Absolute Pardons, 1788-1870 - State Records Authority of New South Wales; Kingswood, New South Wales, Australia; Card Index to Letters Received, Colonial Secretary; Reel Number: 784; Roll Number: 1250
[18] New South Wales, Australia, Gaol Description and Entrance Books, 1818-1930 - State Archives NSW; Kingswood, New South Wales; Gaol Description and Entrance Books, 1818-1930; Series: 2517; Item: 4/6296; Roll: 855
[19] Staffordshire Advertiser - Saturday 27 July 1833 - Page 2
[20] Home Office: Convict Prison Hulks: Registers and Letter Books; Class: HO9; Piece: 4
[21] Staffordshire Advertiser - Saturday 20 July 1833 - Page 2
[22] Staffordshire Advertiser - Saturday 3 August 1833
[23] England & Wales, Criminal Registers, 1791-1892 - Class: HO 27; Piece: 48; Page: 182
[24] Harvard Law School Library, Harvard University - 990022193050203941 - G. Smeeton, Printer, 74, Tooley Street.
[25] Staffordshire Advertiser - Saturday 22 March 1834 - Page 2
[26] Wolverhampton Chronicle and Staffordshire Advertiser - Wednesday 26 March 1834 - Page 3
[27] Staffordshire Advertiser - Saturday 19 March 1836 - Page 3
[28] UK and Ireland, Find a Grave® Index, 1300s-Current

[29] Wolverhampton Chronicle and Staffordshire Advertiser - Wednesday 3 February 1836 - Page 2
[30] England & Wales, Criminal Registers, 1791-1892 - Class: HO 27; Piece: 52; Page: 296
[31] England & Wales, Criminal Registers, 1791-1892 - Class: HO 27; Piece: 54; Page: 231
[32] UK, Prison Hulk Registers and Letter Books, 1802-1849 - Home Office: Convict Prison Hulks: Registers and Letter Books; Class: HO9; Piece: 12
[33] Australia, Convict Records Index, 1787-1867 - State Library of Queensland; South Brisbane, Queensland, Australia; Australian Joint Copying Project. Microfilm Roll 90, Class and Piece Number HO11/11, Page Number 169 (86)
[34] New South Wales, Australia, Convict Indents, 1788-1842 - State Archives NSW; Series: NRS 12189; Item: [X640]; Microfiche: 730
[35] Web: Australia, Convict Records Index, 1787-1867 - State Library of Queensland; South Brisbane, Queensland, Australia; Australian Joint Copying Project. Microfilm Roll 90, Class and Piece Number HO11/11, Page Number 98
[36] Staffordshire Advertiser - Saturday 18 March 1837 - Page 4
[37] Wolverhampton Chronicle and Staffordshire Advertiser - Wednesday 15 March 1837 - Page 3
[38] Staffordshire Advertiser - Friday 14 July 1837 - Page 2
[39] England & Wales, Criminal Registers, 1791-1892 - Class: HO 27; Piece: 54; Page: 267
[40] Staffordshire Advertiser - Saturday 04 February 1837 - Page 3
[41] 1841 England Census - Class: HO107; Piece: 983; Book: 5; Civil Parish: Walsall; County: Staffordshire; Enumeration District: 9; Folio: 15; Page: 22; Line: 1; GSU roll: 474617
[42] Wolverhampton Chronicle and Staffordshire Advertiser - Wednesday 15 February 1837 - Page 3
[43] Wolverhampton Chronicle and Staffordshire Advertiser - Wednesday 22 February 1837 - Page 3
[44] Staffordshire Advertiser - Saturday 11 March 1837 - Page 3
[45] Home Office: Criminal Registers, Middlesex and Home Office: Criminal Registers, England and Wales - Class: HO 27; Piece: 54; Page: 224
[46] Home Office: Convict Prison Hulks: Registers and Letter Books; Class: HO9; Piece: 12
[47] Home Office: Convict Transportation Registers; (The National Archives Microfilm Publication HO11 - Class: HO 11; Piece: 11
[48] Tasmania, Australia, Convict Court and Selected Records, 1800-1899 - Tasmanian Colonial Convict, Passenger and Land Records. Various collections (30 series). Tasmanian Archive and Heritage Office, Hobart, Tasmania.
[49] Australia, Convict Records Index, 1787-1867 - State Library of Queensland; South Brisbane, Queensland, Australia; Australian Joint Copying Project. Microfilm Roll 90, Class and Piece Number HO11/11, Page Number 168
[50] UK, Criminal Records, 1780-1871 - The National Archives; Kew, Surrey, England; HO 13 Home Office: Criminal Entry Books; Reference: HO 13/71
[51] UK, Criminal Records, 1780-1871 - The National Archives; Kew, Surrey, England; HO 19 Home Office: Registers of Criminal Petitions; Reference: HO 19/7
[52] UK, Criminal Records, 1780-1871 - The National Archives; Kew, Surrey, England; HO 17 Home Office: Criminal Petitions: Series I; Reference: HO 17/116
[53] Wolverhampton Chronicle and Staffordshire Advertiser - Wednesday 01 March 1837 - Page 3
[54] UK and Ireland, Find a Grave® Index, 1300s-Current - Bath Street Burial Grounds
[55] UK, Records of the Removal of Graves and Tombstones, 1601-2007 - The National Archives; Kew, London, England; Rg 37: Copies of Records of Local Authorities and Church Commissioners Relating to Burial Ground Removals; Reference: Rg 37/159; Piece Number: 159; Series Number: Rg 37

56 Morning Herald (London) - Tuesday 25 July 1837 - Page 4
57 Staffordshire Advertiser - Saturday 22 July 1837 - Page 2 & 4
58 England & Wales, Criminal Registers, 1791-1892 - Class: HO 27; Piece: 54; Page: 247
59 Staffordshire Advertiser - Saturday 22 July 1837 - Page 4
60 Criminal Registers, Middlesex and Home Office: Criminal Registers, England and Wales; - Class: HO 27; Piece: 54; Page: 251
61 Home Office: Convict Prison Hulks: Registers and Letter Books; Class: HO9; Piece: 12
62 Australian Convict Transportation Registers – Other Fleets & Ships, 1791-1868 - Class: HO 11; Piece: 11
63 New South Wales, Australia, Convict Indents, 1788-1842 - NSW; Series: NRS 12189; Item: [X641]; Microfiche: 733
64 UK, Criminal Records, 1780-1871 - The National Archives; Kew, Surrey, England; HO 17 Home Office: Criminal Petitions: Series I; Reference: HO 17/126
65 UK, Criminal Records, 1780-1871 - The National Archives; Kew, Surrey, England; HO 13 Home Office: Criminal Entry Books; Reference: HO 13/72
66 Australia, Convict Records Index, 1787-1867 - State Library of Queensland; South Brisbane, Queensland, Australia; Australian Joint Copying Project. Microfilm Roll 90, Class and Piece Number HO11/11, Page Number 203 (103)
67 England & Wales, Criminal Registers, 1791-1892 - Class: HO 27; Piece: 54; Page: 250
68 England & Wales, Criminal Registers, 1791-1892 - Class: HO 27; Piece: 74; Page: 135
69 Australian Convict Transportation Registers – Other Fleets & Ships, 1791-1868 - Class: HO 11; Piece: 14
70 Wolverhampton Chronicle and Staffordshire Advertiser - Wednesday 17 January 1838 - Page 3
71 Wolverhampton Chronicle and Staffordshire Advertiser - Wednesday 21 February 1838 - Page 3
72 UK, Criminal Records, 1780-1871 - The National Archives; Kew, Surrey, England; HO 13 Home Office: Criminal Entry Books; Reference: HO 13/84
73 England & Wales, Criminal Registers, 1791-1892 - Class: HO 27; Piece: 56; Page: 241
74 UK, Prison Hulk Registers and Letter Books, 1802-1849 - Home Office: Convict Prison Hulks: Registers and Letter Books; Class: HO9; Piece: 14
75 UK, Criminal Records, 1780-1871 - The National Archives; Kew, Surrey, England; HO 13 Home Office: Criminal Entry Books; Reference: HO 13/78
76 UK, Prison Hulk Registers and Letter Books, 1802-1849 - Home Office: Convict Prison Hulks: Registers and Letter Books; Class: HO9; Piece: 12
77 Staffordshire Advertiser - Saturday 10 March 1838 - Page 3
78 Staffordshire Advertiser - Saturday 6 October 1838 - Page 3
79 England & Wales, Criminal Registers, 1791-1892 - Class: HO 27; Piece: 56; Page: 243
80 Staffordshire Advertiser - Saturday 12 May 1838 - Page 3
81 Wolverhampton Chronicle and Staffordshire Advertiser - Wednesday 16 May 1838 - Page 3
82 Staffordshire Advertiser - Saturday 9 June 1838 - Page 3
83 Wolverhampton Chronicle and Staffordshire Advertiser - Wednesday 13 June 1838 - Page 3
84 Staffordshire Advertiser - Saturday 1 September 1838 - Page 3
85 Staffordshire Advertiser - Saturday 8 September 1838 - Page 3
86 Staffordshire Advertiser - Saturday 22 September 1838 - Page 3
87 England & Wales, Criminal Registers, 1791-1892 - Class: HO 27; Piece: 56; Page: 243
88 Staffordshire Gazette and County Standard - Saturday 27 July 1839 - Page 1
89 Staffordshire Advertiser - Saturday 27 July 1839 - Page 4
90 England & Wales, Criminal Registers, 1791-1892 - Class: HO 27; Piece: 59; Page: 134

[91] Staffordshire Advertiser - Saturday 27 July 1839 - Page 2
[92] England & Wales, Criminal Registers, 1791-1892 - Class: HO 27; Piece: 59; Page: 132
[93] Derbyshire Courier - Saturday 4 January 1840 - Page 2
[94] England & Wales, Criminal Registers, 1791-1892 - Class: HO 27; Piece: 60; Page: 157
[95] Staffordshire Advertiser - Saturday 30 November 1839 - Page 3
[96] Staffordshire Advertiser - Saturday 14 March 1840 - Page 2
[97] Home Office: Convict Prison Hulks: Registers and Letter Books; Class: HO9; Piece: 12
[98] England & Wales, Criminal Registers, 1791-1892 - Class: HO 27; Piece: 62; Page: 134
[99] Australia, List of Convicts with Particulars, 1788-1842 - Colonial Office and Predecessors: Alphabetical list of convicts with particulars 1788-1825; 1840-1842; (The National Archives Microfilm Publication CO 207/9); The National Archives of the UK (TNA), Kew, Surrey, England.
[100] New South Wales, Australia, Convict Registers of Conditional and Absolute Pardons, 1788-1870 - State Records Authority of New South Wales; Kingswood, New South Wales, Australia; Card Index to Letters Received, Colonial Secretary; Reel Number: 795; Roll Number: 1250
[101] England & Wales, Criminal Registers, 1791-1892 - Class: HO 27; Piece: 62; Page: 133
[102] Staffordshire Advertiser - Saturday 14 March 1840 - Page 2
[103] Home Office: Criminal Registers, Middlesex and Home Office: Criminal Registers, England and Wales; Class: HO 27; Piece: 62; Page: 129
[104] Colonial Office and Predecessors: Alphabetical list of convicts with particulars 1788-1825; 1840-1842; (The National Archives Microfilm Publication CO 207/9); referenced as CO207/1-3.
[105] New South Wales, Australia, Convict Indents, 1788-1842 - State Archives NSW; Series: NRS 12189; Item: [X642A]; Microfiche: 743
[106] Australia, Convict Records Index, 1787-1867 - State Library of Queensland; South Brisbane, Queensland, Australia; Australian Joint Copying Project. Microfilm Roll 91, Class and Piece Number HO11/12, Page Number 206
[107] Australia, Convict Records Index, 1787-1867 - State Library of Queensland; South Brisbane, Queensland, Australia; Australian Joint Copying Project. Microfilm Roll 91, Class and Piece Number HO11/12, Page Number 254
[108] Staffordshire Advertiser - Saturday 14 March 1840 - Page 2
[109] Home Office: Settlers and Convicts, New South Wales and Tasmania - Class: HO 10; Piece: 54
[110] New South Wales, Australia, Convict Registers of Conditional and Absolute Pardons, 1788-1870 - Reel Number: 3037; Roll Number: 1250
[111] England & Wales, Criminal Registers, 1791-1892 - Class: HO 27; Piece: 62; Page: 130
[112] Staffordshire Gazette and County Standard - Saturday 28 March 1840 - Page 3
[113] England & Wales, Criminal Registers, 1791-1892 - Class: HO 27; Piece: 62; Page: 160
[114] Staffordshire Gazette and County Standard - Saturday 7 March 1840 - Page 3
[115] Staffordshire Gazette and County Standard - Saturday 23 May 1840 - Page 3
[116] Staffordshire Gazette and County Standard - Saturday 4 July 1840 - Page 1
[117] England & Wales, Criminal Registers, 1791-1892 - Class: HO 27; Piece: 62; Page: 161
[118] Staffordshire Gazette and County Standard - Saturday 23 May 1840 - Page 3
[119] Staffordshire Gazette and County Standard - Saturday 6 June 1840 - Page 3
[120] Staffordshire Gazette and County Standard - Saturday 20 June 1840 - Page 2
[121] Staffordshire Gazette and County Standard - Saturday 4 July 1840 - Page 1
[122] England & Wales, Criminal Registers, 1791-1892 - Class: HO 27; Piece: 62; Page: 161
[123] Wolverhampton Chronicle and Staffordshire Advertiser - Wednesday 24 June 1840 - Page 2

[124] Staffordshire Gazette and County Standard - Saturday 4 July 1840 - Page 1
[125] Staffordshire Gazette and County Standard - Saturday 17 October 1840 - Page 3
[126] England & Wales, Criminal Registers, 1791-1892 - Class: HO 27; Piece: 62; Page: 161
[127] Staffordshire Gazette and County Standard - Saturday 21 November 1840 - Page 3
[128] Staffordshire Gazette and County Standard - Thursday 18 February 1841 - Page 3
[129] Staffordshire Advertiser - Saturday 13 March 1841 - Page 4
[130] Wolverhampton Chronicle and Staffordshire Advertiser - Wednesday 17 March 1841 - Page 4
[131] Tasmania, Australia, Convict Court and Selected Records, 1800-1899 - CON22-1-3
[132] New South Wales and Tasmania, Australia Convict Musters, 1806-1849 - Class: HO 10; Piece: 40
[133] England & Wales, Criminal Registers, 1791-1892 - Class: HO 27; Piece: 65; Page: 115
[134] England & Wales, Criminal Registers, 1791-1892 - Class: HO 27; Piece: 65; Page: 158
[135] UK, Prison Hulk Registers and Letter Books, 1802-1849 - Home Office: Convict Prison Hulks: Registers and Letter Books; Class: HO9; Piece: 12
[136] Australia, Convict Records Index, 1787-1867 - State Library of Queensland; South Brisbane, Queensland, Australia; Australian Joint Copying Project. Microfilm Roll 91, Class and Piece Number HO11/13, Page Number 219 (111)
[137] Staffordshire Gazette and County Standard - Thursday 5 August 1841 - Page 3
[138] Staffordshire Gazette and County Standard - Thursday 12 August 1841 - Page 2
[139] Staffordshire Advertiser - Saturday 14 August 1841 - Page 3
[140] Staffordshire Advertiser - Saturday 23 October 1841 - Page 2
[141] England & Wales, Criminal Registers, 1791-1892 - Class: HO 27; Piece: 65; Page: 144 & 145
[142] UK, Prison Hulk Registers and Letter Books, 1802-1849 - Home Office: Convict Prison Hulks: Registers and Letter Books; Class: HO9; Piece: 13
[143] Staffordshire Advertiser - Saturday 19 March 1842 - Page 2
[144] Staffordshire Advertiser - Saturday 19 March 1842 - Page 4
[145] UK, Prison Hulk Registers and Letter Books, 1802-1849 - Home Office: Convict Prison Hulks: Registers and Letter Books; Class: HO9; Piece: 12
[146] Staffordshire Advertiser - Saturday 13 November 1841 - Page 2
[147] Staffordshire, England, Church of England Deaths and Burials, 1813-1900
[148] England & Wales, Criminal Registers, 1791-1892 - Class: HO 27; Piece: 68; Page: 138
[149] 1841 England Census - Class: HO107; Piece: 984; Book: 1; Civil Parish: Wednesbury; County: Staffordshire; Enumeration District: 1; Page: 5; Line: 14; GSU roll: 474618
[150] 1841 England Census - Class: HO107; Piece: 984; Book: 1; Civil Parish: Wednesbury; County: Staffordshire; Enumeration District: 1; Page: 1; Line: 14; GSU roll: 474618
[151] 1841 England Census - Class: HO107; Piece: 983; Book: 12; Civil Parish: Walsall; County: Staffordshire; Enumeration District: 14; Page: 1; Line: 12; GSU roll: 474617
[152] Staffordshire, England, Church of England Deaths and Burials, 1813-1900 - Indexes created from Anglican Parish Registers held at Staffordshire Record Office; Stafford, Staffordshire, England
[153] UK, Prison Commission Records, 1770-1951 - The National Archives; Kew, London, England; PCOM 2: Metropolitan Police: Criminal Record Office: Habitual Criminals Registers and Miscellaneous Papers
[154] Staffordshire Advertiser - Saturday 2 April 1842 - Page 3
[155] Staffordshire Advertiser - Saturday 9 April 1842 - Page 3
[156] UK, Prison Hulk Registers and Letter Books, 1802-1849 - Home Office: Convict Prison Hulks: Registers and Letter Books; Class: HO9; Piece: 12

[157] Wolverhampton Chronicle and Staffordshire Advertiser - Wednesday 15 December 1841 - Page 3
[158] Staffordshire Advertiser - Saturday 4 December 1841 - Page 3
[159] Staffordshire Gazette and County Standard - Thursday 09 December 1841 - Page 3
[160] Staffordshire Advertiser - Saturday 11 December 1841 - Page 2
[161] Staffordshire Advertiser - Saturday 11 December 1841 - Page 3
[162] Staffordshire Advertiser - Saturday 18 December 1841 - Page 2
[163] Staffordshire Advertiser - Saturday 19 March 1842 - Page 2
[164] Staffordshire Advertiser - Saturday 19 November 1842 - Page 2, 3 & 4
[165] England & Wales, Criminal Registers, 1791-1892 - Class: HO 27; Piece: 68; Page: 141
[166] Tasmania, Australia, Convict Court and Selected Records, 1800-1899 - Tasmanian Colonial Convict, Passenger and Land Records. Various collections (30 series). Tasmanian Archive and Heritage Office, Hobart, Tasmania.
[167] Staffordshire Advertiser - Saturday 26 March 1842 - Page 3
[168] Staffordshire Advertiser - Saturday 9 April 1842 - Page 2
[169] England & Wales, Criminal Registers, 1791-1892 - Class: HO 27; Piece: 68; Page: 192
[170] UK, Prison Hulk Registers and Letter Books, 1802-1849 - Home Office: Convict Prison Hulks: Registers and Letter Books; Class: HO9; Piece: 13
[171] UK, Criminal Records, 1780-1871 - The National Archives; Kew, Surrey, England; HO 19 Home Office: Registers of Criminal Petitions; Reference: HO 19/9
[172] UK, Criminal Records, 1780-1871 - The National Archives; Kew, Surrey, England; HO 18 Home Office: Criminal Petitions: Series II; Reference: HO 18/78
[173] Australia, Convict Records Index, 1787-1867 - State Library of Queensland; South Brisbane, Queensland, Australia; Australian Joint Copying Project. Microfilm Roll 91, Class and Piece Number HO11/13, Page Number 237 (120)
[174] Wolverhampton Chronicle and Staffordshire Advertiser - Wednesday 7 September 1842 - Page 1
[175] 1841 England Census - Class: HO107; Piece: 980; Book: 17; Civil Parish: St Michael Lichfield; County: Staffordshire; Enumeration District: 12; Folio: 6; Page: 7; Line: 5; GSU roll: 474615
[176] Weekly Chronicle (London) - Saturday 25 November 1843 - Page 3
[177] Coventry Standard - Friday 24 November 1843 - Page 4
[178] UK and Ireland, Find a Grave® Index, 1300s-Current - UK and Ireland, Find a Grave® Index, 1300s-Current [database on-line]. Lehi, UT, USA: Ancestry.com Operations, Inc., 2012.
[179] Staffordshire, England, Church of England Deaths and Burials, 1813-1900 - Staffordshire Anglican Parish Registers. Stafford, Staffordshire, England: Indexes created from Anglican Parish Registers held at Staffordshire Record Office.
[180] Wolverhampton Chronicle and Staffordshire Advertiser - Wednesday 3 January 1844 - Page 4
[181] Staffordshire Advertiser - Saturday 13 January 1844 - Page 3
[182] Staffordshire Advertiser - Saturday 20 January 1844 - Page 3
[183] England & Wales, Criminal Registers, 1791-1892 - Class: HO 27; Piece: 71; Page: 187
[184] England & Wales, Crime, Prisons & Punishment, 1770-1935 - HO18 - Piece number 123
[185] England & Wales, Crime, Prisons & Punishment, 1770-1935 - HO13 - Correspondence And Warrants, Piece number 83, Page number 421
[186] Staffordshire Advertiser - Saturday 5 April 1845 - Page 2
[187] Lincolnshire Chronicle - Friday 18 July 1845 - Page 4
[188] Staffordshire Advertiser - Saturday 19 July 1845 - Page 3
[189] Staffordshire Advertiser - Saturday 26 July 1845 - Page 3

[190] Coventry Standard - Friday 25 July 1845 - Page 4
[191] Wolverhampton Chronicle and Staffordshire Advertiser - Wednesday 23 July 1845 - Page 3
[192] Wolverhampton Chronicle and Staffordshire Advertiser - Wednesday 1 September 1847 - Page 1
[193] Wolverhampton Chronicle and Staffordshire Advertiser - Wednesday 28 June 1848 - Page 4
[194] Staffordshire Advertiser - Saturday 29 July 1848 - Page 8
[195] England & Wales, Criminal Registers, 1791-1892 - Class: HO 27; Piece: 86; Page: 146
[196] England & Wales, Criminal Registers, 1791-1892 - Class: HO 27; Piece: 86; Page: 144
[197] UK, Criminal Records, 1780-1871 - The National Archives; Kew, Surrey, England; HO 19 Home Office: Registers of Criminal Petitions; Reference: HO 19/11A
[198] Tasmania, Australia, Convict Court and Selected Records, 1800-1899 - Tasmanian Colonial Convict, Passenger and Land Records. Various collections (30 series). Tasmanian Archive and Heritage Office, Hobart, Tasmania.
[199] Web: Australia, Convict Records Index, 1787-1867 - State Library of Queensland; South Brisbane, Queensland, Australia; Australian Joint Copying Project. Microfilm Roll 92, Class and Piece Number HO11/17, Page Number 415 (210)
[200] Australian Convict Transportation Registers – Other Fleets & Ships, 1791-1868 - Class: HO 11; Piece: 17 - Home Office: Convict Transportation Registers; (The National Archives Microfilm Publication HO11); The National Archives of the UK (TNA), Kew, Surrey, England.
[201] UK, Criminal Records, 1780-1871 - The National Archives; Kew, Surrey, England; HO 13 Home Office: Criminal Entry Books; Reference: HO 13/95 & Entry Books; Reference: HO 13/95
[202] UK, Criminal Records, 1780-1871 - The National Archives; Kew, Surrey, England; HO 24 Home Office: Prison Registers and Statistical Returns; Reference: HO 24/4
[203] UK, Prison Commission Records, 1770-1951 - The National Archives; Kew, London, England; PCOM 2: Metropolitan Police: Criminal Record Office: Habitual Criminals Registers and Miscellaneous Papers
[204] Wolverhampton Chronicle and Staffordshire Advertiser - Wednesday 9 August 1848 - Page 3
[205] Staffordshire Advertiser - Saturday 22 December 1849 - Page 8
[206] Staffordshire Advertiser - Saturday 23 March 1850 - Page 7
[207] England & Wales, Criminal Registers, 1791-1892 - Class: HO 27; Piece: 94; Page: 97
[208] England & Wales, Criminal Registers, 1791-1892 - Class: HO 27; Piece: 94; Page: 100
[209] England & Wales, Criminal Registers, 1791-1892 - Class: HO 27; Piece: 86; Page: 152
[210] England & Wales, Criminal Registers, 1791-1892 - Class: HO 27; Piece: 94; Page: 106
[211] UK, Criminal Records, 1780-1871 - The National Archives; Kew, Surrey, England; HO 19 Home Office: Registers of Criminal Petitions; Reference: HO 19/11B
[212] Staffordshire Advertiser - Saturday 6 July 1850 - Page 7
[213] Birmingham Journal - Saturday 29 December 1849 - Page 7
[214] Wolverhampton Chronicle and Staffordshire Advertiser - Wednesday 9 January 1850 - Page 4
[215] Staffordshire Advertiser - Saturday 6 July 1850 - Page 7
[216] England & Wales, Criminal Registers, 1791-1892 - Class: HO 27; Piece: 94; Page: 89
[217] England & Wales, Criminal Registers, 1791-1892 - Class: HO 27; Piece: 94; Page: 107
[218] Wolverhampton Chronicle and Staffordshire Advertiser - Wednesday 1 May 1850 - Page 3
[219] Staffordshire Advertiser - Saturday 22 March 1851 - Page 7
[220] England & Wales, Criminal Registers, 1791-1892 - Class: HO 27; Piece: 98; Page: 97
[221] England, Criminal Lunatic Asylum Registers, 1820-1876 - The National Archives; Kew, Surrey, England; HO 8: Home Office: Convict Hulks, Convict Prisons and Criminal Lunatic Asylums: Quarterly Returns of Prisoners; Class: HO 8; Piece Number: HO 8/121

[222] Staffordshire Advertiser - Saturday 21 September 1850 - Page 5
[223] Wolverhampton Chronicle and Staffordshire Advertiser - Wednesday 2 October 1850 - Page 4
[224] England & Wales, Criminal Registers, 1791-1892 - Class: HO 27; Piece: 94; Page: 121
[225] Staffordshire Advertiser - Saturday 28 September 1850 - Page 8
[226] Staffordshire Advertiser - Saturday 7 December 1850 - Page 5
[227] England & Wales, Criminal Registers, 1791-1892 - Class: HO 27; Piece: 94; Page: 121
[228] Staffordshire Advertiser - Saturday 22 March 1851 - Page 5
[229] Staffordshire Advertiser - Saturday 5 April 1851 - Page 5
[230] Wolverhampton Chronicle and Staffordshire Advertiser - Wednesday 30 April 1851 - Page 2
[231] Sussex Advertiser - Tuesday 6 May 1851 - Page 2
[232] England & Wales, Criminal Registers, 1791-1892 - Class: HO 27; Piece: 59; Page: 128
[233] England & Wales, Criminal Registers, 1791-1892 - Class: HO 27; Piece: 98; Page: 123
[234] UK, Prison Commission Records, 1770-1951 - The National Archives; Kew, London, England; PCOM 2: Metropolitan Police: Criminal Record Office: Habitual Criminals Registers and Miscellaneous Papers
[235] England & Wales, Criminal Registers, 1791-1892 - Class: HO 27; Piece: 118; Page: 186
[236] Wolverhampton Chronicle and Staffordshire Advertiser - Wednesday 18 March 1857 - Page 7
[237] Home Office: Old Captions And Transfer Papers - PCOM5 - Piece number 48
[238] Staffordshire Advertiser - Saturday 14 June 1851 - Page 5
[239] Staffordshire Advertiser - Saturday 6 September 1851 - Page 5
[240] Worcester Journal - Thursday 4 March 1852 - Page 4
[241] Wolverhampton Chronicle and Staffordshire Advertiser - Wednesday 25 February 1852 - Page 2
[242] Staffordshire Advertiser - Saturday 6 March 1852 - Page 4
[243] Staffordshire Advertiser - Saturday 10 April 1852 - Page 5
[244] Staffordshire Advertiser - Saturday 24 April 1852 - Page 5
[245] Staffordshire Advertiser - Saturday 1 May 1852 - Page 5
[246] England & Wales, Criminal Registers, 1791-1892 - Class: HO 27; Piece: 102; Page: 123 & 124
[247] Staffordshire Advertiser - Saturday 18 June 1853 - Page 8
[248] Staffordshire Advertiser - Saturday 23 July 1853 - Page 6
[249] Wolverhampton Chronicle and Staffordshire Advertiser - Wednesday 3 August 1853 - Page 4
[250] England & Wales, Criminal Registers, 1791-1892 - Class: HO 27; Piece: 106; Page: 109
[251] UK, Criminal Records, 1780-1871 - The National Archives; Kew, Surrey, England; HO 13 Home Office: Criminal Entry Books; Reference: HO 13/102
[252] UK, Criminal Records, 1780-1871 - The National Archives; Kew, Surrey, England; HO 19 Home Office: Registers of Criminal Petitions; Reference: HO 19/12
[253] UK, Criminal Records, 1780-1871 - The National Archives; Kew, Surrey, England; HO 24 Home Office: Prison Registers and Statistical Returns; Reference: HO 24/13
[254] UK, Criminal Records, 1780-1871 - The National Archives; Kew, Surrey, England; HO 18 Home Office: Criminal Petitions: Series II; Reference: HO 18/365
[255] England & Wales, Crime, Prisons & Punishment, 1770-1935 - PCOM4 - Piece date 1864 Feb 29 - May 31 - Item reference 10
[256] Wolverhampton Chronicle and Staffordshire Advertiser - Wednesday 04 January 1854 - Page 6
[257] England & Wales, Criminal Registers, 1791-1892 - Class: HO 27; Piece: 109; Page: 281
[258] England & Wales, Criminal Registers, 1791-1892 - Class: HO 27; Piece: 109; Page: 281

[259] Wolverhampton Chronicle and Staffordshire Advertiser - Wednesday 22 February 1854 - Page
[260] Staffordshire Advertiser - Saturday 25 February 1854 - Page 5
[261] Staffordshire Advertiser - Saturday 8 April 1854 - Page 7
[262] England & Wales, Criminal Registers, 1791-1892 - Class: HO 27; Piece: 109; Page: 252
[263] England & Wales, Criminal Registers, 1791-1892 - Class: HO 27; Piece: 109; Page: 281
[264] UK, Criminal Records, 1780-1871 - The National Archives; Kew, Surrey, England; HO 24 Home Office: Prison Registers and Statistical Returns; Reference: HO 24/8
[265] Staffordshire Advertiser - Saturday 10 June 1854 - Page 5
[266] Staffordshire Advertiser - Saturday 17 June 1854 - Page 5
[267] Staffordshire Advertiser - Saturday 24 June 1854 - Page 3
[268] Globe - Monday 26 March 1855 - Page 4
[269] Staffordshire Advertiser - Saturday 21 April 1855 - Page 7
[270] England & Wales, Criminal Registers, 1791-1892 - Class: HO 27; Piece: 112; Page: 245 & 246
[271] Staffordshire Advertiser - Saturday 3 November 1855 - Page 6
[272] England & Wales, Criminal Registers, 1791-1892 - Class: HO 27; Piece: 112; Page: 247
[273] Staffordshire Advertiser - Saturday 15 December 1855 - Page 5
[274] England & Wales, Criminal Registers, 1791-1892 - Class: HO 27; Piece: 115; Page: 194
[275] England & Wales, Criminal Registers, 1791-1892 - Class: HO 27; Piece: 115; Page: 194
[276] Staffordshire Advertiser - Saturday 2 February 1856 - Page 5
[277] Staffordshire Advertiser - Wednesday 19 March 1856 - Page 3
[278] Home Office: Criminal Registers, England and Wales: Class: HO 27; Piece: 115; Page: 196
[279] Birmingham Journal - Wednesday 21 May 1856 - Page 2
[280] Staffordshire Sentinel and Commercial & General Advertiser - Saturday 4 October 1856 - Page 6
[281] Staffordshire Sentinel - Saturday 11 October 1856 - Page 6
[282] Staffordshire Sentinel - Saturday 6 December 1856 - Page 5
[283] England & Wales, Criminal Registers, 1791-1892 - Class: HO 27; Piece: 115; Page: 203
[284] UK, Prison Commission Records, 1770-1951 - The National Archives; Kew, London, England; PCOM 2: Metropolitan Police: Criminal Record Office: Habitual Criminals Registers and Miscellaneous Papers
[285] Wolverhampton Chronicle and Staffordshire Advertiser - Wednesday 10 December 1856 - Page 4
[286] Staffordshire Advertiser - Saturday 13 September 1856 - Page 7
[287] Birmingham Journal - Saturday 13 December 1856 - Page 7
[288] Staffordshire Advertiser - Saturday 31 January 1857 - Page 5
[289] Wolverhampton Chronicle and Staffordshire Advertiser - Wednesday 8 October 1856 - Page 3
[290] England & Wales, Criminal Registers, 1791-1892 - Class: HO 27; Piece: 115; Page: 205
[291] England & Wales, Criminal Registers, 1791-1892 - Class: HO 27; Piece: 112; Page: 245
[292] England & Wales, Criminal Registers, 1791-1892 - Class: HO 27; Piece: 118; Page: 183
[293] Staffordshire Advertiser - Saturday 13 December 1856 - Page 6
[294] Birmingham Journal - Saturday 20 December 1856 - Page 7
[295] England & Wales, Criminal Registers, 1791-1892 - Class: HO 27; Piece: 118; Page: 183, HO 27; Piece: 121; Page: 73 and HO 27; Piece: 130; Page: 89
[296] The National Archives; Kew, London, England; PCOM 2: Metropolitan Police: Criminal Record Office: Habitual Criminals Registers and Miscellaneous Papers.
[297] England & Wales, Criminal Registers, 1791-1892 - Class: HO 27; Piece: 118; Page: 183

[298] England & Wales, Criminal Registers, 1791-1892 - Class: HO 27; Piece: 121; Page: 73
[299] England & Wales, Criminal Registers, 1791-1892 - Class: HO 27; Piece: 130; Page: 89
[300] Australian Convict Transportation Registers – Other Fleets & Ships, 1791-1868 - Class: HO 11; Piece: 18 14 Dec 1861
[301] UK, Prison Commission Records, 1770-1951 - The National Archives; Kew, London, England; PCOM 2: Metropolitan Police: Criminal Record Office: Habitual Criminals Registers and Miscellaneous Papers
[302] Web: Australia, Convict Records Index, 1787-1867 - State Library of Queensland; South Brisbane, Queensland, Australia; Australian Joint Copying Project. Microfilm Roll 93, Class and Piece Number HO11/18, Page Number 532
[303] Western Australia, Australia, Convict Records, 1846-1930 - State Records Office of Western Australia; Perth, Australia; Convict Records
[304] Bells Life in London and Sporting Chronicle - Sunday 7 March 1858 - Page 7
[305] Birmingham Journal - Wednesday 22 April 1857 - Page 3
[306] Walsall Free Press and General Advertiser - Saturday 2 May 1857 - Page 4
[307] Walsall Free Press and General Advertiser - Saturday 9 May 1857 - Page 6
[308] Wolverhampton Chronicle and Staffordshire Advertiser - Wednesday 22 July 1857 - Page 5
[309] UK, Criminal Records, 1780-1871 - The National Archives; Kew, Surrey, England; HO 24 Home Office: Prison Registers and Statistical Returns; Reference: HO 24/8
[310] England & Wales, Criminal Registers, 1791-1892 - Class: HO 27; Piece: 118; Page: 188
[311] Walsall Free Press and General Advertiser - Saturday 2 May 1857 - Page 4
[312] Walsall Free Press and General Advertiser - Saturday 11 July 1857 - Page 4
[313] England & Wales, Criminal Registers, 1791-1892 - Class: HO 27; Piece: 118; Page: 183
[314] Walsall Free Press and General Advertiser - Saturday 6 June 1857 - Page 4
[315] Walsall Free Press and General Advertiser - Saturday 15 August 1857
[316] Staffordshire Advertiser - Saturday 12 December 1857 - Page 5
[317] Criminal Registers, England and Wales: Class: HO 27; Piece: 118; Page: 191
[318] England & Wales, Criminal Registers, 1791-1892 - Class: HO 27; Piece: 118; Page: 191
[319] UK, Prison Commission Records, 1770-1951 - The National Archives; Kew, London, England; PCOM 2: Metropolitan Police: Criminal Record Office: Habitual Criminals Registers and Miscellaneous Papers
[320] England & Wales, Civil Registration Death Index, 1837-1915 - Ann Smart died Walsall Q4/1857 (Volume 6b, Page 33b)
[321] Walsall Free Press and General Advertiser - Saturday 31 October 1857 - Page 4
[322] Staffordshire Advertiser - Saturday 28 August 1858 - Page 7
[323] Wolverhampton Chronicle and Staffordshire Advertiser - Wednesday 1 September 1858 - Page 2
[324] Staffordshire Advertiser - Saturday 4 December 1858 - Page 7
[325] England & Wales, Criminal Registers, 1791-1892 - Class: HO 27; Piece: 121; Page: 81 & 82
[326] Staffordshire Advertiser - Saturday 2 September 1854 - Page 5
[327] Walsall Free Press and General Advertiser - Saturday 21 May 1859 - Page 4
[328] Walsall Free Press and General Advertiser - Saturday 25 February 1860 - Page 4
[329] Wolverhampton Chronicle and Staffordshire Advertiser - Wednesday 29 February 1860 - Page 7
[330] Walsall Free Press and General Advertiser - Saturday 10 March 1860 - Page 4
[331] Walsall Free Press and General Advertiser - Saturday 5 May 1860 - Page 4
[332] Bell's Life in London and Sporting Chronicle - Sunday 6 May 1860 - Page 6
[333] Bell's Life in London and Sporting Chronicle - Sunday 29 April 1860 - Page 7
[334] Walsall Free Press and General Advertiser - Saturday 27 October 1860 - Page 4

335 Walsall Free Press and General Advertiser - Saturday 22 December 1860 - Page 4
336 England & Wales, Criminal Registers, 1791-1892: Class: HO 27; Piece: 127; Page: 63
337 Walsall Free Press and General Advertiser - Saturday 5 January 1861 - Page 4
338 Walsall Free Press and General Advertiser - Saturday 16 March 1861 - Page 4
339 England & Wales, Criminal Registers, 1791-1892 - Class: HO 27; Piece: 130; Page: 85
340 Walsall Free Press and General Advertiser - Saturday 29 March 1862 - Page 4
341 Walsall Free Press and General Advertiser - Saturday 5 July 1862 - Page 5
342 England & Wales, Criminal Registers, 1791-1892: Class: HO 27; Piece: 133; Page: 86
343 Walsall Free Press and General Advertiser - Saturday 7 April 1866 - Page 4
344 Walsall Free Press and General Advertiser - Saturday 14 April 1866 - Page 4
345 Walsall Free Press and General Advertiser - Saturday 28 July 1866 - Page 4
346 England & Wales, Criminal Registers, 1791-1892: Class: HO 27; Piece: 145; Page: 90
347 UK, Prison Commission Records, 1770-1951 - The National Archives; Kew, London, England; PCOM 2: Metropolitan Police: Criminal Record Office: Habitual Criminals Registers and Miscellaneous Papers
348 Walsall Free Press and General Advertiser - Saturday 9 February 1867 - Page 4
349 Walsall Free Press and General Advertiser - Saturday 20 November 1869 - Page 4
350 Walsall Free Press and General Advertiser - Saturday 27 November 1869 - Page 4
351 Walsall Free Press and General Advertiser - Saturday 4 December 1869 - Page 4
352 Walsall Free Press and General Advertiser - Saturday 15 January 1870 - Page 4
353 England & Wales, Criminal Registers, 1791-1892: Class: HO 27; Piece: 157; Page: 49
354 UK, Prison Commission Records, 1770-1951 - The National Archives; Kew, London, England; PCOM 2: Metropolitan Police: Criminal Record Office: Habitual Criminals Registers and Miscellaneous Papers
355 England & Wales, Criminal Registers, 1791-1892 - Class: HO 27; Piece: 157; Page: 49
356 Walsall Free Press and General Advertiser - Saturday 15 January 1870 - Page 4
357 Walsall Free Press and General Advertiser - Saturday 22 January 1870 - Page 4
358 Walsall Free Press and General Advertiser - Saturday 19 March 1870 - Page 4
359 UK, Calendar of Prisoners, 1868-1929: Reference: HO 140/12
360 UK, Prison Commission Records, 1770-1951: PCOM 2
361 England & Wales, Criminal Registers, 1791-1892: Class: HO 27; Piece: 157; Page: 31
362 Walsall Free Press and General Advertiser - Saturday 8 July 1871 - Page 4
363 Walsall Free Press and General Advertiser - Saturday 9 March 1872 - Page 4
364 England & Wales, Criminal Registers, 1791-1892: Class: HO 27; Piece: 163; Page: 29
365 UK, Calendar of Prisoners, 1868-1929: Reference: HO 140/20
366 England & Wales, Civil Registration Death Index, 1837-1915 - Sarah Ann Perrins died Walsall Q2/1908 (Volume 6b, Page 375)
367 England & Wales, Civil Registration Death Index, 1837-1915 - Samuel Cotterell died West Bromwich Q4/1934 (Volume 6b, Page 686)
368 England & Wales, Civil Registration Death Index, 1837-1915 - Elizabeth Whittick died Walsall Q4/1874 (Volume 6b, Page 413)
369 Walsall Free Press and General Advertiser - Saturday 10 October 1874 - Page 4
370 Cannock Chase Examiner - Saturday 27 February 1875 - Page 8
371 Walsall Observer - Saturday 6 March 1875 - Page 3
372 Walsall Observer - Saturday 13 March 1875 - Page 3
373 England & Wales, Criminal Registers, 1791-1892: Class: HO 27; Piece: 172; Page: 59
374 UK, Calendar of Prisoners, 1868-1929: Reference: HO 140/32
375 Walsall Observer - Saturday 19 August 1876 - Page 3
376 Walsall Observer - Saturday 26 August 1876 - Page 3

273

[377] County Express; Brierley Hill, Stourbridge, Kidderminster, and Dudley News - Saturday 10 March 1877 - Page 6
[378] England & Wales, Criminal Registers, 1791-1892: Class: HO 27; Piece: 178; Page: 63
[379] UK, Calendar of Prisoners, 1868-1929 - The National Archives; Kew, London, England; HO 140 Home Office: Calendar of Prisoners; Reference: HO 140/40
[380] England, Marriages, 1538–1973. FHL Film Number: 1526109
[381] England & Wales, Civil Registration Birth Index, 1837-1915 - John Thomas Lines born Walsall Q2/1879 (Volume 6b, Page 746)
[382] Walsall Observer - Saturday 3 May 1879 - Page 3
[383] Walsall Observer - Saturday 10 May 1879 - Page 3
[384] Walsall Observer - Saturday 17 May 1879 - Page 3
[385] Walsall Observer - Saturday 26 July 1879 - Page 3
[386] Walsall Observer - Saturday 9 August 1879 - Page 3
[387] Walsall Observer - Saturday 17 May 1879 - Page 4
[388] Metropolitan Police: Criminal Record Office: Habitual Criminals Registers and Miscellaneous Papers; Reference: MEPO 6/10
[389] Census Returns of England and Wales, 1901. Kew, Surrey, England: Class: RG13; Piece: 2726; Folio: 43; Page: 40
[390] Birmingham Daily Post - Thursday 3 August 1882 - Page 5
[391] Walsall Observer - Saturday 26 April 1884 - Page 5
[392] Walsall Observer and South Staffordshire Chronicle - Saturday 10 May 1884 - Page 7
[393] Haverfordwest & Milford Haven Telegraph: Wednesday 4 September 1889 - Page 3
[394] Manchester Courier - Tuesday 3 September 1889 - Page 3
[395] Birmingham Weekly Post - Saturday 7 September 1889 - Page 8
[396] Brecon and Radnor Express and Carmarthen Gazette - Friday 20 December 1889 - Page 8
[397] West Midlands, England, Criminal Registers, 1850-1933 - West Midlands Police; Birmingham, England; Criminals Offences Registers 1880- 1910
[398] Birmingham, England, Calendar of Prisoners, 1880-1922 - Library of Birmingham; Birmingham, UK; General Sessions of the Peace; Reference Number: Qs/B/20/13
[399] UK, Calendar of Prisoners, 1868-1929 - The National Archives; Kew, London, England; HO 140 Home Office: Calendar of Prisoners; Reference: HO 140/110
[400] Walsall Observer - Saturday 2 May 1885 - Page 5
[401] Walsall Observer - Saturday 16 May 1885 - Page 8
[402] Walsall Observer - Saturday 18 July 1885 - Page 5
[403] UK, Calendar of Prisoners, 1868-1929 - The National Archives; Kew, London, England; HO 140 Home Office: Calendar of Prisoners; Reference: HO 140/84
[404] England & Wales, Criminal Registers, 1791-1892 - Class: HO 27; Piece: 202; Page: 83
[405] UK, Calendar of Prisoners, 1868-1929 - The National Archives; Kew, London, England; HO 140 Home Office: Calendar of Prisoners; Reference: HO 140/117
[406] England & Wales, Civil Registration Marriage Index, 1837-1915 - Benjamin Thorp married Sarah Ann Claydon or Mary Burk at West Bromwich Q3/1868 (Volume 6b, Page 835)
[407] England & Wales, Civil Registration Death Index, 1837-1915 - Sarah Thorpe aged 22 years died at West Bromwich Q4/1871 (Volume 6c, Page 127)
[408] England & Wales, Civil Registration Marriage Index, 1837-1915 - Benjamin Thorp married Harriet Ingram at Wolverhampton Q1/1872 (Volume 6b, Page 673)
[409] England & Wales, Civil Registration Death Index, 1837-1915 - Harriet Thorpe aged 29 years died at Bromsgrove Q4/1871 (Volume 6c, Page 292)
[410] England & Wales, Civil Registration Marriage Index, 1837-1915 - Arthur Benjamin Thorp married Hannah Long at Walsall Q1/1874 (Volume 6b, Page 806)

[411] England & Wales, Civil Registration Marriage Index, 1837-1915 - Arthur THORP married Emma RUSSELL at West Bromwich Q1/1882 (Volume 6b, Page 838)
[412] Birmingham Daily Post - Thursday 24 February 1887 - Page 7
[413] Walsall Observer - Saturday 19 February 1887 - Page 5
[414] Walsall Observer - Saturday 26 February 1887 - Page 5
[415] England & Wales, Criminal Registers, 1791-1892 - Class: HO 27; Piece: 208; Page: 66
[416] UK, Calendar of Prisoners, 1868-1929 - The National Archives; Kew, London, England; HO 140 Home Office: Calendar of Prisoners; Reference: HO 140/100
[417] Walsall Observer - Saturday 14 May 1887 - Page 5
[418] England & Wales, Civil Registration Death Index, 1916-2007 - Arthur B Thorp died aged 75 years at Wolverhampton Q4/1922 (Volume 6b, Page 491)
[419] England & Wales, Civil Registration Death Index, 1916-2007 - Emma Thorpe died aged 69 years at Wolverhampton Q2/1926 (Volume 6b, Page 571)
[420] England & Wales, Civil Registration Birth Index, 1837-1915 - Emma Valentine Thorp born Walsall Q4/1882 (Volume 6b, Page 712), Evelyn Matilda Thorp born Walsall Q4/1884 (Volume 6b, Page 728), Gertrude Beatrice Thorp born Walsall Q3/1886 (Volume 6b, Page 725), Louis Nelson Thorpe born Dudley Q3/1889 (Volume 6b, Page 725), Arthur Clifford Thorp born Dudley Q3/1894 (Volume 6b, Page 74), Florence Eugenia Thorp born Dudley Q3/1894 (Volume 6b, Page 78)
[421] England & Wales, Civil Registration Death Index, 1837-1915 - Maria Bullers died aged 31 years at Walsall Q3/1870 (Volume 6b, Page 368)
[422] England & Wales, Civil Registration Marriage Index, 1837-1915 - Mary Ann Bullers died aged 29 years at Walsall Q1/1876 (Volume 6b, Page 524)
[423] England & Wales, Civil Registration Birth Index, 1837-1915 - Joe Bullers born Walsall Q1/1879 (Volume 6b, Page 756). Charles James Bullers born Walsall Q4/1881 (Volume 6b, Page 658). Ernest George Bullers born Walsall Q1/1884 (Volume 6b, Page 707). Howard William Allen Bullers born Walsall Q4/1885 (Volume 6b, Page 699). Mothers name for all was Long.
[424] England & Wales, Civil Registration Marriage Index, 1837-1915 - James Thompson married Hannah Delagrade Thorp at Walsall Q4/1890 (Volume 6b, Page 1248)
[425] England & Wales, Civil Registration Marriage Index, 1837-1915 - Dinah Thompson died aged 50 years at Walsall Q1/1890 (Volume 6b, Page 527)
[426] England & Wales, Civil Registration Death Index, 1837-1915 - James Thompson died aged 61 years at Walsall Q4/1891 (Volume 6b, Page 462)
[427] England & Wales, Civil Registration Marriage Index, 1837-1915 - Joseph Bullers married Hannah Delagrade Thompson at Walsall Q1/1892 (Volume 6b, Page 766)
[428] England & Wales, Civil Registration Death Index, 1837-1915 - Hannah Delegarde Bullers died age 46 years at Walsall Q3/1898 (Volume 6b, Page 485)
[429] Walsall Observer - Saturday 12 January 1889 - Page 5
[430] Birmingham Daily Post - Saturday 16 March 1889 - Page 6
[431] Walsall Observer - Saturday 18 May 1889 - Page 3
[432] Walsall Observer - Saturday 24 October 1891 - Page 5
[433] Walsall Observer and South Staffordshire Chronicle - Saturday 31 October 1891 - Page 8
[434] Walsall Observer - Saturday 7 November 1891 - Page 7
[435] Walsall Observer - Saturday 14 November 1891 - Page 3
[436] England & Wales, Criminal Registers, 1791-1892 - Class: HO 27; Piece: 220; Page: 76
[437] Lichfield Mercury - Friday 18 December 1891 - Page 7
[438] England & Wales, Civil Registration Marriage Index, 1837-1915 - William Joseph Bate married Charlotte Busst at Walsall Q4/1883 (Volume 6b, Page 1152)

[439] Henrietta Rebecca Eliza Bate born Walsall Q2/1885 (Volume 6b, Page 695)
[440] William Thomas Bate born Walsall Q1/1891 (Volume 6b, Page 777)
[441] England & Wales, Civil Registration Death Index, 1837-1915 - William Joseph Bate died aged 31 years at Walsall Q4 (Volume 6b, Page 419)
[442] England & Wales, Civil Registration Death Index, 1837-1915 - Charlotte Bate died aged 28 years at Walsall Q4 (Volume 6b, Page 418)
[443] Walsall Observer - Saturday 24 December 1892 - Page 3
[444] Walsall Observer - Saturday 13 October 1894 - Page 5
[445] Walsall Observer - Saturday 10 November 1894 - Page 5
[446] England & Wales, Civil Registration Marriage Index, 1837-1915 - Walter Frank Kendrick married Sarah Jane Bache at Walsall Q1/1893 (Volume 6b, Page 762)
[447] England & Wales, Civil Registration Birth Index, 1837-1915 - Grace Janette Kendrick was born Walsall Q2/1893 (Volume 6b, Page 783)
[448] England & Wales, Civil Registration Birth Index, 1837-1915 - Dorothy Mary Kendrick was born Walsall Q4/1894 (Volume 6b, Page 767)
[449] England & Wales, Civil Registration Death Index, 1837-1915 - Dorothy Mary Kendrick died age 0 at Walsall Q1/1895 (Volume 6b, Page 514)
[450] England & Wales, Civil Registration Death Index, 1837-1915 - Grace Janette Kendrick died aged 2 years at Walsall Q2/1895 (Volume 6b, Page 439)
[451] Walsall Observer - Saturday 4 May 1895 - Page 7
[452] Walsall Observer - Saturday 27 July 1895 - Page 5
[453] UK, Calendar of Prisoners, 1868-1929 - The National Archives; Kew, London, England; HO 140 Home Office: Calendar of Prisoners; Reference: HO 140/164
[454] England & Wales, Civil Registration Marriage Index, 1837-1915 - Albert Edward Kendrick married Phoebe Bache at Walsall Q3/1895 (Volume 6b, Page 1049)
[455] Walsall Observer - Saturday 17 November 1896 - Page 5
[456] Walsall Advertiser - Saturday 21 November 1896 - Page 5
[457] Walsall Advertiser - Saturday 28 November 1896 - Page 8
[458] Walsall Observer - Saturday 5 December 1896 - Page 3
[459] Walsall Advertiser - Saturday 5 December 1896 - Page 2
[460] Walsall Advertiser - Saturday 12 December 1896 - Page 8
[461] Walsall Observer - Saturday 19 December 1896 - Page 2
[462] Walsall Observer - Saturday 18 February 1899 - Page 2
[463] England & Wales, Civil Registration Death Index, 1837-1915 - John J Reddick died at Walsall aged 47 years Q4/1912 (Volume 6b, Page 783)
[464] Walsall Advertiser - Saturday 30 November 1912 - Page 7
[465] Walsall Observer - Saturday 30 November 1912 - Page 7
[466] Walsall Observer - Saturday 19 March 1898 - Page 2
[467] Walsall Observer - Saturday 26 March 1898 - Page 5
[468] Walsall Observer - Saturday 16 April 1898 - Page 2
[469] Regimental & Service Records - WO 96 - Militia Service Records 1806-1915 - Box 905, Record 103
[470] England & Wales, Civil Registration Marriage Index, 1837-1915 - Sidney John Charlesworth married Annie Maria Froggatt at Oxford Q3/1898 (Volume 3a, Page 1654)
[471] UK, Calendar of Prisoners, 1868-1929 - The National Archives; Kew, London, England; HO 140 Home Office: Calendar of Prisoners; Reference: HO 140/182
[472] UK, Registers of Habitual Criminals and Police Gazettes, 1834-1934 - The National Archives; Kew, London, England; MEPO 6: Metropolitan Police: Criminal Record Office: Habitual Criminals Registers and Miscellaneous Papers; Reference: MEPO 6/10

[473] UK, British Army World War I Pension Records 1914-1920 - War Office: Soldiers' Documents from Pension Claims, First World War (Microfilm Copies); (The National Archives Microfilm Publication WO364)
[474] England & Wales, Civil Divorce Records, 1858-1918 - The National Archives; Kew, Surrey, England; Court for Divorce and Matrimonial Causes, later Supreme Court of Judicature: Divorce and Matrimonial Causes Files, J 77; Reference Number: J 77/898/7274
[475] Staffordshire Newsletter - Saturday 6 July 1907 - Page 4
[476] Walsall Observer - Saturday 27 August 1898 - Page 5
[477] UK, Calendar of Prisoners, 1868-1929 - The National Archives; Kew, London, England; HO 140 Home Office: Calendar of Prisoners; Reference: HO 140/260
[478] UK, Registers of Habitual Criminals and Police Gazettes, 1834-1934 - The National Archives; Kew, London, England; MEPO 6: Metropolitan Police: Criminal Record Office: Habitual Criminals Registers and Miscellaneous Papers; Reference: MEPO 6/22
[479] UK, Registers of Habitual Criminals and Police Gazettes, 1834-1934 - The National Archives; Kew, London, England; MEPO 6: Metropolitan Police: Criminal Record Office: Habitual Criminals Registers and Miscellaneous Papers; Reference: MEPO 6/29
[480] England & Wales, Civil Registration Marriage Index, 1916-2005 - Sidney J Charlesworth married Mary Jane Holbrow at Bath Q1/1918 (Volume 5c, Page 933)
[481] England & Wales, Crime, Prisons & Punishment, 1770-1935 - The National Archives, MEPO6, Police Gazette Supplement 'A'